W9-BMM-965

CRUCIBLES
OF LEADERSHIP

CRUCIBLES OF LEADERSHIP

[HOW TO LEARN FROM EXPERIENCE
TO BECOME A GREAT LEADER]

ROBERT J. THOMAS

HARVARD BUSINESS PRESS

Boston, Massachusetts

Copyright 2008 Harvard Business School Publishing Corporation
All rights reserved
Printed in the United States of America
15 14 13 12 11 10 9 8 7

No part of this publication may be reproduced, stored in or introduced into
a retrieval system, or transmitted, in any form, or by any means (electronic,
mechanical, photocopying, recording, or otherwise), without the prior
permission of the publisher. Requests for permission should be directed to
permissions@hbsp.harvard.edu, or mailed to Permissions, Harvard Business
School Publishing, 60 Harvard Way, Boston, Massachusetts 02163.

Library of Congress Cataloging-in-Publication Data
Thomas, Robert J. (Robert Joseph), 1952–
    Crucibles of leadership: how to learn from experience to become a great
  leader / Robert J. Thomas.
      p. cm.
    ISBN 978-1-59139-137-1
    1. Leadership 2. Executive ability. I. Title.
  HD57.7.T467 2008
  658.4'092—dc22

                                                                2007037462

The paper used in this publication meets the requirements of the American
National Standard for Permanence of Paper for Publications and Documents
in Libraries and Archives Z39.48-1992.

CONTENTS

FOREWORD

By Warren G. Bennis

Bob Thomas and I began discussing the central themes of this fascinating new book on leading and learning almost a decade ago. I was struck then by Bob's passion and distinctive ideas on this critically important subject, which we believe is central to how leaders develop and how individuals learn to lead meaningful lives, whatever they do professionally. Those lively talks over several years led to our 2002 collaboration *Geeks and Geezers: How Era, Values, and Defining Moments Shape Leaders*, recently published in paperback with a new introduction and a new title, *Leading for a Lifetime*. In light of that shared history, it is a special pleasure for me to read Bob's *Crucibles of Leadership* and to see how deftly he has built on and then significantly extended those earlier discoveries to create an indispensable handbook for would-be leaders and the organizations that need them so.

Central to both books is the powerful idea of the crucible. When we first looked at scores of leaders, we found over and over again that each had had some sort of transformative experience. These were sometimes tragic losses, sometimes immersion in a new culture, sometimes a relationship with a life-changing mentor. Whatever the experience, no matter how harsh, the future leader extracted from it a new sense of self and a new panoply of tools and strategies for leading others.

The term that best seemed to fit these varied experiences was *crucible*, the vessel in which medieval alchemists attempted to

turn base metals into gold. The crucibles that our leaders under-
went were sometimes fiery ordeals, including frontline service in
wartime, but they were also magical experiences that lifted the individuals to new levels of understanding and mastery. In every
case, the crucible was also an education, one that gave the newly
minted leader an appreciation of how learning is the great gift
given to those who are tested and survive. As Bob writes so in-
sightfully, the ability to learn is "the all-purpose tool, the Swiss
Army knife, that leaders need to carry at all times."

What Bob and I didn't do in our earlier work was to explore
what life is like inside a crucible. We speculated about how people
made sense of their crucibles and learned from them, but we only
scratched the surface on critical issues like how individuals actually
harness the power of experience and whether organizations can
more effectively use crucibles to accelerate leader development.

Crucibles of Leadership creatively extends and enriches the
crucible concept to serve as a guide for aspiring leaders. As aca-
demics, we respect, even treasure, theory. We are always striving
to find the overarching pattern that weaves disparate data into an
illuminating whole. Bob did a great deal of original research for
Crucibles of Leadership into such important matters as how leaders
learn from experience and learn even as they lead. Among his key
insights is that "practice and performance are part of the same
process." Genuine leaders, he points out, are expert performers who
have developed and continue to benefit from a Personal Learning
Strategy, a highly individual plan for leveraging hard-won insights
about learning from adversity and using practice to improve
performance.

Perhaps the most valuable quality of Bob's book is its wise
pragmatism. In business as in the rest of life, we need wisdom we
can act on, and this book is filled with truths that can be put into
action. Through original exercises, Bob shows readers how to
take such essential steps toward both leadership and continued
learning as finding their passion. By the end of the book, the engaged reader will have developed his or her own Personal Learning Strategy. At its heart, this is a book of self-discovery, but

self-discovery in the broadest sense—the kind of deeper understanding of self that then turns outward rather than inward and results in better understanding of others and the organizations that matter to us.

Bob reveals how everyday experiences—including those numbing meetings that most organizations continue to be addicted to—can be turned into opportunities to hone such leadership abilities as becoming an expert observer. But much of what makes Bob's book such a delightful read are the wonderful stories he tells. It is fascinating to learn, for instance, how Boston Celtics legend Bill Russell discovered the centrality to greatness of a personal "signature." That critical part of Russell's education came not on the basketball court, but in the local library that young Bill's mother encouraged him to frequent. His unlikely teachers were Michelangelo and Leonardo da Vinci. Russell loved the art of the Renaissance and could competently copy the works of the masters. All that Russell's drawings lacked, he realized, was the uniqueness that distinguishes the truly great from the merely adept. That insight ignited in him a lifelong search for a signature style in his play *and* in his team leadership.

Crucibles of Leadership holds powerful and actionable insights for organizations as well as for individuals. We seem to have been talking forever about the great leadership crisis, the paucity of leaders worldwide that threatens us as surely as global warming, terrorism, and endemic poverty in much of the world. Yet the crisis is clearly getting worse instead of better. That is the context in which we must think about leadership development, not simply in terms of training the next CEO of General Electric or some other commercial enterprise. More than personal ambition is at stake. Preparing future leaders is as critical to our shared survival, if somewhat less fashionable at the moment, as any green initiative. We desperately need to grow more leaders as well as trees.

As a passionate believer and practitioner of experience-based leadership development, Bob includes a couple of unexpected, and engrossing, models of top-notch training programs. They are the missionary experience required of every young member of the

Church of Jesus Christ of Latter-day Saints and the group motorcycle runs held by the Hells Angels motorcycle club. As Bob explains, the Mormons prepare their future leaders by teaching them not only the language of the country where they will seek converts, but such subtle skills as how to tell whether a potential convert's interest is genuine. And what better way to learn resilience—a key element in adaptive capacity, one of the essential attributes of every great leader—than by surviving the thousands of rebuffs that make up such missionaries' experience as they travel the world knocking on every door. As for the Hells Angels, they, too, give their future leaders an educational experience tailored to their needs. In planning the typical interstate run, for example, the future leader must negotiate boundaries with rival gangs, take into account the potential for parole violations, and navigate city, state, and federal laws while addressing members' preference to live by their own rules.

Evidenced by the lessons he draws from the education of leading figures in business, government, social movements, religious organizations, and the arts, Bob is a wide-ranging thinker and writer. But, as readers will discover, he always returns to the practical implications of the provocative idea. This, I believe, is a product of his unique career as academic, adviser to top management teams, and leader of a widely respected R&D organization. This invaluable book reminds us that talent is only the beginning of greatness, that leading and learning are inextricably linked, and that the crucibles that break some people can give rise to serial leaders and learners as well. Because Bob's volume extends and expands on many of the same themes, it is a perfect companion to our *Leading for a Lifetime*. And in providing readers with opportunities to actively engage with the material, Bob's book reflects the timeless wisdom of Galileo's observation: "You cannot teach a man anything; you can only help him find it within himself."

Whatever the context in life and work and whatever your gender, *Crucibles of Leadership* can help you find the leader within.

PREFACE

This exploration of how leaders learn had its origins in two fortu-itous events—one quite pleasant and the other rather chilling. The first event was breakfast with Warren Bennis at Shutters in Santa Monica on a bright morning in December 1999. While shar-ing our thoughts on the way experience shapes a leader's persona, I described to Warren an insight I'd gotten while observing a master class led by acclaimed choreographer Twyla Tharp at City Center in Manhattan. During the question and answer period following the class, I'd asked Tharp what was to her mind the biggest difference between practice and performance. She looked at me quizzically, as if I'd asked a truly boneheaded question. But then, patiently, she explained that practice and performance were part of the same thing . . . that when a dancer practices she thinks about the per-formance and when she performs she notices the things she ought to practice more. In fact, Tharp added, the key is to practice while you perform, and vice versa. I told Bennis that I thought the same thing ought to apply to leaders. He leaned forward over the rem-nants of our breakfast and fixed me with his steely eyes. "Kid," he said, "you've got something there. Build on it."

The second event preceded the first by several months, but it wasn't until the breakfast with Bennis that I began to understand the meaning of the first. I had been granted an interview with a young man who had been regaled by the national press as an emerging leader in the world of corporate finance. In the middle of the interview, I asked about a topic that had recently come to interest me, a topic that had to do with friendship and advice net-works. I asked who he turned to for advice when facing difficult situations, choices that he'd never imagined having to make. He answered without hesitation: "Myself." It struck me even then that either he was supremely self-confident, a poster child for American independent thinking, or he was supremely foolish, not unlike the lawyer who takes himself on as a client . . . or both. My gut argued for the second interpretation. And, as it turns out, so did the grand jury that later issued an indictment for fraud with his name on it.

The education of a leader is a complex thing. Certainly, talent matters. But even the most naturally gifted still have a lot to learn, and one of the most important things a leader needs to learn is what he or she stands for: what he is made of, what she believes in, what lines he will not cross. Crucible events and relationships have the potential to reveal what a leader stands for. Sometimes the revelation is immediate and obvious, but it can just as easily take years to figure out. The key is being able to notice, to be open to learning. Perhaps two years in federal prison will prove a crucible through which a young financial wizard learns what he stands for.

The education of a leader rarely takes place in the classroom. That doesn't mean we shouldn't offer classes in leadership or that we shouldn't organize workshops for aspiring leaders. I am a big fan of leadership research in all the disciplines—psychology, sociology, economics, history, political science—and in every facet of life—in politics, business, the arts, athletics, families. But the study of others cannot supplant the study of self. We need to find ways to leverage the critical formative and transformative experiences that men and women have in their own lives that can reveal to them who they are and where they stand. Not knowing what she stands for (and against) can leave a leader ill equipped to act in the circumstances in which we need leaders most: when time is short, stakes are high, and alternatives are not easy to discern.

Nearly three decades of teaching, consulting, coaching, and leading have brought me to the conclusion that the ability to learn is the all-purpose tool, the Swiss Army knife, that leaders need to carry at all times if they hope to fulfill the expectations they've set for themselves and that others have of them. The ability to learn is bolstered by self-confidence, and successful learning enhances self-confidence; but self-confidence without openness to learning new things and to disconfirmation of things once believed to be true is an empty vessel, arguably a dangerous one, too.

This book strives to illuminate the process by which leaders learn and the skills and circumstances that accelerate their learning. I was inspired to research the topic by several leaders with whom I'd had the honor to work (or work for) and by the hundreds of young men and women who took classes on leadership with me—during which we tried collaboratively to figure out how leaders learn. In that respect, I may be the nominal author of the book, but I owe a huge debt to the people who by interview or by discussion invited me to learn from them.

METHODS AND DATA

The data analyzed in this book comes from three major sources. Interviews with leaders in business, government, military, social movements, and the performing arts represent the bulk of the raw material from which the arguments are derived. Over the course of the project, eighty-eight leaders were selected for interview on the basis of their proven ability to grow and sustain an organization during times of trial. These included men and women in both the public and the private sector, in organizations as diverse as Marriott International, the United Parcel Service, the U.S. Marines, the PLO, the Girl Scouts of America, City Year, the Central American chapters of the Young Presidents' Organization, the Mormon Church, and the Hells Angels motorcycle club. In addition, I interviewed executives and professional staff involved with leader development in twenty-three business enterprises, voluntary and civic organizations, music school faculty, sports psychologists, and others who could provide insight on how talented people learn.

An additional 110 interviews were conducted opportunistically. These included people who had read my book (coauthored with Warren Bennis), *Geeks and Geezers,* or who had attended presentations I gave on that book and related themes (including talks and workshops conducted at nearly two dozen *Fortune 500* companies and twenty academic institutions).[1] Students at Tufts University's Fletcher School of International Affairs and at MIT's Sloan School of Management provided nearly one hundred crucible stories that I analyzed—and occasionally excerpted. In addition, Warren Bennis and Steve Sample generously contributed forty-eight crucible stories from their senior seminar on leadership at the University of Southern California.

Finally, I reviewed and analyzed the content of the biographies and autobiographies of sixty-three contemporary business leaders and performing artists with a public reputation for having pioneered new organizational forms and business models (such as Internet-based, multinational, or networked enterprises) or new artistic genres (e.g., jazz fusion, world music, postmodern architecture, modern dance). Throughout, I sought insight and examples as to how leaders and performers learned their craft and how they transcended conventions in their fields.

ACKNOWLEDGMENTS

Writing this book was not a crucible . . . though it came close. It took longer to research and write than I ever believed it would, and the fact that it is in print is testimony to my indebtedness to many, many people. First in line among my colleagues would have to be Warren Bennis. Warren considered me and my ideas about practice and performance with the discerning ear of a music critic. Fortunately, he liked what he heard and encouraged me to keep at it until I got it right. He kept on encouraging me for the better part of seven years. With friends like Warren, anything is possible.

I owe special thanks to the people who read the manuscript in its various iterations and who provided trenchant criticism and advice when I needed it most. Among them I include my former

Harvard Business Press editor Suzanne Rotondo, who asked remarkably helpful questions and listened to endless retellings of the stories as I searched for the threads that connected them; and Rosanna Hertz, who more than anyone else endured the spew of drafts, challenged me to be more inventive, and kept me firmly focused on completing a task that meant so much to me.

My colleagues at Accenture and in the Institute for High Performance Business and my students at the Fletcher School at Tufts University have been a constant source of support and inspiration. Jim Benton, Tim Breene, Sue Cantrell, Peter Cheese, Tom Davenport, Ana Dutra, Jeanne Harris, Paul Nunes, and Walt Shill challenged me with great ideas and counterexamples and urged me to keep the book relevant to practicing leaders. Chi Pham found the wheat among the chaff of leader development programs, and Karen O'Brien and Amy Burkhardt were relentlessly cheerful as they helped me produce a readable manuscript. Fred Harburg, Ed Schein, John Van Maanen, Tom Kochan, Jan Klein, Rob Cross, Joe Raelin, and Paul Lagace—colleagues and friends from other careers—could always be counted on to answer a question or to prompt me with an example to enrich my thinking.

I have nothing but praise and warm thanks for my Harvard Business Press editor, Jeff Kehoe, who endured (too) many rambling lunches and guided me with a steady hand as I plodded along. His faith gave me mine. Lucy McCauley dove into the near-final manuscript with remarkable editing skill and patience and helped me take it up a notch. The rest of the team at the Press, including Hollis Heimbouch, demonstrated once again the utmost professionalism in bringing the book across the finish line.

This book is dedicated to the leaders who have inspired me in my journey: Cesar Chavez, Ernesto Loredo, Bill Friedland, Arun Maira, Warren Bennis, and Rosanna Hertz . . . and to a future leader who already inspires me, Alyssa Thomas.

PART ONE

EXPERIENCE MATTERS— BUT THEN WHAT?

[1]

HOW DO YOU FIND WHAT MATTERS IN EXPERIENCE?

Leadership and learning are indispensable to each other.

—John F. Kennedy (speech prepared for delivery
in Dallas, Texas, November 22, 1963)

ARE YOU THE MOST EFFECTIVE LEADER you can be? Most people will admit they aren't. They read books and articles and attend the occasional workshop. In moments of doubt, they will search out a coach or a mentor. Like Tony Soprano, a surprising number watch the History Channel, hoping to glean some insight about how leaders are born and grown. Their intentions are good, but still they struggle to find a way to increase their leadership acumen—and that frustrates them.

The struggle is understandable. Time is scarce. People in management roles, whether in business, in government, or in nonprofits, work so hard and so long that they just don't have time to spare, even for things that they might truly value, like developing themselves as leaders. It's hard to learn just from books and seminars. A classroom is a sterile environment, and the half-life of most training is notoriously short. Learning styles vary enormously, and too often there isn't a good fit between teaching style and learning style. Off-site workshops may be good for clearing the head, and a barefoot stroll over hot coals may boost self-confidence, but it's tough to keep the learning fresh when you go back to a situation that's completely unchanged. And finally, it's difficult to learn just through observation. Too often people say they can only snatch a glimpse of good leadership in action; and hearing someone deliver a great speech is not the same as sitting them down and picking their brains about how they do what they do.

Still, some people do grow and improve as leaders. Like consummate actors and athletes, they find ways to take it up one notch and then another and another. If they're not reading more or attending more classes or they don't have loads of free time to reflect, how do they become more proficient? The answer is *experience*. For all the wide-ranging theories of effective leadership, almost everyone agrees that anyone who seeks to lead must get firsthand experience: get their feet wet and their hands dirty, seek out challenging assignments, volunteer for foreign postings, work for great leaders (and even for bad ones)—and learn as much as possible.

But there's a hitch. Two people can have the same experience and come away with profoundly different reactions: one may blossom and grow while the other is unchanged or even depleted. The same can be said for any pair of fired CEOs, successful project leaders, failed entrepreneurs, rookie supervisors, and those on international duty.

Experience by itself guarantees nothing.

To complicate matters, many memorable leadership experiences don't occur at scheduled times or in convenient places, like work or school. For instance, when pressed to identify an experience in which they learned something important about leadership or about themselves as leaders, the men and women interviewed for this book rarely pointed to events experienced in conventional training courses and MBA curricula. Instead, they described transformative events that occurred outside their professional lives as often as they cited ones that happened on the job. The most profound among those experiences—the *crucibles* that led to a new or an altered sense of identity—were nested in family life, wartime trauma, athletic competition, and/or personal loss far more often than in work assignments.

What exactly is a crucible? In medieval times it was the vessel in which alchemists attempted to turn base metals into gold. In a leadership context, then, we can think of a crucible as a transformative experience from which a person extracts his or her "gold": a new or an altered sense of identity. A crucible is not the same as a life stage or transition, like moving from adolescence to adulthood or from midlife to retirement. Life stages can be stressful, even tumultuous; but, unlike crucibles, they tend to be gradual, reasonably predictable, and patterned.[1] Crucibles are more like trials or tests that corner individuals and force them to answer questions about who they are and what is really important to them.

Consider Bob Galvin, Motorola's visionary former CEO and chairman of the board, who shepherded the company from analog to digital technology and into the coveted status of preferred supplier to auto giants like Toyota. When I asked him to tell me about a time when he learned an important lesson about leading, Galvin remembered an event from his early years when he worked in one of his father's factories.

Galvin was just seventeen, and he'd just made his first big mistake—one that shut down an assembly line. He knew that the plant supervisors could easily have had great fun at the expense of the boss's son. Instead, they helped him resolve the problem in minutes and said something that encouraged him to keep learning for the rest of his life: "I overheard one foreman saying to another, 'No problem with Bob. If he happens to screw it up, we can point it out to him and we can get on and get the job done right. Hopefully he does it right most of the time.'"[2] A small compliment, perhaps, but one that had a lasting effect on Galvin and on the company. Galvin credits that factory foreman for helping him gain the confidence to make mistakes and to learn from them.

The moral of Galvin's story? While experience matters, what matters more is what one *makes* of experience: how a person comes to recognize in a crucible experience that something new or important is happening, to see beyond the discomfort, perhaps even the pain, of new and unexpected information and to incorporate that information as useful knowledge, not just about the world but, as likely, about oneself. Extracting insight from experience is a competence especially relevant to men and women in leadership positions in business and government, and to those who aspire to leadership, because their professional lives so often consist of complex, uncertain, and fluid situations for which there is no practical guide and where resolution depends on the exercise of judgment. Judgment can only be acquired through experience.

What distinguishes men and women who grow through a crucible experience is not breeding or intellect. Talent plays a role, undoubtedly, but it is a supporting role. No amount of native talent can prepare a leader for the infinite variety of circumstances she will face or the challenges she must surmount. No gene for resilience ensures that gems of wisdom will suddenly appear amid the turmoil of a crucible.

Instead, what sets these leaders apart is their approach to learning. Rather than wait for the right moment to arrive, they discover and exploit learning opportunities. Rather than partition their lives into periods of action and periods of reflection, they do both, often on a daily basis, sometimes in precisely the same moment. Rather than complain about the scarcity of time to learn, they make time. Like accomplished performers in sports or music or the arts, *they practice as strenuously as they perform*. And when, as often happens to organizational leaders, they find themselves onstage much of the time, they learn how to *practice while they perform*—not simply to learn by doing, but to learn *while* doing.

This is a book *about* leaders who are skilled at transforming crucible experiences into lessons that make them personally more effective and that, more importantly, result in improved performance on the part of the organizations they lead. But this is a book *for* anyone who aspires to leadership. I say that because one of the most important findings of the research on which this book is based is that the ability to mine crucible experiences for insight *can be learned.* In fact, intensive, long-term conscious practice at it can trump native talent. Practice establishes a state of continuous preparedness: awareness of oneself and one's capabilities and alertness to important events, like crucible experiences, so that they can be learned from.

Crucible experiences are not only defining moments; they can also be a valuable starting point for discovering a form of practice closely attuned to an individual's aspirations and motivations—something I refer to as a *Personal Learning Strategy.* That is, crucibles trigger a search for meaning: Why did this happen? Why did it happen to *me*? What should I learn from this for the future? Handled properly, crucibles can catalyze a vigorous and sustained interior dialogue that leads to deeper self-understanding and enhanced performance.

By paying close attention to the words and stories of a wide variety of leaders, we can gain skill in recognizing the context and the trajectory of a crucible experience. Moreover, we can become alert to the "warning signs" of an impending crucible and identify the skills necessary to cope, respond, and learn. The goal of this book is to render that process visible and practical.

CRUCIBLES AND THE LESSONS THEY OFFER

This exploration of crucibles—what they teach and how leaders learn—builds on a foundation that Warren Bennis and I set in our book, *Geeks and Geezers.* That research was designed to uncover the ways that *era* (or the social, political, cultural, and economic milieu of one's maturing years) influences a leader's motivations and aspirations. We interviewed forty-three of today's top leaders in business and the public sector, limiting our subjects to people born in or before 1925, or in or after 1970.

To our delight we learned a great deal about how age and era affect leadership style (for a brief summary of key findings, see the box, "Geeks and Geezers"). Our older and younger leaders had very different ideas about paying your dues (interestingly, not about whether they should be paid, but *how*), work-life balance, the role of heroes, and more. But they also shared some striking similarities—among them a love of learning and a strong sense of values. Most intriguing was the fact that both our geeks and geezers told us again and again how certain experiences inspired them, shaped them, and, indeed, taught them to lead.

"Geeks and Geezers"

I N *Geeks and Geezers* (published in paperback as *Leading for a Lifetime*), Warren Bennis and I had the opportunity to interview at length a group of remarkable leaders who taught us a great deal about what distinguishes truly outstanding leaders from the rest. Three qualities, in particular, stood out as common to outstanding leaders, young and old (see table 1-1):

- *Adaptive capacity* is the ability to learn—about yourself, about the world around you, about what it takes to adjust to, and to make, change.

- *Engaging others through shared meaning* is teaching and, in turn, listening—being an interactive leader, one who can enlist as well as command, and one who is capable of mobilizing the best in people through shared vision.

- *Integrity* is about knowing what you stand for—possessing a strong moral compass—and having the courage of your convictions; it is a process of self-knowledge that provides a core identity and a spine that remains strong even when circumstances demand that you adapt. Integrity is what keeps the leader from becoming a hollow dissembler or a leaf in the wind.

Adaptive capacity, the ability to engage others, and integrity are qualities that characterize outstanding leaders. They are not static, however. They are not achieved once and forever. They must be renewed continuously because the circumstances that leaders face change constantly—and change demands a continuous demonstration of each quality if it is to remain a legitimate description of the leader.

TABLE 1-1

Qualities of outstanding leaders

Qualities	Attributes
Adaptive capacity	• Resilience
	• Creativity
	• Openness to new experience and a willingness to learn
	• Acute observational skill
Engaging others through shared meaning	• Deep sense of purpose and focus
	• Self-awareness and emotional intelligence
	• Obsessive and skilled communication
	• Comfort with dissent
Integrity	• Clear values and voice
	• Balance among ambition, technique, moral compass
	• Able to work with value conflicts
	• Knowledge of when to lead and how to follow

We came to call the experiences that shape leaders "crucibles," and for the leaders we interviewed, the crucible experience was a trial and a test, a point of deep self-reflection that challenged them to step up and be someone or do something they'd never been or done before. In some instances, crucibles were momentous events shared by many people, like World War II or the Great Depression; in others, crucibles were far more individual and private, like the loss of a loved one or a bankruptcy. Either way, crucibles required these leaders to examine their values, to question their assumptions, to hone their judgment. And in virtually every instance, they emerged from the experience stronger and more sure of themselves and their purpose—enhanced in some fundamental way.

Although we found the stories of our leaders studded with insight, we barely lifted the lid on the box of crucible experiences. We could not say, for example, whether crucibles followed a similar trajectory or whether, since some people reported being oblivious to what they were enduring at the time, conscious recognition of crucibles was necessary at all. And we only speculated as to whether the qualities that we found among learning leaders were themselves capable of being learned.

We also did not anticipate the resonant chord that the crucible concept struck with readers and listeners. Many wanted to share their own stories. Inadvertently, we'd tapped a rich vein of common experience—a highly personal and consequential event or relationship—that people felt not only shaped them, but also helped *explain* them. Sometimes their stories were emotional, cathartic even, and other times they were quite sublime. Sometimes they were told in private, over coffee, and other times they were shared in classrooms, boardrooms, or auditoriums. But in every instance, we found people driven to convey their own distinctive meaning, in much the same way an artist might employ light, color, and shape or a musician might invoke pitch and rhythm to articulate something deeply personal and yet also profoundly universal.

PUTTING CRUCIBLES AT CENTER STAGE

In this book, I examine crucibles from several different angles as I search for answers to the challenging questions readers and leaders have raised. For example, what is life like inside a crucible? Is it possible to spot a crucible approaching or to divine when one has arrived? How do people make sense of their crucibles, much less learn from them? If, as we argued in *Geeks and Geezers*, adaptive capacity—or the ability to transcend adversity—is a defining quality of lifelong leaders, then is it possible for anyone to harness the power of experience? And finally, can organizations more effectively use crucible experiences to accelerate leader development?

A recurring point of comparison in this book will be between the crucibles experienced by organizational leaders and those experienced by men and women in other pursuits—for example, accomplished performers in the arts and athletics. While mindful that leading an organization is not the same as commanding a football team or choreographing a ballet, we will find a great deal to be gained from comparing the arc of learning and mastery that characterizes the careers of outstanding athletes, performing artists, and organizational leaders. In fact, my research provides valuable clues about expert performance and how it is the product of talent, experience (large and small, crucible and day-to-day), and disciplined practice.

HOW THIS BOOK IS ORGANIZED

I have organized this book around four major findings from the research I've done since the publication of *Geeks and Geezers*. First, that *crucibles contain two vital lessons, not just one*. Second, that *practice can trump talent*. Third, that *outstanding leaders—consciously or unconsciously—devise a personal strategy for recognizing and transforming crucible experiences into lessons that keep them refreshed and responsive*. And finally, that *organizations can grow more leaders—and grow them faster—by helping individuals learn from experience*.

The three parts of this book address those findings to varying degrees. Part I explores how effective leaders learn from experience. Therefore, chapter 2, Extracting Insight from Experience, reveals the first finding, that *crucibles contain two lessons*: one lesson is about *leadership* and the other is about *learning*. Leadership lessons, while intensely meaningful on a personal level, are usually idiosyncratic: most are fascinating, but what they teach is rarely profound except, of course, to the person who endured them. Lessons about learning, on the other hand, are more subtle *and* more powerful: they reveal flaws or, in some instances, hidden strengths in the way one deals with new, perhaps even disconfirming, information. When addressed in a disciplined way, lessons can accelerate learning in the future—not just in learning from crucibles, but in learning from everyday experiments.

For example, many people struggle with the question of whether they should trust instinct or rely solely on reasoning and empirical evidence. A college president I know struggled with just that dilemma when faced with the threat of a violent confrontation between student groups during the Vietnam War. In the end, rather than calling in the police, he listened to his inner voice and interceded with an unconventional proposition that diffused the situation.

Crucible stories like his provide rare glimpses into the way instinct operates—for example, how and why memory, freighted as it often is with strong emotions and associations, can activate gut-level responses, premonitory thoughts, and all the other trappings of instinct. Knowing that a sense of foreboding is intimately related to how one makes sense of the world can help tremendously when it comes to assessing how to read people and situations and make decisions—that is, all the things leaders are expected to do. More commonly, lessons about learning—for example, coming to understand that you only learn when your fear of learning is surpassed by your fear of the consequences of not learning—can encourage an individual to create conditions in the future that increase the odds of learning something new or to keep on learning despite all the traps (personal as well as structural) that might argue for relaxing on a bed of prior knowledge.

In chapter 3, Inside the Crucible, we go in search of clues as to why crucibles make some people better leaders and sap the energy and vitality from others. Along the way, we will see that crucibles vary in significant ways—not just in their magnitude but in the choices they present and the opportunities for learning they contain. Such insights help explain why some leaders will put themselves directly in the path of crucible experiences in order to enhance their likelihood of learning.

Chapter 4, Leaders as Expert Performers, offers examples from a growing body of research that corroborates the book's second major finding, that *practice can trump talent*, in leadership just as much as in sports and the performing arts. Without a doubt, talent matters. But the right kind and combination of ambition, instruction, and feedback can turn someone with modest talent into a viable competitor with so-called natural talents. In business as well as in the arts, outstanding performers are remarkably attentive to the opportunities for polishing basic skills—and testing new ones—that crop up in the midst of crucible experiences *and* day-to-day work. For them, the seam between practice and performance is invisible.

Part II shifts the focus to practice—that is, it translates ideas grounded in the research into positive actions that individuals can take to enhance their performance as leaders. Thus chapter 5, The Core of a Personal Learning Strategy, illuminates the book's third major finding, that *outstanding leaders—consciously or unconsciously—devise a personal strategy for recognizing and transforming crucible experiences into lessons that keep them refreshed and responsive* to the demands of a changing world. Paradoxically, although this personal strategy sets outstanding leaders apart from their peers, no one talks about it. It's a secret because for some, the competence is unconscious; they've incorporated it to the point that it's virtually impossible to articulate. For others, it's so much a part of their art, they rarely talk about it. However, it's possible to crack the code and put such a strategy within reach of every aspiring leader. This chapter, therefore, offers a practical, actionable guide to devising a Personal Learning Strategy (PLS).

Creating and applying a PLS begins with the examination of one's own crucible experiences, aspirations, and learning style and concludes with a rigorous plan to increase individual skill at learning from experience—from crucibles as well as everyday situations. Chapters 6 and 7, therefore, show how a PLS can create a bridge between an individual's unique experiences, aspirations, and learning styles (things that only he or she can truly know) and the skills (e.g., communication, evaluation, decision making, and the like) and competencies (which often vary by industry and culture) expected of those selected to move into key leadership roles. Drawing from our interviews with outstanding leaders who have been tested through years of practice, chapter 6, Exploring Your Capabilities, provides a set of structured self-assessments that enable individuals to get a better sense of their strengths and weaknesses in the qualities that distinguish outstanding leaders: adaptive capacity, engaging others, and integrity. Chapter 7, Creating Your Own Personal Learning Strategy, in turn offers a very practical format for organizing and documenting a PLS.

Part III delves into the fourth major finding of this book: that *organizations can grow more leaders—and grow them faster—by helping individuals learn from experience.* In other words, organizations have a vital supporting role to play in helping individuals develop their Personal Learning Strategies and making the most of their crucible experiences. Despite the fact that a PLS is, by its very nature, an individual obligation and crucibles are difficult to schedule, organizations *can* create events and relationships, prepare and support participants to make the most of what they offer, and help them embed the critical things they have learned into their lives. They needn't jettison traditional approaches, but they will need to reorient them.

Chapter 8, Experience-Based Leader Development, then, examines innovations in a number of organizations, including Toyota, General Electric, Accenture, and Boeing, intended to leverage experience to grow leaders. Finding those to be positive but partial solutions, I widen the focus to include organizations like the Massachusetts Institute of Technology's Leaders for Manufacturing program and Ford Motor Company's Virtual Factory, where more systemic solutions are being developed. But for insight into the way experience-based learning has been thoroughly integrated into organizational functioning—to such an extent that leader development is a fortuitous by-product—I examine an unlikely pair of organizations: the Church of Jesus Christ of Latter-day Saints (the Mormons) and the Hells Angels motorcycle gang. Distant though they may be from the mainstream of business (and certainly from each other), the Mormons and the Angels provide valuable clues as to how business and government might leverage experience to grow more leaders faster.

On that foundation, and incorporating the insights from research at the level of individuals, chapter 9, Invigorating the Practice of Leadership, proposes an original approach to leader development that leverages crucible experiences and establishes an important new role for senior management in the process of preparing, deploying, and renewing leaders. The goal of this concluding chapter is to show that it is both possible and essential for organizations to do more than just draft technical specifications for leaders in terms of competencies, courses, and criteria. Employers must also encourage individuals—or, at a minimum, those individuals who aspire to leadership—to craft Personal Learning Strategies and to use them as living documents or operating manuals, not something written once and forgotten.

Let's now take up the transformative experience of a crucible, first from the outside in and then from the inside out. A close examination from the outside in will reveal that not all crucibles are the same; they vary in texture, in duration, and, most importantly, in the lessons they offer. From the inside out—that is, from the perspective of the participant—we'll explore the experience of encountering and surmounting a crucible. Both perspectives are introduced in the following chapters, as part I continues.

[2]

EXTRACTING INSIGHT
FROM EXPERIENCE

To be thrown upon one's own resources is to be cast into the very lap
of fortune; for our faculties then undergo a development and
display an energy of which they were previously unsusceptible.

—Benjamin Franklin

PEOPLE WHO UNDERGO A CRUCIBLE and grow through the experience all share something vital: they don't become stuck. No matter how much they struggle, no matter how much they may grieve, and no matter how much they may chafe at finding themselves in situations they cannot immediately control, they are not paralyzed by difficult situations. Where others see chaos and confusion, they see opportunities to learn and grow.

This chapter explores the role of crucibles in the education of a leader and begins to examine the first of the four major findings from my recent research—specifically, that *crucibles contain two valuable lessons, not just one: lessons in leadership and lessons in learning.* Here we search for answers to core questions about how leaders learn, like What is life like inside a crucible? How do people make sense of their crucibles, much less learn from them? And perhaps most importantly, Can anyone harness the power of experience—or is that a reward reserved for a favored few?

I have already defined a crucible as a transformative experience through which an individual comes to a new or an altered sense of identity. But look closely at the crucible experience, and you will see distinctive contours and trajectories. Crucibles invariably rupture the status quo. Sometimes they sever a comfortable web of relationships, as in the case of war, insurrection, or terrorist attack. Sometimes they change a person's expectations dramatically and unpredictably, such as when a policeman is thrust into the role of wartime commander or when a consummate insider is expelled by her comrades. Other crucibles challenge an individual's identity, like the wrenching episodes of self-doubt occasioned by bankruptcy, loss of an election, or the death of a loved one. People experience crucibles most commonly as a profound tension or conflict between opposing forces.

Despite their differences, a powerful unifying theme emerges from close study of the variety of crucible stories: crucibles catalyze the process of learning *from experience*. Consider, for example, the following story from Major Joe Rupp, U.S. Marine Corps and a commander in Desert Storm.

Early in his career, Rupp took leave from the military to fulfill his missionary obligation to the Mormon church—where he would learn things about leading that he'd overlooked in officer candidate school (OCS). Assigned to a village in Mexico, he and a companion were making their rounds, meeting church members on a particularly hot day. "This was really unfamiliar territory to me," he recalled. "Despite having been through boot camp and OCS, I was basically still this kid from Utah." So when a village woman offered the young men some refreshing papaya water, they eagerly accepted. "She chopped that papaya up and threw it in a bucket of water and threw some sugar in there and gave it to us," Rupp said. "And I drank three glasses. I was thirsty and didn't want to offend anyone."

His politeness cost him dearly. He got a case of dysentery that made him drop twenty pounds within a week. He was so sick that at one point he asked his zone leader whether he could call his mother. "I'd been a Marine. I was strong," he recalled. "I knew all about going on a mission. And there I am in front of my zone leader crying. All I want to do is just call my mom because I feel absolutely miserable. But he said, 'No. I'm not going to let you call your mom. That's not why you're here. You didn't come here so you can get sick and feel sorry for yourself and call your mom. When Christ was here on earth, he suffered the same things that the people on earth suffered. And these type of infirmities are what these people down here deal with every day. This isn't about you. It's about them.'"

Rupp said his leader's words had such an effect on him that he wrote them down. "That situation taught me a great lesson: that I should not be so focused on myself and look at situations only as how they affect me."

While in OCS, Rupp had been advised repeatedly to put his people ahead of his own needs (and to avoid untreated water), but those lessons never really took root. That bout of dysentery put his view of himself into stark relief—in a way that classroom instruction and even Marine training couldn't. He "mattered," as he was reminded by his zone leader, but not in the way Rupp had thought: not at the center of the situation, but as a part of the situation. A mild rebuke, perhaps, and certainly not an earth-shattering experience, but it forced Rupp to both recognize and resolve a tension between his vision of himself and his role and the expectations that others had of him.

Later, as a helicopter pilot and commander in Desert Storm, he recalled his experience in that little Mexican town and counseled his peers as well as his direct reports about the importance of attending to the needs of the local population before grousing about the heat, dust, and sand. It is also important to note that Rupp, like many leaders we studied, did not go through his crucible alone. The lessons he learned were intensely personal, but in his case (and others I'll explore later), a teacher, a guide, a mentor, or a coach played an essential role in helping him sharpen his focus, to see what truly mattered in the situation he faced.

Crucible experiences like Rupp's teach something deep and enduring about how to behave (or how not to) in the face of real impairment and demoralization. In fact, my analysis of nearly two hundred crucible experiences pointed to three major types, each with its own unique signature. (See the box, "Crucibles in a Career Perspective.") Some involve encounters with the new or unknown, which I refer to as *new territory*. These crucibles *sharpen an individual's alertness to new information and his or her skill at sense making in the midst of confusion.* A second type of crucible involves loss, impairment, defeat, or failure of the kind that Rupp faced; I refer to this as *reversal*. Reversal teaches both *endurance and imagination.* Finally, there are the crucibles that involve an extended period of contemplation or deliberation, which I refer to as *suspension*. Suspension challenges a leader to *clarify his or her values and purpose in life.*

Crucibles in a Career Perspective

THE SAMPLE OF CRUCIBLE STORIES was assembled in the following way: (1) individuals were asked to identify an event or a relationship through which they learned something important about leadership or about themselves as leaders; (2) they were then asked to locate that event or relationship in time and space. The stories counted here were, for the most part, the first or the second story an individual offered. Reasoning that these stories are likely to be the most salient to that individual, I then tallied them by type and career stage.

While further testing of these results is clearly warranted, several interesting interpretations are possible, and as I will argue in later chapters, they have important implications for how individuals and organizations use crucible experiences for the purpose of leader development. Several observations are worth noting.

FIGURE 2-1

Crucible types throughout career stages

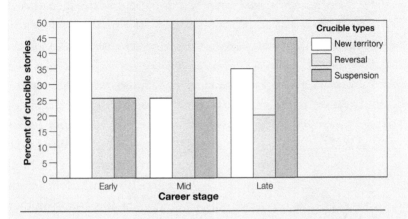

First, the association between crucible type and career stage is striking. That is, crucibles involving new territory were much more likely to occur in early career (even before one's entry into the labor market). This makes sense because one would expect new locales and relationships to be more frequent among people just starting out. The high frequency of stories about reversal among men and women at midcareer are also understandable. That is, they are more likely to have arrived at a position where mistakes, failures, or losses on the job and in relationships would be more consequential; more is at stake, in other words. Finally, the largest fragment of crucibles described by older, late-career leaders involved some sort of suspension or time-out from routine affairs. One possible explanation could have to do with the increased likelihood of voluntary or involuntary breaks caused by illness, unemployment, or job change.

Second, the more frequent experience of new territory among leaders at the beginning and toward the end of their careers suggests that they share something in common. In *Geeks and Geezers*, Warren Bennis and I drew attention to *neoteny*: a characteristic of older leaders who'd remained active and vital across eras and organizations. Neoteny, we argued, is the quality of retaining youthful habits and behaviors, like curiosity, and openness to experience, and surprise, well into one's later years. The collection of crucibles seems to suggest that those who continue to explore new territory as they age are likely to remain vital and active as leaders. This was borne out in the interviews with people like Walter Sondheim, John Wooden, Sidney Harman, Warren Bennis, and Frances Hesselbein, who recounted for us new territory crucibles they had experienced over the past ten years.

This restless urge to learn new things by being exposed to new territory, as we will see in the next chapter, is shared by performing artists who continue to excel even as they age.

All three types of crucible test an individual's adaptive capacity and resilience in the face of trying circumstances. Each crucible represents a different kind of problem, but what they share in common is a fundamental tension. Like a stretched rubber band, a crucible embodies potential energy—energy that can be released productively or unproductively. In the following sections, we'll consider examples of each type of crucible, first in the context of lessons they have to teach about *leadership* and then through the lens of lessons that each type has to teach about *learning*.

LESSONS ABOUT LEADERSHIP

Crucibles teach powerful leadership lessons. Repeatedly, the lessons people extract from their times of trial became touchstones they carry with them for the rest of their lives. Crucible stories are, in many respects, the raw material from which outstanding leaders derive their core qualities—that is, these are lessons about adapting and growing, about discovering new ways to engage or enroll others in a shared pursuit, and about recognizing the right thing to do and summoning the courage to do it.

Let's begin by looking at the kinds of leadership lessons that crucible experiences in new territory can foster.

New Territory

Being thrust into a new terrain—an overseas assignment, an unexpected turn of events in business or family life, a new social or
organizational role—carries with it a challenge not simply to survive
but also to prosper in unfamiliar soil. The challenge is to overcome
the disorientation and weave it into one's own experiential tapestry, rather than being consumed in the newness, confusion, and
deluge of foreign sensations. For many of the leaders with whom
we spoke, the crucible was a dividing line that, once crossed, forever heightened their alertness to the power of experience.

Consider the example of Patrick Mellon (not his real name),
an executive highly regarded for his track record as a leader of
corporate turnarounds. Over the course of nearly three decades
and in a dozen companies, he has earned a reputation as a tough-
as-nails negotiator who can stare down creditors, soothe anxious
investors, and rally the spirits and the energies of employees and
pensioners with the greatest personal stakes to lose.

When asked about a time in his life in which he learned something important about leadership, Mellon paused and took a breath
before describing an event that occurred when he was a teenager
pledging membership in a high school honor society. "They dropped
me in the woods in what had to be the darkest, the most isolated
corner of this huge forest," he began, "and they made me swear
on my mother's grave to not remove the blindfold until I could no
longer hear them. This was part of the test. If I could find my way
back to camp, I'd be accepted into the society." When Mellon finally removed the blindfold, he found himself in complete dark-
ness, in a place so pitch-black that he couldn't see the hand in front
of his face. "I didn't dare move because I couldn't tell if I was on
the edge of a cliff or at the bottom of a pit," he recalled.

That's when it hit him: he was utterly alone, in a way he'd
never been before in his fifteen years. "I started to shiver and
panic," he said. "I moaned out loud. I broke down and cried. It's
embarrassing to tell you this. Gone completely was the Eagle

Scout who had all these merit badges. I was totally, completely panicked and sure that I would never find my way back to camp, that I would be lost there, fall off a cliff, break my leg . . . or worse, that they would have to mount a search and it would be on TV and I would be embarrassed beyond belief."

After about two hours, Mellon recalled, he finally calmed down. "It was like one half of me—the rational half—had to talk the other, irrational half through a crisis. I'd never had to calm myself like that before." That night he learned two important things about himself, he said: that he is capable of panic—and of leading himself out of panic.

Still, the fact that he's capable of panic is why he preferred to use a pseudonym for his interview: for fear that his direct reports might lose confidence in him. Today when he starts to feel panic coming on, he said he stops and takes a few deep breaths. "And I recall what I learned when I was 15. I walk myself mentally back through situations where I've faced that kind of stress and uncertainty before. And I recall what I did to sort things out, how I behaved, how I enlisted other people to help me, and how we created a solution where it didn't look like one was possible."

Given that Mellon was in the midst of a difficult turnaround assignment at the time of our interview, his choice of crucibles to relate was probably not coincidental. But in that story, he revealed how he had transformed his own sense of weakness and shame—a profound tension between the way he'd always thought about himself and the young man immobilized by fear in that dark corner of a forest—into a strategy for managing himself and others around him in times of distress bordering on panic.

But what real impact did Mellon's experience have on his later behavior as a leader? He said, "It made me a more compassionate leader. Up until that time, I'd never met a challenge I couldn't take on and beat. But here was a situation where the stakes turned out to be much, much higher than I'd ever faced before. I just suddenly realized that this was real—not an exercise, not a classroom test, not me scampering down a rock wall with a belay rope there to save my ass if I did something stupid. There was no walking away." He understood for the first time what it meant to be face-to-face with forces he couldn't control. As a leader today, Mellon said, that experience as a teenager later helped him understand how people, from executives to blue-collar workers, feel when higher-ups make a radical change that affects their lives.

"I realized something about the panic that other people must feel when things just suddenly fall apart—like losing your job or seeing your pension evaporate. I learned that panic can be real, that I could experience it, and that fortunately I could also work my way out of it. And so could other people," Mellon said. "It's a truth I've tried to pass along to the people I mentor."

His memory of that crucible—and the way he resolved the tension and he drew himself out of it—have enabled him to cope with the vexing, contentious, and worrisome situations that beset an organization or a community in crisis, situations he faced dozens of times over the years. Indeed, that night in the woods alerted him to the learning opportunities that are so often deeply embedded in crisis.

Another leader whose crucible experience involved new territory was Ling Yun Shao, a sergeant in the U.S. Army Reserve. Shao, named by a leading women's magazine as one of the top ten women leaders in U.S. colleges, initially applied for an ROTC scholarship in order to pay for college. However, after a year of what she dismissed as "simulated soldiering," she enlisted in the regular army and went through basic training. As it was for the millions of men and women who preceded her, boot camp was an eye-opener for Shao. Even though she learned a great deal about American diversity (having grown up in a fairly sheltered suburban environment after her parents emigrated from China), the leadership crucible she nominated as most influential in her life occurred in her first assignment.

Trained as a medic but aspiring to be a doctor, Shao found herself thrust into a netherworld between hurricane relief and military "police action" when, in the wake of Hurricane Mitch, she was dispatched to a field hospital on the border between El Salvador and Nicaragua—which was considered a hostile-fire zone.

She recalled, "I was supposed to have an officer who ran a battalion aid station. But the day before we left, she got sick, so for the time I was there I was left to run the battalion aid station alone. And it was the best leadership experience I've ever had." Although she didn't do any highly skilled medical procedures, she felt she helped people take care of themselves.

"All I had was bandages and ointments, but I felt like I had made this enormous difference," she said. "And these people lined up for literally a mile outside of the base, just to come in and have someone look at their wound."

Providing care, solving problems, and mobilizing people to do great things with limited resources emerged for Shao to be a compelling definition of what it meant to be a leader—especially when contrasted with the nightmare of insurance forms and bureaucratic regulation she knew to be the norm in U.S. medical care. The experience of doing familiar things in an unfamiliar territory opened her eyes to the tension between the results she truly wanted to achieve and the limits of conventional practice in the U.S. medical establishment. Shao therefore reset her sights: her goal after gaining her medical degree is to establish a clinic in South Boston for immigrants who lack insurance but who are, in her words, "contributing members to society."

A crucible experience in new territory both demands and teaches an almost preternatural alertness. It encourages an openness to signals and guidance, often from unanticipated sources, that makes it possible over time to get more skilled at detecting impending traps and diversions. See table 2-1 for more leadership lessons drawn from interviews about crucible experiences in new territory.

Reversal

The loss of a loved one, a divorce, bankruptcy, or failure in a major assignment can be profoundly disruptive and disconfirming. At its core is another form of tension: something thought to be permanent turns out to be transient, or something believed to be

TABLE 2-1

New territory: lessons about leadership*

- Don't assume anything about a situation; you'll likely be wrong if you rely on your first impression.
- Leaders need to ask questions as often as they give answers.
- Be aware of the lenses you bring to a situation; a leader needs to question himself or herself.
- Learn to rely on others; a leader needs to be able to trust other people.
- When you're new to a leadership situation, find common ground by telling stories and getting people to share theirs.
- Remember that sometimes events can conspire to make you a leader.

*These lessons were extracted from interviews.

true turns out to be false. A reversal can bring a leader to understand her situation in a fundamentally new—and more comprehensive—way.

Case in point: Jeff Wilke, senior vice president of online retailer Amazon.com and widely regarded for his rare combination of being both people savvy and numbers driven, recalled a major reversal that became a turning point in his education as a leader: at a chemical plant where he worked before joining Amazon.com, one of his employees died on the job. He said he went through a lot of soul-searching. "How could this happen? Who's responsible? Or are we in some way responsible?" he wondered. "You start to question all these things. And to go to the town, to meet his widow, to speak at the plant, to spend a week with these folks and to understand their pain and to try to help them through what's happened. It's a transformational experience. So you can convince yourself in an industrial environment that leadership is about making money, making the quarter—and at the end of the day you get to go home to your nice cushy urban or suburban life style. But in the end it's all these lives that are all wrapped up together, and every so often an event happens that isn't just about whether we made the quarter. It hits you square in the face."

Though Wilke had always prided himself on his analytical skills, he recognized that he and his coworkers faced events that could not be resolved through detached calculation. There was a profound tension induced by the need to reconcile two very different modes of thinking and behaving. Within weeks he began to notice a profound change in the way he thought about his job: "I was no longer willing to focus on the business as detached from everything else that happened along with it. I began to give myself permission to have emotion about my work. At the end of the day leadership is about people, and you can't separate their lives from their work or your work."

The ability to find meaning and strength in adversity distinguishes leaders from nonleaders. When terrible things happen, less-able people feel singled out, powerless, even victimized. Leaders find purpose and resolve. The experience of reversal, like Wilke's, challenges the individual to transcend narrow self-regard and reflect on the self in relation to others. Reversals are often places where one becomes intensely aware of his or her connectedness. Above all, they are experiences from which one extracts meaning that leads to new definitions of self and new competencies that better prepare one for the next crucible.

Sometimes the tension at the core of reversal is not loss or failure, but profound disconfirmation, even contradiction. Consider a story from Edwin Guthman, now professor emeritus at the University of Southern California's Annenberg School of Communications, and widely acclaimed for both his reporting at the *Seattle Times* (where he won a Pulitzer Prize) and his leadership as national editor at the *Los Angeles Times* and the *Philadelphia Inquirer*. He was working as a press secretary for Attorney General Robert F. Kennedy in the early 1960s when he had his crucible experience that taught him something important about leadership.

The time was September 1962, and the place was Oxford, Mississippi, on the campus of the University of Mississippi. Guthman was stationed by a pay phone along with other Justice Department officials in a campus building while an angry and armed crowd threatened to riot in opposition to the registration of

James Meredith, a young black man, at the university. According to Guthman, "There were about 300 marshals and five or six of us from the [Justice] Department. And we are besieged by a mob of a couple thousand people. And we have tear gas and we're armed and we're able to hold off the mob, although ultimately 29 of the marshals are wounded by gunfire. The injured are laying on the floor of the Lyceum Building. And there's an Army division on its way down from Memphis."

That's when he and other members of his group decided it was time to ask permission to use their weapons. Deputy Attorney General Nick Katzenbach made the call to Robert Kennedy. The answer? An unequivocal "No!" Guthman recalled, "And there's a discussion about this. We're really pissed off because we think we're going to get killed!" Most of all, Guthman himself felt outraged that Kennedy, this young thirty-five-year-old attorney general—with no previous military experience, at that—was leaving his own staff people in such a vulnerable position.

But of course none of them were killed, and a few hours later the army showed up and things quieted down. Later, the group involved met in the Justice Department to critique how they'd handled that situation. They realized that if Robert Kennedy had given them permission to fire, it would have been an utter disaster. "Imagine if we'd fired into this mob!" said Guthman. He and his colleagues met several times in subsequent days, on their own and with no prompting from Kennedy, to try to understand how they got to a point where they were urging the attorney general to take arms against fellow citizens.

That painful and in many ways embarrassing process of reflection proved fateful to Guthman. Despite his initial anger at Kennedy—an anger fueled as much by Kennedy's youth and lack of military experience as by Guthman's fear of impending harm—Guthman volunteered Kennedy's decision as a powerful influence on his behavior as a leader in years to come. In his words: "We realized how important that decision was, but we also realized that we had made some mistakes . . . Looking back, I've often learned from this. When something happens, go in and try to figure it out, not to blame somebody, but so you don't make the same mistakes. You should always take the time to confront the problem; face up to it."

It was a powerful lesson about the need to recognize the tension between personal ego and the welfare of others that can accompany high-stakes decision making. Guthman's resolve as a leader to think decisions through and to ask the tough questions of himself and the people who worked for him was tested several times over the course of his career. For example, when the *Philadelphia Inquirer* published an editorial criticizing Israel's invasion of Lebanon, and Guthman and his staff were roundly chastised for their position, he spent weeks meeting with Jewish organizations in his own investigation to determine whether the paper had made the right decision.

Reversal tests both wherewithal and imagination. It stretches to the limits an individual's self-confidence. At the same time, reversal sharpens the ability to see beyond or through bleak circumstances to another set of outcomes. Reversal teaches leaders the power of optimism and the courage to reflect honestly on one's own shortcomings. See table 2-2 for more examples of leadership lessons learned through reversal.

TABLE 2-2

Reversal: lessons about leadership*

- Leaders need to remember the importance of interdependence—that life is not just about the business; an organization is a community of human beings.
- Leaders need to care about interpersonal relationships and be willing to be cared about.
- A leader doesn't have to be superhuman or have all the answers, no matter how much people may wish it to be so.
- Failing is only a step on the path to success.
- Trouble doesn't last forever.
- Know what you stand for as a leader before crisis hits; when things are crashing down around you and people are looking for your leadership, it's too late to figure things out.
- Integrity is the only thing you have that's truly yours.

* These lessons were extracted from interviews.

Suspension

Crucibles of this type involve a hiatus, often one that is unanticipated, during which a well-known set of behaviors and routines is
set aside, sometimes forcibly, and replaced with a regimented
structure or no structure at all. Suspension has at its core a tension between realities—old and new, immediate and indeterminate,
comforting and uncomfortable—and with that tension an opportunity for both exploration and reflection. College, prolonged unemployment, and jail time can be crucibles, particularly as they
afford time and space to explore other possible selves and lifestyles.
The same can also be said for entry into more severely structured
settings—"total institutions" like a boot camp or a convent—that
demand a wholesale change in identity.[1]

Suspension challenges leaders to clarify—or, in some instances,
to create—their personal mission and purpose; to cement their own
personal foundation of beliefs and values.

Ali Omar, a captain in the Palestinian security forces who had
been active in the Fatah branch of the Palestinian National Liber-
ation Movement since the age of fifteen, recalled a time in the
heat of battle and its aftermath when he realized that he could be
imperfect and yet still be an effective leader. From an early age, he
had looked to the commanders under whom he served for his
models of leadership. One leader in particular, the acting commander of a major city force, had a profound effect on him. "He
had joined the forces after the Israeli occupation of the West
Bank," Omar recalled. "I believed that he knew everything, that
he had the answer to all questions, the solution to all the problems, and the knowledge to lead us in critical situations."

At a decisive juncture, however, this commander faltered—
hesitating and looking confused—leaving Omar and his comrades to their own devices. With the commander unable to lead
them, Omar suddenly found himself in charge of leading a group
of men to defend a neighborhood. "[The commander] sent me a
message saying simply that I had to depend on myself and to stop
sending correspondents asking for orders," he said. "I recognized

then how difficult it is to be a leader, especially when defending a city and protecting civilians and trying to give the right orders to the soldiers without making a mistake that I would regret to the last day in my life."

Importantly, the order for Omar to make his own decisions came not from a commander too busy to attend to the pestering of an underling; it came from a man who had suddenly lost his will to lead, who had withdrawn into a shell from which pleas could not extract him.

Captain Omar described the feeling as a "slap in the face," akin to being rejected by a father figure. Even worse, this father figure had revealed himself to be a coward, afraid, self-absorbed, and completely without regard for those in his charge. Omar felt acute pain in those moments. He felt both empathy for and fury toward his commander. He questioned his own ability to lead but would not walk away from his men. He concluded, "I learnt from this great experience that nothing can change the fact that all of us are human beings who may make mistakes any moment that can cause a lot of losses. But a man can also take the risk and act in an unexpected way and develop himself to a certain level where he surprises everybody, including himself. And I think this is what happened to me."

Among other things, Omar decided in the wake of that crucible to dedicate himself to something he'd never considered possible previously: to become an active participant in the process of creating a viable Palestinian state and to help secure its place in the international community through diplomatic service.

Suspension challenges individuals to create structures, first for themselves and then, potentially, for others. By snatching people out of a familiar web of relationships that appear self-sealed and lasting and inserting them into what can feel like free fall, suspension calls forth the ability to impose meaningful rules on oneself—to create a foundation of values and meaning on which to stand and then perhaps to extend that foundation into organizing principles for one's life, one's pursuits, and one's relationships. Table 2-3 offers further examples of leadership lessons learned through the experience of suspension.

TABLE 2-3

Suspension: lessons about leadership*

- It is crucial for you, as a leader, to have a purpose or mission; people respond to your earnestness and authenticity as much as to your logic.
- Leaders need to be at peace with themselves before they can ask others to be peaceful; leaders need to be clear about what they value if they expect others to be driven by their values.
- Leaders don't need to be bulletproof: although it's scary not to have all the answers, it can help engage others in the decision-making process.
- Leaders need to roll with the punches and be ready to acknowledge when they're wrong.

*These lessons were extracted from interviews.

Each story just recounted about crucibles involving new territory, reversal, and suspension had at its core a tension, a kind of potential energy, that demanded a behavior or maybe an answer that either did not exist previously or went unrecognized. Although some of the lessons in leadership learned from these crucible experiences may not seem particularly new or noteworthy, the manner in which these leaders recounted them was dramatic indeed—and therein lies a key aspect of effective leadership.

As the scholar Noel Tichy argues, leaders must be teachers— and the leaders in this chapter offer precisely what Tichy calls a "teachable point of view."[2] He argues that leaders' responsibility is not only to provide direction or judgment in the moment, but to strive continuously to develop leadership in others, now and into the future. Stories, especially stories of trial and transcendence, provide a foundation for a teachable point of view. They provide the grit and detail, the suspense, and the credibility that turns what might otherwise sound like a homily into something that screenwriter Robert McKee once termed "advice with substance."[3]

Let's turn now to the lessons that each of the three types of crucibles have to teach about learning itself.

LESSONS ABOUT LEARNING

Although leadership lessons gained from crucible experiences are valuable enough in themselves, crucibles go a step further to offer lessons in learning as well: the subtext to virtually every crucible story reveals the conditions associated with gaining new, useful knowledge. The men and women who recounted their stories in this chapter, then, also gained deep insights *about how they learn*—about what it takes for them as capable and accomplished people to learn new things, to resolve the tensions inherent in a crucible, and to raise the level of their performance. They each described a powerful flywheel effect: once alerted to what it takes to draw insight from experience, they began seeing learning opportunities all around them.

Lessons about learning are arguably *more valuable* than leadership lessons, per se, because learning is what enables an individual to grow and adapt to changing circumstances. Indeed, lessons about learning make it possible to even recognize that circumstances are changing, that adaptation is needed, and that growth is possible. Liken it to the difference between a novice and an expert in virtually any artistic or athletic domain (a theme to which we return in the next chapter): a neophyte delights in accidentally executing a difficult move, be it a dance step, a chess maneuver, or a tricky approach shot in golf; but an expert appreciates the combination of skill and practice it takes to execute consistently and notices the learning opportunity in even the most elegant and seemingly flawless move. Learning about learning makes it possible to take control of one's education, to learn better and faster, and to adapt and grow across time, across circumstances, and across organizations.[4]

Lessons about learning often had to be teased out of offhand remarks, such as Bob Galvin's comment (from the example in chapter 1) about the encouragement he received from a factory foreman.[5] Sometimes these lessons are overlooked or taken for granted—but that doesn't mean they're not critically valuable. Some leaders, like performers in other domains, are unconsciously competent. They literally cannot describe what they do when they lead or how they learned to do it. That doesn't make them less effective or less likely to learn from experience. However, those who are aware of how they learn—and learn best or most deeply and durably—seem to learn with greater economy and speed. They are also better at explaining what they know to apprentices and protégés, meaning that they are likely to leave *more* leaders in their wake. Their conscious competence does not slow them down or render them paralyzed by self-analysis. In fact, it enhances their ability to spot learning needs and opportunities in themselves and in others.

How does learning about learning manifest itself? In my interviews and in discussions with leaders about crucibles, I would ask not only what they learned but *how* they learned it. I asked, "What made it possible for you to learn what you learned? If I were to change one thing about your story that would have made it ordinary, what would that be?"

Answers to those questions yielded valuable and sometimes surprising clues as to how some leaders learn from experience. Most importantly, learning from crucibles (and, I'll later argue, learning from any experience) tended to occur when the individual could identify a connection among three things: their personal *aspirations* (i.e., what they pictured as their best or ideal self), their *motivations* (what they most deeply valued), and their *learning style* (how they learned best or most effectively).[6]

For example, Jeff Wilke earlier recounted the epiphany that occurred to him with the tragic loss of an employee at a plant he managed. He described it as an insight about the connectedness among people that a leader needs to comprehend, honor, and support. He also talked about the insight that crucible had teased out of him *about himself*—how he needed to more effectively resolve the tension between the emotional aspects of work (and himself) and the analytical. When pressed to "go deeper" and explore the conditions surrounding that learning, he began to talk about the importance of being out of his comfort zone, to be confronted with facts and with feelings that were unfamiliar, and to acknowledge that the whole package—situation, resources, emotions—created an opening for better understanding the world and himself.

Ling Yun Shao's experience as a medic in El Salvador clarified her self-perception. Moreover, in comparing her role in that village with what she knew she'd do as a doctor in an American hospital, Shao got a rare glimpse into both her core motivations (healing, not prestige) and her preferred learning style (hands-on, interactive, kinesthetic).

Sidney Harman, founder of Harman International (previously Harman-Kardon) and former deputy secretary of commerce about whom Warren Bennis and I wrote at length in *Geeks and Geezers*, talked about two important insights he had regarding his own learning style. First, he believed that through his daily journal entries, he could literally see what was on his mind: what questions he needed to answer and what answers were forming. (Brandeis University president Jehuda Reinharz and legendary UCLA basketball coach John Wooden also told me that writing helped clarify their own learning.) Second, Harman claimed that by spending time with masters in a given field—working alongside them, interviewing them as a journalist or historian might—he "borrowed energy" from their passion and depth of understanding to aid him in gaining insight into that field quickly and effectively. For example, in order to deepen his understanding of what jazz trumpeter Wynton Marsalis wanted his horn to sound like when reproduced by Harman-Kardon stereo equipment, Harman studied and questioned Marsalis the way a music critic might.

But how do the seeds for such lessons about learning come about in the first place—and how does a leader learn to recognize and cultivate them? Engaging in what I call a *Personal Learning Strategy* is key.

The Personal Learning Strategy

The ability to recognize the tension at the core of a crucible and to convert the energy of a crucible to productive uses through awareness of one's own aspirations, motivations, and learning style—these represent the foundation of a Personal Learning Strategy. Such a strategy enables two things: (1) it guides an individual in identifying learning needs and opportunities, and (2) it provides insights about what conditions, resources, and supports are most likely to result in improved performance.

For some leaders, the interviews I conducted about crucible experiences turned into explorations of the contours of the individual's Personal Learning Strategy: what an individual might have described as "restlessness" or "entrepreneurial spirit" would, on closer inspection, reveal an intuitive self-understanding that learning can be either pleasant or unpleasant but that it most likely occurs under fairly specific circumstances. For example, Bill Porter, founder of the first completely online brokerage, E*TRADE, prided himself on the "problem-finding" skills he applied with as much gusto to organization building as he did to helping develop satellite stabilizers, measurement devices, and electronic exchanges.

In other instances, the people interviewed clearly recognized how they learned best—and they routinely engaged that knowledge as a guide for their next project or assignment or personal challenge. Sometimes, as in the case of former SEC chair Arthur Levitt Jr., they became seekers of crucibles, constantly looking for the kinds of challenges that would stretch them. In a career of more than fifty years, Levitt served in the air force, was both a cattle rancher and an editor at *Look*, and served, under President Clinton, as chairman of the U.S. Securities and Exchange Commission. "What I believe is important in life is to keep as many doors open as possible," Levitt explained. "You close a door when you fall in love with a community and say you won't move. I'll move any place. I couldn't care less where. And I think that's important. You re-pot yourself."

A Personal Learning Strategy, then, is an individualized routine or recipe for learning, with a special quality to it: its function is to challenge other routines—that is, to uncover patterns of activity that can, through repeated use, become habitual, stagnant, resistant to change, obsolete, ineffective, and, ultimately, destructive. The ability to *engage* this unique routine is nearly as important as the routine itself. The same attentiveness to situations that enables some people to spot trends, to see market opportunities, or to discern openings for negotiating through an impasse gets applied *internally*. The same resolve to act that propels an organization to move when an opportunity is spotted gets applied to the self. Warren Bennis, interviewed about his experience as a university president, talked about learning as a spark of insight, sometimes a "premonition about what I need to do or to be in order to avoid getting mired in habit." People attuned to learning are what Saul Bellow once described as "first-class noticers"—not just of the world, but of themselves, too.

On the other hand, a Personal Learning Strategy is not just the state of self-awareness or situational awareness described in recent writings as "emotional intelligence." Those qualities are real and important, but they do not quite capture the potential of a Personal Learning Strategy: the potential it contains for propelling an individual, a leader, forward into situations and relationships that will cause him or her to put to the test enduring, but potentially obsolete, ideas and behaviors, or to encounter things (relationships, cultures, technologies, and worldviews) that are not only unfamiliar but potentially antagonistic to a comfortable current reality.

But how exactly do Personal Learning Strategies connect to crucible experiences? On one level, crucibles are quite often the catalyst not only to learning important things about leadership but also to insights about learning—about the conditions and resources in and through which learning is most likely to occur. At another level, once a person recognizes his or her Personal Learning Strategy, that strategy can guide the individual to detect the need for challenge and learning, for growth and adaptation, and for situations in which they are possible. A Personal Learning Strategy leads, perhaps inevitably, to future crucibles.

A Personal Learning Strategy can also alert one to learning opportunities that are far less special (or extreme) than the crucibles we've been describing to this point. It can enhance a person's alertness to the myriad opportunities for learning that occur in everyday life—opportunities for conscious experimentation and testing in real time. Mellon, the turnaround specialist who earlier described how panic had taught him to calm himself and others, explained it this way:

> *Whether I am at the podium at an investor conference, with all these razor-sharp analysts trying to reveal some hidden weakness, or in a small group with a bunch of junior people who want desperately to believe that we're going in the right direction and that somebody—anybody—has a plan they can trust, I feel like I'm on stage and I've got to perform. I've got to project confidence even when I'm unsure. I've got to truly believe that what I am asking people to do is possible, that it's going to lead to results we want and need. I'm acting— for sure—but I'm not pretending. I am walking a tightrope with all the confidence of a professional, knowing fully well that if I fall I'm in serious trouble, but never looking down. That's the work of leading.*

How did Mellon get to a point where he felt confident in his ability to perform? "It takes practice," he said. "I've learned a lot from experience and reflecting on that experience."

The ability to experiment in real time is not exclusively a product of crucible experiences. It is an ability, however, that seems unusually common among leaders who have had a crucible experience that caused them to reflect on their own Personal Learning Strategy. Once aware of the way they learned from experience, they saw opportunities for learning all around them. Not unlike stage actors repeating their performance of a particular play, they could be "in role" but still able to improvise in tone or emphasis and thus to judge the reaction of the audience or their fellow actors. Not unlike martial artists Bruce Lee or Jackie Chan, who perform exquisitely complicated bodily contortions with speed and grace, these leaders are intensely aware of themselves and their surroundings even as they seem to observers to be a blur of motion. And not unlike consummate musicians who tune themselves and their instruments in midperformance, these leaders demonstrate that they can *practice while they perform.*

Table 2-4 lists more lessons on learning extracted from interviews about crucible experiences. Notice as you read through them the very individual and yet practical quality to the lessons people gained from a wide variety of experiences.

One thing that came across during the interviews for this book is that many, if not all, of these leaders are what I call "egoless" learners. They are constantly in search of new ideas and new

TABLE 2-4

Lessons about learning

Crucible type	Lessons about learning*
New territory	• Leaders learn through tests and challenging situations—not from things with which they're already familiar.
	• Leaders learn best when out of their comfort zones and forced to try on new behaviors.
	• Leaders learn best from the best: search out the leading practitioners, and try to find out both what they do that's different and what they can teach you about the inner game.
	• Everything is theoretical until you've been there. Seek out new places and experiences to build a stockpile of examples.
Reversal	• Face your fears: rather than sidestep or delay, address your deepest worries and concerns directly; then gather yourself up to move on.
	• Recognize that panic often precedes learning—and that calm often comes after panic.
	• Don't fail to learn from failing.
	• While not endangering yourself, sometimes it's good to put yourself to the test.
	• Be willing to fail in order to learn.
Suspension	• Practice before you preach: take the time to practice a new skill or behavior alone—in quiet and without fanfare—before you take it public.
	• Learn to use every moment to reflect; i.e., if you take a deep breath or meditate, you can engage in short but relaxing bursts of creative thought.
	• Recognize that there are times, like being fired or laid off, when you may get an unexpected opportunity to think, to sort out your priorities, and to explore what you could be—rather than being shackled to who you *were*.

*These lessons were extracted from interviews.

ways of thinking about and solving perennial problems. Like trapeze artists, they let go in order to move forward—even when they're uncertain that the swing will be there to catch hold of at the precise moment it's needed. Calling them egoless doesn't mean they don't have egos—not by a stretch. Rather, it means that they refuse to let what they know get in the way of learning new things. Morgan McCall underscored this point in his study of successful executives: "[They] took responsibility for their own learning. Instead of denying critical feedback that hurt, they swallowed their pride and took it to heart. Instead of blaming everything on an intolerable boss, they dug out messages for themselves. Instead of dismissing other people because they were too old or too young or too abrasive or too soft or too different, they adopted the attitude that you can learn something from everyone."[7]

Experiences, crucible experiences most profoundly, may provide the opportunity and the reason to learn, but, like a horse drawn to water, individuals won't learn from experience if they are not prepared to learn. Thus, a crucial precondition for mining experience for insight is awareness of what it takes to learn. To understand how people achieve this awareness and how the flywheel of learning starts to move, we must venture deeper into what goes on inside a crucible—the topic of the next chapter.

$$\begin{bmatrix} 3 \end{bmatrix}$$

INSIDE THE CRUCIBLE

Learning and Leading with Resilience

Success is how high you bounce when you hit the bottom.

—General George S. Patton

I N HIS SHORT STORY "A Descent into the Maelstrom," Edgar Allan Poe offers a marvelous literary evocation of life inside a crucible.[1] The story's narrator, one of three brothers who achieved success as fishermen by sailing through waters made treacherous by a periodic whirlpool or maelstrom, tells of a fateful day when he lost track of the time and tides and his ship was sucked into the circling waters. In the clamor and rush of water pulling the boat to the ocean floor, he confesses that he fell into the grip of an overpowering panic. In the moment of greatest confusion, however, with the sky narrowing above him, he was suddenly enveloped in an unearthly calm, a revelation that everything was beyond his control. No matter what he did, it seemed he was going to die. And in those minutes of calm, he let loose his death grip on one reality and recognized another.

The noise and the fog that had impaired his senses receded. He stepped outside the part of him that had panicked and saw with astonishing clarity that some debris caught up in the whirlpool wasn't descending as fast as his ship. In fact, some empty barrels seemed to hang suspended above him as he and the ship sank deeper and deeper. He realized that if the barrels hung there long enough, they might escape being pulled to the bottom altogether. His chance for salvation was to lash himself to a barrel and step off the ship. He did, and he survived.

Like Poe's protagonist, most people I interview recalled life inside a crucible as a time of turbulence and profound tension—sometimes depressing, sometimes giddy, sometimes chaotic, sometimes all three. Wendy Kopp, founder of Teach For America, described how, as a college senior struggling to define a thesis topic, she descended into a "funk that I had never been in before and will hopefully never be in again." She emerged out of it with the idea of a national teacher corps. Tara Church, who founded a nationwide conservation organization, told of her inner struggle as an eight-year-old when she realized that drought robbed trees of their sustenance—but that activities aimed to save water (like using disposable paper plates) consumed trees. The seeming contradiction between conservation and destruction puzzled and then terrified her as a child. Would humans have to live underground if there were no trees and water? she wondered. Out of that nightmare came an organization she formed as a child (with help from her mother) made up of children who planted trees.

Leaders I spoke with also experienced their time inside the crucible as a seemingly intractable double bind. They often looked back in wonder that they survived the turmoil at all. Some spoke ruefully (and occasionally with embarrassment) about how long it took them to see and understand what they'd actually been through. But the lessons they recounted were as immediate as if they had occurred just days before.

Even when they dismissed their survival as so much luck or good fortune, each person said their crucibles invoked as well as strengthened something crucial: their adaptive capacity. Adaptive capacity is all about learning—about oneself, about the world, and about what it takes to adjust to, and make, change. Adaptive capacity is what makes it possible to live with the doubt that accompanies a double bind, to open up to possibilities rather than shutting down and retreating.

Defensive reactions like tensing up, on the other hand, as Richard Boyatzis and Annie McKee remind us in *Resonant Leadership*, can increase vulnerability. Such reactions make it difficult to flex—to sidestep an attacker or to see an opportunity for escape, for example—and, worse yet, they dissipate energy rather than unleash it.[2] "Fight or flight" may be an instinct rooted in a part of the brain evolved over tens of thousands of years of survival in the wild, but the ability to learn—and to learn quickly—is an essential part of successful adaptation to the challenges of living in human society, especially in the twenty-first century.

Resilience, a central facet of adaptive capacity, makes it possible for leaders to find calm in the face of tension and to begin the search for answers. According to psychologist Frederic Flach, resilience is about resolving the tension between opposing forces: "Each period of change is necessarily stressful, for it involves conflict between a powerful force that operates to keep things exactly as they've been, and another powerful force that commands us to move forward and embrace new conditions."[3] (See the box, "Resilience: Inner Strengths and Interpersonal Strengths.")

Resilience: Inner Strengths and Interpersonal Strengths

Inner Strengths

Two sources of strength—internal and interpersonal—make resilience possible.[a]

- A strong, supple sense of self-esteem

- A high level of personal discipline and a sense of responsibility

(continued)

- Recognition and development of one's special gifts and talents

- Creativity: open-mindedness, receptivity to new ideas, willingness to dream

- A wide range of interests

- A keen sense of humor

- High tolerance for distress

- Focus and a commitment to life

- Faith: a philosophical and spiritual framework within which personal experiences can be interpreted and understood with meaning and hope, even at life's seemingly most helpless moments

Interpersonal Strengths

- Independence of thought and action, without being unduly reluctant to rely on others

- The ability to give and take in human interactions

- A well-established network of family and friends, including one or more who serve as confidants

- The willingness and skill to let go of resentments and forgive others as well as oneself

- Proficiency in setting limits

- Healthy self-interest

- Freedom from one's own selfishness and protection against the selfishness of others

- Generosity

- The ability to easily give and receive love

a. Adapted from Frederic Flach, *Resilience: Discovering a New Strength at Times of Stress* (Long Island City, NY: Hatherleigh Press, 2004).

My interviews about crucibles and their lessons—especially the lessons people learned about learning—suggest that resilience is perhaps better understood as a process rather than an inherited trait. In other words, while resilience may be innate to some individuals, it can also be practiced much like a deliberate sequence of moves or enacted like a diagnostic routine. As I'll show in more detail later in this book, that kind of practice is vital to an individual's Personal Learning Strategy.

Resilience manifested itself in different moments in leaders' crucible stories. The following examples illustrate three key moments in the process of resilience: recognizing the tension (sometimes even the pain) that accompanies a crucible, reframing the tension as something knowable and manageable, and resolving the tension constructively.[4]

RECOGNIZING THE TENSION

Muriel Siebert, founder of Siebert Financial and the first woman to own a seat on the New York Stock Exchange, came to New York in the 1950s after her father died broke from three years of illness. She marveled at the money she was making: $12,500 a year. But after several years of work and despite distinguishing herself as the lead airlines analyst in the NYSE Analysts Society, she was refused the title of "trader" and was denied the commissions routinely due to someone who dealt in blocks of stock the way she did.

She remembers, "I was a partner of a small firm, Finkel & Co., because I could not get hired by a large firm and get credit on the business. They did not have women. We just were not there. They had women as secretaries; sometimes they had an analyst or two; but we were secretaries. This was a period of time that was not nice on Wall Street." When she realized that the men in her firm were being paid twice her wages, she sent her résumé to every firm downtown—but didn't get a single bite. It wasn't until the Analysts Society sent around her résumé with only her initials on it (rather than her full name) that she got an interview at a major brokerage house—and she got the job.

Still, she continued to earn only a fraction of the proper commission on her sales. She recalled in vivid detail the conflict she felt between her pride at making a sale and the deep-seated inequity she experienced. "When I learned how to trade and put the blocks together, that changed everything," she said. "One day, the Madison Fund gave me a 10,000 share order. And I went to my boss, and I said, 'Isn't this great?' And he looked at me and said, 'That's shit!' We didn't have negotiated rates, so I think the commission was maybe $4,000, but I made only $1,600 that day. On one hand, I thought I was doing well. That was a good month's pay. On the other hand, I was being cheated. I had to decide what I was going to do about it."

Siebert thought long and hard about her double bind: the inequity of her situation was maddening, but the risk of starting her own firm and thus deftly sidestepping the game rigged against her was enormous. Not only could she fail, but she could thoroughly alienate herself from future employers who would always question her allegiance. In the end, she chose to transform the tension that might have consumed her into a resolution to create her own firm—and ultimately also to train women and minorities to be world-class performers.

Her success in setting up her own firm (a fascinating story in itself) emboldened her to take her ideas public (e.g., as superintendent of banks for the state of New York) and to create a high school curriculum to teach teenagers about money, focused on budgeting and prudent use of credit.[5] "Do you know there is nowhere, on any credit card bill, that says if you make only the minimum payment you will be paying for last night's dinner for fifteen to twenty years? That's the way it's designed," Siebert said. Her goal is to make sure that young people understand all the ins and outs of money and financial well-being, and she hopes to make the course mandatory for high school graduation. Siebert also launched one of the first Web sites dedicated to women and finance.

For leaders like Siebert and others I interviewed, recognizing the tension inside a crucible situation was often not easy. It requires one to distinguish between the force that is driving for change and the force that is trying desperately to sustain the status quo. It requires an awareness of one's vulnerability (difficult things are happening *to me*), and yet it demands a relentless sense of agency (I *can* do something in, or despite, these circumstances). The next step, then, involves taking that recognition and reframing or reshaping it into a new perception of reality.

REFRAMING THE TENSION

Growing up in the African American community on Baltimore's West Side, Brian Morris recalled being "not the poorest of the poor, but clearly not the richest of the rich." Truth is, his family just scraped by. Close friends and relatives were claimed as victims of drugs and gang violence. But because of some strong adult models, including a grandmother with high aspirations for young Brian, Morris was able to reshape that early adversity into opportunity: today he heads his own community-based building and investment company, and he serves on the Baltimore city school board.

Asked to recall a time when he learned something important about being a leader, Morris talked about an incident at age eleven that "shaped who I am and why I behave the way I do." His story centered on what for many children is the ultimate nightmare: he found his father lying face down on the apartment floor, unconscious from an apparent drug overdose. Morris called his mother, who summoned an ambulance, but as he recalled, "It seemed like hours, me standing there just staring at him. I don't know if I ever blinked the whole time."

The tension confronting Morris—between life and death, between life as he'd known it with a family and the specter of losing his father, between his grandmother's aspirations for him and his everyday experience of the West Side's mean streets—came at him like a freight train. "When you're young, you don't have a sense of your own existence," he said. "You don't have a sense that one day this thing ends. And not until that point did I have an understanding that this thing called my life, or this thing called the life of other people, could actually end." He began then and there to feel his own mortality, that he only had a certain amount of time allotted to him—a lesson that typically happens to people much later in life.

With that crucible experience came the realization that he wanted to make something of his limited time on earth, helping Morris to reframe his circumstances as he moved through adolescence into manhood. Describing himself as a "glass half-full kind of guy," he influenced his friends too. When his pals complained about the lack of basketball hoops in the neighborhood, he got their help to nail up milk crates. When they needed jerseys, he scavenged T-shirts and lettered them by hand.

Morris modeled himself on several heroes, Martin Luther King Jr. and John F. Kennedy among them. But Malcolm X came the closest to being a kindred spirit. "Malcolm X came from nothing," Morris said. "He was a criminal, a burglar, a pimp, a drug dealer and then made this miraculous metamorphosis into this guy who led a nation in understanding themselves, understanding how to clean yourself up from whatever vices that you have and be a stand up guy who can be respected." Clearly, Morris took that understanding to heart, given his own transformation from that boy staring at his father lying on the floor to the leading Baltimore citizen and community member he later became.

Sometimes the process of reframing becomes a communal activity. Many of the leaders whose crucibles involved reversal—bankruptcy, loss of an election, or a major project failure—worked their way out of an untenable situation by enlisting the aid of others facing similar straits. A marvelous example can be found in the Island Moving Company, a contemporary ballet company based in Newport, Rhode Island, and founded by Miki Ohlsen. Classically trained in the Netherlands, Ohlsen experienced a deep and abiding love for ballet since her earliest days as a dancer. As she progressed in her training, however, earning more prominent roles and artistic acclaim, she also experienced what she termed the "brutal hierarchy" of the traditional ballet company, with the harsh and "ego-crushing" domination of the ballet master and the mindless subservience expected of even the most accomplished dancers.

Determined to pursue her passion for dance in an environment more consistent with personal expression, Ohlsen assembled a small but like-minded group of dancers into a company dedicated, in the words of its mission statement, "to the belief that *collaboration and a supportive environment* enhance the creative process, producing great works of art representing profound expressions of the human spirit and experience."[6] The Island Moving Company, now more than twenty-five years old, has done what few regional dance organizations have done: established a permanent home, maintained a continuous schedule of performances over two decades, successfully recruited and retained a stable cast of dancers, and offered a living salary to all members of the company.

Reshaping and reframing tension is not illusion—or self-delusion. It is a purposive reframing: finding an angle or a lens through which the current reality can be reshaped into a healthier and more productive outcome. In Ohlsen's case, a principal tenet of the Island Moving Company is personal responsibility, which includes the responsibility to articulate one's own values and aspirations and to find ways to productively resolve the conflicts that will inevitably result. When, for example, individual dancers feel that they have been relegated too often to supporting roles, and they desire to be out in front, it is their obligation to say so, even if that means an uncomfortable confrontation with the artistic director or other dancers.

RESOLVING THE TENSION CONSTRUCTIVELY

Resolving the tension of any crucible experience means finding a way to mend the tear that has occurred between life as one has known it and life as it now presents itself. George Vaillant, in his long-term studies of a cohort of men, concluded that the core attribute of mental health is the ability to adapt and adjust.[7] He identified some eighteen forms of adaptation—what he referred to as defense mechanisms—and argued that five were characteristic of healthy, mature means by which people cope with the challenges that life presents: altruism, humor, suppression, anticipation and sublimation. I found ample evidence for each in the stories I heard about learning from crucible experiences.

For example, Bob Donohue, who leads the Fire and Rescue Department for the Massachusetts Port Authority (Massport), which includes Boston's Logan International Airport, spoke of the challenges of leading in a complex, interdependent environment. The emergencies that are so much a part of his department's mission do not respect organizational boundaries. But there are emergencies and then there are frame-busting events that toss convention out the window. On September 11, 2001, when two commercial airliners out of Logan were hijacked and sent hurtling into the World Trade Center in New York City, Donohue was one of a very few people who understood just how complicated the task would be of coordinating several dozen local, municipal, airport, state, and federal agencies and nearly as many businesses in their response to this unprecedented crisis.

"As the news began to filter in I was stunned, absolutely stunned," he recalled. "How could anyone do this? Why would they do it? And then: what are *we* going to do?" Fortunately, his department had a set of agreements and rules about how to behave in an emergency—even if none were truly matched to the scale of that one. "But even more important, we had a network of people I knew well. It was a bad situation, but I knew I could trust these people to do the right things when they were called on to do them."

Donohue called on his network that day in ways he never imagined he'd have to, and like the unanticipated leaders who emerged in the days following the devastation—particularly midlevel managers in the Port Authority of New York and New Jersey—they kept order at the airport; coordinated operations to accommodate dozens of grounded aircraft, flight crews, and thousands of passengers; mobilized staff to meet and console the families of the hijacking victims; and began a methodical search for clues to the events of the day.

What did a crucible experience like 9/11 teach Donohue about himself as a leader and his own learning style? He replied that though he did gain some confidence in himself as a leader, the real resolution from this crucible event for him came when he realized he'd become more willing to ask for help from others.

Donohue makes a powerful point: awareness of tension or the demand for adaptation is an empty vessel if you are not disposed to learn from it. Seeing others act or, in this instance, seeking out others to lend assistance is something that individuals can learn to do. In other words, resilience is not an accident of birth. It can be learned.

A resolution to the tension is not always the product of conscious deliberation. Once in a while it seems to happen spontaneously, as Jack Coleman, former president of Haverford College in Pennsylvania, suggests in a crucible story he chose to share. Coleman described how one day, during the Vietnam War, he heard that a group of students was planning to pull down the American flag and burn it. He also knew that members of the school's football team were determined that the protesters would not succeed. As both factions gathered around the flagpole, Coleman suddenly had an idea to preempt the showdown. With a voice quavering with the depth of emotion the experience still held for him, he explained, "From somewhere a voice came to me, gave me a message. And I went to the peace faction and said, 'Instead of burning the flag, why not get a bucket of soap and water? Wash the flag and put it back up.' That's what happened. The troops dispersed. I don't know where that message came from or why."

Whether spontaneous or the product of a prepared mind, resolutions of the sort Coleman and Donohue described are the work of leaders. But success at resolving tension does not always take place on the stage of world events, of course. As they say, sometimes healing the universe is an inside job. Certainly that would be the case with the leaders I encountered who overcame learning disabilities through creative adaptations.

For example, Virgin Group founder Richard Branson suffers from dyslexia, is bad at math, and, by his own admission, has a terrible memory. He never made it through high school. But, he says, "At some point, I think I decided that being dyslexic was better than being stupid."[8] Knowing how he learns—and learns best—he set about creating things he could be proud of, leveraging lessons learned in one product or service to grow another and another (forty-nine at last count).

The list of business leaders with learning disabilities is formidable—and I mention it here because it seems imminently appropriate in a discussion about learning. They include business leaders John Chambers (CEO of Cisco Systems), Charles Schwab, John Reed (formerly of Citibank), Craig McCaw (who pioneered the cellular industry), Paul Orfalea (founder of Kinko's), Diane Swonk (chief economist of Bank One), and attorney David Boies. Orfalea failed second grade and spent part of third in a class of mentally retarded children. He could not read. As his peers read aloud in class, Orfalea described it as if "angels whispered words in their ears." Each in his or her own way resolved the conflict between a learning disability that threatened to sideline them at an early age and an overpowering urge to succeed.[9]

Resolution can be accomplished by shifting the focus from a disability to an ability to confront and overcome challenges. Finding a way to cope with dyslexia or navigate a path to normalcy after September 11 does not necessarily mean the underlying tension has been eradicated. It has, however, been rendered manageable. And importantly, finding resolution is almost never done in complete isolation.

No One Learns Alone

The journey that transforms an individual into a leader is often a lonely one. We only truly know one side of any conversation: our own. We know every torturous turn and pang of our own ordeals and rites of passage, but we never know more than a cartoon version of anyone else's. Unable to hear another's interior monologue, you may not realize that he or she is struggling at all.

Yet, the leaders I interviewed were rarely alone in their crucibles. Mentors, coaches, teachers, spouses, peers, bosses, and friends played critical advisory or "sense-making" roles during crucible experiences. They helped most by putting events in context, in helping others create a more robust awareness of the things that were going on around them. As Vaillant concluded in his study of lifelong adaptation, "Both as children and as adults, we learn to anticipate pain effectively only if someone first sits beside us while we learn to bear current anxiety."[10]

For example, and as I will show in detail in the next chapter, outstanding performers often seek out the best available teachers—even when, to the rest of us, it appears that they are at the peak of their game or their profession. A great coach or mentor can contribute a wealth of experience and an objective eye. The same finding applies to effective leaders, especially because of the central role that experience plays in their matriculation and their maturation.

Consider the case of the 1970s congressman and priest, Father Robert Drinan. He was the first member of the House to file a resolution of impeachment on President Nixon (on July 31, 1973). Although by that point he was a seasoned religious and political leader, he told me that during this particular crucible experience, he leaned heavily on a network of Jesuit peers and moral leaders to convince him that he was doing the right thing by publicly accusing the president of the United States of illegal acts. The community of Jesuits with whom he lived in Washington, D.C., many of whom were on the faculty at Georgetown University, provided a critical sounding board.

For leaders in the midst of a crucible, one of the most important things that their coaches and mentors did was to help them to "step out of role" temporarily, to accomplish what management educator Janice Klein argues is a vital skill for leaders and change agents: the ability to be both an insider and an outsider.[11]

The insider is entirely in the game, in the action as it unfolds, but the outsider looks around, questions what is being taken for granted, and assesses his or her own performance from a more dispassionate perspective. In crucible situations, coaching tends to be more effective than mentoring: unlike mentors, coaches do not offer answers, they offer perspective.

Coaches and mentors rarely just appeared—as if by magic or destiny—though that would have lent a more dramatic flair to some of the crucible stories. More often, coaches and mentors were recruited as part of a strategy for managing and/or resolving the tension induced by a crucible situation. Family members, most commonly parents and grandparents, tended to be more easily at hand, and in many instances they were more attractive because they'd already proved themselves to be understanding and accepting of the individual and his or her prior quandaries.

Some leaders enlarged the role of coach by impaneling for themselves the equivalent of a personal board of directors whom they call on periodically for advice, feedback, and perspective. Amazon.com's Jeff Wilke has done just that. As a result of a crucible early in his career (described in chapter 2), Wilke said he recognized the value of having a group of people—friends, former bosses, and teachers—to whom he could refer for advice and counsel and who, in turn, cared enough about him and his success to tell him the unvarnished truth.

What distinguishes learning from a crucible and simply surviving it (or, worse yet, not surviving it) is partly a product of personality and partly a product of learned behavior. Some people are constitutionally optimistic. The roots of their resilience go deep—so deep, in fact, that beyond a certain point, a search for origins becomes a purely metaphysical exercise.

The crucible stories in these last two chapters, however, offer strong evidence that both helplessness and resilience can be learned.[12] Repeatedly, people attributed to their crucible experiences an enriched understanding of how they lead, and then used that understanding, in the words of one, "to put themselves in the path of more crucibles"—so that they could continue to learn, adapt, and improve.

That's why, for example, I found these leaders to be resolute in their curiosity, what I refer to as their proclivity to be egoless learners. To a person, they denied suffering from boredom, whether on the job or in the rest of life. There is always something new to explore: a new technique, a colleague's or an employee's new idea, a new way to look at an old problem. Each challenge refines, sharpens, and/or improves understanding of the world and of the self and, in many instances, enhances appreciation of the fact that there is still so much more to learn. Practice makes perfect—and as I'll show in the next chapter, it can even overcome any perceived limits in the talent department.

[4]

LEADERS AS EXPERT PERFORMERS

Practice Can Trump Talent

The fight is won or lost far away from the witnesses,
behind the lines, in the gym, and out there on the road;
long before I dance under those lights.

—Muhammad Ali

INTELLECT, BREEDING, BEAUTY—none of these things has much to do with whether or not you develop as a leader through a crucible experience. Talent plays a role, undoubtedly, but it is a supporting role. No amount of native talent can prepare a leader for the infinite variety of circumstances she will face or the challenges she must surmount. No gene for resilience ensures that gems of wisdom will suddenly appear amid the turmoil of a crucible.

What distinguishes these leaders who do continue to learn and grow is their approach to learning. Each person I spoke with offered evidence, whether explicit or implicit, that they had fashioned a Personal Learning Strategy that enabled them to notice the tension that accompanies a crucible, to manage it, and, in virtually every instance, to resolve it productively. But these leaders don't wait for crucible situations to call on their heightened level of awareness. Rather, they find it becomes part of the fabric of their everyday life so that, like accomplished performers in sports or music or the arts, these leaders *practice as strenuously as they perform*. And since they find themselves onstage much of the time, they extend that skill so that they *practice while they perform*— not simply to learn by doing, but to learn *while* doing.

In fact, the comparison between learning to lead and learning to perform in the arts or athletics ought not be an idle allusion. Business commentators often suggest that leadership is a performing art.[1] But missing from prior writing has been an active investigation of how leadership performance is related to, or enhanced by, leadership practice—and whether the distinctions so often used to grade performers, like novice and amateur versus eminent or outstanding, ought not also be applied to leaders.

This chapter explores more deeply the education of leaders and other performing artists. In it you will find some surprising similarities between the two and, more importantly, additional clues for how aspiring leaders can leverage crucibles to enhance their growth and to improve their performance.

PRACTICE AND PERFORMANCE

Talent is rarely enough to explain who becomes an eminent performer. Chess masters, for instance, differ from beginners not because they are blessed with superior memory or because of the way their brains are wired, but because they have what researchers describe as "a richer store of familiar moves."[2] In other words, they have played more matches and therefore have literally seen more patterns and the strategies associated with them. Clearly, they haven't seen every possible situation, but chess masters have acquired a way to do what psychologists call *chunking*: making a smaller number of units of information out of a vast number of discrete bits. Increased experience and practice enhances skill at reading situations (like chessboards) quickly and accurately.

Penn and Teller, a headline act in Las Vegas, blend comedy with magic by revealing how magicians create the effects we refer to as magic. They invite audiences behind the scenes to learn the fundamentals of magic—the so-called seven basic magic moves—so that they can understand how effects like mind reading and levitation are accomplished through dedicated practice.[3] They demonstrate something very important about magic and, as I will suggest, about leadership, too: the moves that compose the foundations of magic should not be confused with magic itself. *Mastering* the moves makes it possible to do magic. The same goes for leading: the underlying moves are not leadership, though mastery and adroit combination can make someone a leader.

Actor Kevin Spacey, who is artistic director of London's Old Vic Theatre Company and a winner of both a Tony Award and an Oscar, is one of many stage actors who have described acting as walking a tightrope: "An actor cannot connect with an audience until the audience comes to believe that—in that space and time, that theatre, that stage, and in that scene—he is who he portrays," he said. "It's not unlike walking a tightrope. It takes an incredible amount of practice. You can slip and when you do you fall—you lose your audience and probably your job."[4]

So, what does this have to do with leadership? All an actor has to do is memorize his lines and emote, while an organizational leader faces a daily onslaught of unpredictable events and a constant tugging at his sleeve from any of a hundred stakeholders wanting his time. Right?

Yes and no. Consider Mike Eskew, CEO of United Parcel Service (UPS), one of the world's largest employers and the world's ninth-largest airline. Eskew has ushered in nothing short of a revolution in the global delivery business by means of new technology and new work practices. I asked him to explain how he stays on top of such a complex operation. His answer bore a distinct resemblance to Spacey's: "I learn a lot by talking to people, just asking them what works and what doesn't," he said. "And I constantly remind people of something I believe deeply: we are part of something special, something noble. People make their customers better. They connect people. They make business run better. They keep assembly lines running. They save lives. Of course, I would be lying if I didn't think I have some talent. But I've learned a lot from experience and from practicing a few skills in a disciplined way."

Leaders like Eskew put a lot of stock in *practice*—yet you'll rarely find that concept in the lexicon of leader development, and certainly not in the way medical doctors or athletes or musicians use it. For example, in his chronicle of medical education, surgeon Atul Gawande underscores the central role of practice: "People often assume that you have to have great hands to become a surgeon, but it's not true," he writes. "When I interviewed to get into surgery programs, no one made me sew or take a dexterity test or checked if my hands were steady . . . [A]ttending surgeons say that what's most important to them is finding people who are conscientious, industrious, and boneheaded enough to stick at practicing this one difficult thing day and night for years on end."[5]

Yet, in business, practice tends to be regarded as something one undertakes outside the mainstream of work—something you do "that doesn't count." Alternatively, a manager will complain, "I don't have time to practice. I have to perform *all the time*." But if you don't have time to practice, it's hard to imagine how you can improve your performance. There can only be one solution: *when you don't have time to practice and yet you seek to improve your performance, you have to learn how to practice while you perform.*

THE EXPERT PERFORMANCE MODEL

Sporting analogies are hugely popular in business, but most books by retired athletes and coaches miss the mark when it comes to answering very fundamental questions at the heart of leader development, such as *How* do exceptional performers and coaches learn to achieve the results that made them famous? *How* do they mine experience for the gems of wisdom they proffer so glibly? *Why* have some lessons stuck with them while others have melted away? And finally, *what* do they do to keep in tune with the changes taking place around them?

The problem is not with comparing business or government leaders with athletes or artists or with misleading comparisons between sports and business (which has no time limits, goalposts, or players with numbers on their backs). Problems arise when we focus solely on *outcomes*—for example, the championship game, the stellar performance, or the brilliant stratagem—and overlook the activities that made those outcomes possible. Retired UCLA basketball coach John Wooden made this point to me emphatically: "Winning is a by-product of preparation. I'd tell the young men who played for me that my job is during the week. Their job is to play the game and try to be the best they can be," he said.

Coach Wooden's teams won ten national championships in twelve years and seven in consecutive years. Wooden himself reflected the dedication to personal improvement that characterizes eminent performers when I asked when he thought he got the hang of coaching basketball: "I never got the hang of it," he said. "I hope I was a better teacher my last year than I was the year before. Ten years before I retired, I wondered if I knew anything. Twenty years before that, I knew I didn't."

Performance, particularly high-stakes performance, cannot be left to chance—whether the game is sports or business leadership. (See the box, "Practice and Play.") That's why it is essential to be attentive to the rigor and absolute dedication to personal improvement that drives expert performers. If preparedness is a vital precondition for making the most of crucible experiences, then, like consummate athletes, leaders need to be as prepared to exploit learning opportunities as they are to exploit business opportunities or chances to enhance the performance of their organizations.

Practice and Play

When I meet people who say they have no time to devote to improving themselves as leaders, I often ask them to tell me about their hobbies. Not surprisingly, people perk up when they start talking about what they do for fun. When they do, I ask a dumb question: did they always know how to do what they now love to do? Of course not. So how did you learn? The answers, though again not surprising, are nonetheless revealing. People buy books, take classes, find a coach, join others with similar interests, swap stories, partake of their hobbies together, learn the language and lore, buy better equipment, devote more time, talk about it incessantly, and practice, practice, practice. And what do they practice? The dance steps, the golf stances, the stroke of the brush, the smell of the wine, the chords and finger placements, and so on, all the building blocks of the avocation that, once mastered, make you a master.

Practice is integral to play. If, as naturalist Diane Ackerman has described it, play is "the brain's way of maneuvering and learning," then practice may hold the key to preserving what play has uncovered.[a] Pianists, golfers, dancers, and amateur magicians practice all the time. Why? Because they recognize that practice is a time for absorption and for controlled experimentation. Musicians and dancers, in particular, talk about the importance of *muscle memory*, the seemingly effortless ability to bow (or to finger) or to palm a card that comes from thousands of repetitions of the same basic moves. Practice allows you to experiment: start, stop, and start again without disrupting anyone's play but your own. You can isolate the things you do well from the things you don't.

What do people do when they practice? Two things, basically. First, they *master* the moves that underlie their particular form of play. A magic trick may elicit awe from an audience, but the effect is really just a combination of basic moves (e.g., misdirection, feint, and switch). And one trick does not a magician make. What's required is a level of mastery that enables a magician (or a player of tennis, golf, or chess) to effortlessly combine the underlying moves.

Second, people *discover* new, hidden, and often captivating things about play when they practice. Virtually every one of the leaders I interviewed found something deeper and more meaningful in their play once they seriously committed themselves to the notion of practice. An accomplished professor who energetically leads an important university research center told me that when she restarted cello lessons after a hiatus of more than twenty years, she discovered an appreciation for practice—the discipline as well as the feeling of accomplishment—bordering on joy that she'd never known as a teenager.

The moral: *learning in any domain, leadership included, is not likely to occur without a desire to learn and the willingness and discipline to practice, practice, practice.*

a. Diane Ackerman, *Deep Play* (New York, Viking Press, 2000).

Fortunately, recent research in the field of expert performance provides a stimulus to expanding our thinking well beyond conventional models of how leaders learn and how leadership is taught—beyond simple models of increasing span of control, responsibility, and authority.[6] Scale and scope are undoubtedly important, but what's missing from extant research is a trajectory for leaders themselves: something that takes into account the fact, as the performing arts do, that deep-seated aspirations drive outstanding performers, that individuals need coaches at every stage of their careers, that both inspiration and knowledge can be mined from a wide variety of experiences (not just classroom teaching), that disciplined practice is essential, and that to plateau as a performer is to stagnate—no matter how big the stage is on which you play.

Rather than sustaining a tired leadership debate between "born and made," research on expert performance provides an empirically based guide to identifying the specific structured, intentional activities that can accelerate performance improvement. Moreover, models of expert performance suggest a shift away from excessive reliance on tests of innate talent and punch lists of "developmental assignments" and toward activities that *leverage experience* (off the job as well as on the job). Finally, research on expert performance suggests that "effortful study"—something very similar to a Personal Learning Strategy—plays an essential catalytic role in the evolution of outstanding performers. That is, just as a decathlete or a violinist needs a training regimen tailored to the demands of their profession and to their bodies and minds as individual performers, leaders need a Personal Learning Strategy that engages them as individuals and that charts for them (and the organizations they work for) appropriate opportunities to learn and grow.

NOVICE, ADEPT, AND EMINENT

How performers move up to the next level of achievement is a central question for students of expert performance—and one that ought to be of far greater concern to leaders, as well. Distinct levels of achievement are recognized in the study of expert performance (see figure 4-1).[7]

FIGURE 4-1

Levels of achievement in performance

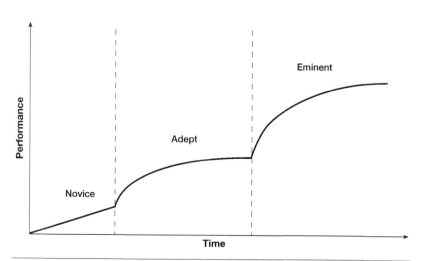

Novices are beginners who have a limited repertoire of skills from which to select. They need explicit guidance in method and technique, no matter how talented, ambitious, or motivated they may be. *Adept* performers have mastered technique in key facets of performance but tend to be constrained to a limited array of styles or genres. Though they may perform at a high level in a given style or genre, they tend not to be innovators or originators of genres. *Eminent* performers demonstrate the greatest range and creativity. They are innovators who stretch boundaries and transcend the limits of a given style or genre. Eminent performers are almost entirely intrinsically motivated, and, paradoxically, they often consider themselves to be beginners though most everyone *else* sees their performances as the greatest expression of maturity.

Are these distinctions relevant to leaders?

They are, in two very important ways. First, novice, adept, and eminent performances are clearly distinguished by the results they produce—just as leaders are. Audiences and commentators are able to see, hear, smell, or touch the outcomes that distinguish one performer or performance from another. "Promise" or potential is not enough. Even when differences in levels of performance are difficult to judge in any objective way, critics and/or markets will eventually rank or assign value to the work.[8]

Second, the distinction between novice, adept, and eminent underscores important differences in ability to adapt and to innovate—clearly critical for leaders as well. An adept performer may shine consistently but prove unable to move between genres or to bring an original interpretation to a script or a musical score.

By focusing equal attention on results, adaptation, and innovation, expert performance points to a definition of eminence in leadership similar to the one Bennis and I offered in *Geeks and Geezers*: the ability to achieve outstanding results over the course of a lifetime by generating—through continuous learning—new responses to changing conditions.[9] "Adept" leaders, then (to use the language of expert performance), recycle and repeat patterns of behavior virtually unchanged over the course of their lives. Think of an ensemble player, a method actor who's on the big screen but never earns a leading role, or a semipro baseball player. They may achieve notable success, but they tend to be successful when they are not forced to develop beyond their current capacity—for example, when they find a domain that doesn't change very often (or deeply) or when they move out of a place that is beginning to change (and find another that matches their style). This is more common than we're led to believe among senior executives and CEOs. When the heat gets turned up, these leaders exit for other organizations that play to their strengths without exposing their weaknesses. For aspiring, highly motivated leaders, this is a losing formula.

Eminent or outstanding leaders, by contrast, resemble the Picassos, the Tiger Woodses, and the Martha Grahams, who relentlessly push forward the boundaries of their fields and, in the process, raise the bar for everyone with whom they work and/or compete. These leaders not only excel in times of turbulence and change, but they also make a habit of refreshing and renewing themselves—and often the organizations they lead—to achieve superior results over long stretches of time, even through the progression of very different eras.[10]

For example, Sidney Harman guided his audio and electronics company, Harman International (formerly Harman-Kardon), through a massive shift from analog to digital technology over many years. He later reflected, "One of the things I tend to do, which seems to me is an appropriate thing to do whether you're a leader or not, is to contemplate the changes that are taking place in the world in which I participate and make a genuine effort to understand and interpret them."

NOT BY TALENT ALONE

Leaders don't become leaders on talent alone, any more than Jack Nicklaus "naturally" came to dominate the game of golf or Jerome Robbins was preordained to lead the world of dance. According to research in expert performance, four additional ingredients are essential for progressing from novice to adept: thorough grasp of method, ambition, instruction, and feedback.[11] A fifth ingredient, deliberate practice—or, in our terms, a Personal Learning Strategy—holds the key to eminence.

Grasp of Method

Individuals with great native talent will progress only so far—or so fast—without mastering the fundamental methods that define a domain of expertise. By method, I mean knowledge and technique for accomplishing what are agreed on as the desired results or effects. In magic these are called "moves," in music they are the building blocks of chords and scales, and in ballet they are the basic "positions," like first, fourth, and fifth position. Without a grasp of method, students may well spend precious time inventing tools and approaches that already exist, and risk blunting their ambition in the frustration of trial and error.

For example, Rock and Roll Hall of Fame guitarist Eric Clapton described the great frustrations of being self-taught: "Not knowing, for instance, when I picked up a six-string guitar, how to tune it," he recalled. "In quite an arrogant way, I refused to buy those 'teach yourself how to play basic guitar' books. So I had to learn how to tune the guitar on my own. Then, the next step was to put your fingers on different frets and try to make a chord . . . I was under the impression I was inventing all this stuff, you see. In actual fact, it had all been done before."[12] To Clapton's mind, it took much longer than he would have liked to learn the basics; he invented methods, certainly, but they weren't always the best, and arriving at them took up valuable time.

What's needed in order to grasp a method, according to studies of expert performers, is easily accessible knowledge and there's plenty of it.[13] For instance, to understand the boundaries of music, one must begin to study the work and style of various composers and other experts. So, Elvis Presley, for example, studied gospel music and blues musicians B. B. King and Furry Lewis to get a firm grounding in the most innovative music styles of the time.

Later, raw talent, combined with incessant practice and a deep understanding of gospel, rhythm and blues, and country music, allowed Presley to pioneer a new kind of music: rock and roll. Repeatedly, Presley credited those deep musical roots for his success, not his innate talent.[14] Likewise, chess players are strongly advised to assemble a capacious library of commentaries and analyses of great masters and their matches in order to create a richer store of familiar moves.

Most performing arts—and most active professions—maintain a "practice field" as a permanent feature of the work environment. Musicians, dancers, artists, and architects all have their studios where real works get done but where it is also possible to experiment, even play, as a legitimate part of work. Actors have rehearsal space, professional athletes have literal practice fields, and airline pilots and nuclear power plant operators have simulators—all dedicated to the sort of deliberate, intense, and meaningful practice essential to achieving and then maintaining a solid grasp of method.

The relevance of a firm grasp of method to leadership is obvious, but the implications are complex. HR departments and leadership consultancies are great places to look for both descriptions of the competencies that leaders should have and the catalogs of the underlying skills they have to master, such as observational and listening skills, self-awareness, communication, and the ability to resolve disputes (among others).[15] These skills are akin to the moves to which Penn and Teller draw attention in their study of magic. That is, by themselves, they will not create the effects that people recognize as leadership (or magic); yet mastering them individually and gaining dexterity in their combination can create those effects.

However, naming skills is not the same as creating the conditions to master them. What's often not clear is how leaders (whether novice, adept, or eminent, or at whatever position in the formal hierarchy) are supposed to master those skills. It's essential not only to name the skills that underlie the competencies, but to illustrate how they can be systematically practiced inside and outside of work.

Ambition

Ambition, like talent, is essential both for sustained superior performance and for the dedication necessary to continue learning. Even when loosely defined (like the dream of winning a championship), the desire for accomplishment can propel a person through the early and often trying stages of learning as a novitiate. *Amateur* is, after all, derived from *amare*, the Latin verb "to love," and clearly some measure of passion for your subject is what's needed to sustain you in the early stages of learning.[16] But ambition gets stoked by encouragement as well. Singer-songwriter Johnny Cash recalled how at seventeen, after cutting wood all day with his father, he'd come in the door singing old gospel songs. His mother would say, "Is that you?" and then she'd hug him and say, "God's got his hands on you."[17]

But, like talent, ambition alone is not sufficient for superior performance. Desire might run deep, but it is rarely limitless. Thus, performing artists must manage their ambition and, quite importantly, renew it. For instance, ambition quite often gets sapped in the demand for practice. Among novices (as well as many adept performers), practice is something to be endured in order to simply play and, once they are playing, something to do to improve performance (win).[18] Competitions and public exhibitions can provide a short-term encouragement to practice, of course. But until practice actually becomes part of the fabric of performance—where the artist recognizes that practice, rehearsal, and performance are moments in the same process—ambition will be consumed in just overcoming continual inertia.

In fact, in many fields it takes ten years of deliberate, intentional practice to achieve the status of expert, according to research on expert performance. So for anyone who has taken up and dropped a dozen or more hobbies or sports, it's painfully obvious why we don't practice: our desire to improve isn't high enough to drive us to continue the routine, repetitive grind. And practice does not end once someone has achieved public acclaim.[19] Even when we have an admirable personal goal planted firmly in our minds, the specter of mind-numbing repetition without a sip from the victory cup can shrivel that vision in seconds flat.

For anyone hoping to make the leap from novice to eminent performer, continued evolution requires something richer than just winning a contest, for example. It may mean finding a way to gain deeper insight into the dynamics of your topic, including its aesthetics, or it may mean facing challenges like transcending established convention. In their studies of leaders, James Champy and Nitin Nohria describe this trajectory as the *arc of ambition*: the upward incline of an idea and its originator with accompanying struggles, the peak of success, and the inevitable decline that eventually occurs.[20] The challenge for eminent artists and leaders—and for adept artists and leaders who have experienced success once—is in repeating the arc, first by letting go of an idea or a mode of performance that has lost its luster and then by continually searching out new genres to master.

Consider the case of Mayo Shattuck. Before joining Constellation Energy Group's board and eventually becoming its CEO, Shattuck had risen in the ranks of Deutsche Bank Alex. Brown on the basis of a combination of personal ambition, analytical skill, and raw imagination. Taking over the reins of a 150-year-old utility known for its conservatism in a period of dramatic change was nothing if not an audacious move: this was in the early days of deregulation, when Enron's creative accounting practices were first drawing suspicious looks. But Shattuck felt deep down that tremendous human and financial potential resided just beneath the surface of the organization. It was his ambition to unleash that potential. According to Shattuck, that could not be accomplished without top-to-bottom change. Specifically, he knew he needed to develop among his managers a sense of competitive, commercial behavior in a company where, in his words, "no one had ever had to market or sell anything." He took a chance and hired people from outside the organization for their functional rather than industry expertise.

The results have been astounding, and clearly Shattuck's ambition helped his company buck the odds in a volatile environment. Not only has Constellation chalked up a record string of profitable quarters—while many competitors reeled in the wake of Enron's collapse—but also the company has achieved broad-scale change in under five years, a turnaround comparable to GE's resurrection under Jack Welch.

As with grasp of method, ambition too connects to leadership in organizations—but, again, looking at leadership through the lens of expert performance reveals some interesting twists. Most important among them is the content of individual ambition and how it is shaped. The content of an individual's ambition is rarely questioned in the early stages of their career. Of course, it's routine for a job interviewer to ask an applicant where he or she plans to be in five to ten years. But it's quite unusual in those situations to ask what a young man or woman wants to do with their life, what they want to be known for, what mark they want to leave on the world. It's unfortunate that those questions—questions often prompted by suspension crucibles as we discussed them in chapter 2—are not asked, because they might encourage organizations to more closely examine what they want from leaders (current and future). What's more, such questions could force young managers to ask themselves whether they truly want to lead—and why. In the absence of a definition made richer by such reflection, ambition can quickly get focused solely on "winning."[21]

In any case, in order to prevent stagnation, organizations will most likely need to help individuals clarify and evolve their personal ambitions over time. And individuals, like adept and eminent performers, will need to find ways to enrich their ambitions if they are to renew themselves as leaders, a topic I'll address in more detail in chapter 5.

Instruction

A great teacher or coach can bring a wealth of experience, an objective eye, and an ability to match instruction and pace to the personality and learning style of the performer. People who achieve eminence routinely seek out the best teachers they can find—regardless of their demonstrated native ability. For example, actress Jodie Foster, who by age twelve had been acting professionally for nearly a decade, credited the Academy Award nomination she received for her role in *Taxi Driver* to the light-handed coaching she got from fellow actor Robert De Niro. "It wasn't until I met Robert De Niro . . . that I understood that there was more to acting than just being a puppet," she recalled. De Niro would take her to coffee shops in Spanish Harlem, where they would rehearse their lines and, more importantly, where they could immerse themselves in the social context called for by the script. "Having been a child actor, of course, I knew my lines, so now I was really bored," she said, "because I'd have to do these lines over and over again with this adult." But later he'd begin to improvise here and there. "Suddenly I learned that improvisation was about knowing the text so well that you could deviate from it in a meaningful way, as if you had been living this conversation, and always find your way back to the text. That's a lesson that most young actors don't really get."[22]

But the relationship often goes both ways: clever students know how to make good teachers even better. They can do a great deal to engage, enlist, or as psychologist Robert Kegan aptly puts it, "recruit" mentors. Not only do they convince mentors to work with them, but they make mentors/teachers want to do the best job they can—often because of the protégé's genuine rapt interest that encourages the mentor to reveal aspects to the topic that are linked to his or her passion.[23]

Michael Klein's mentor was his grandfather, a man who had left a blue-collar job with General Motors with $5,000 in savings and bought a tiny company that pioneered paint-by-numbers kits. Within three years, his grandfather grew the business from five employees to over eight hundred. Klein recalled how his grandfather instilled both the knowledge and the confidence that would help him become a millionaire by the age of nineteen and then a successful CEO of several Internet-based companies. He took young Michael aside one day and told him that, rather than money, he wanted to pass on to him the knowledge he'd gained in business. "'I'll tell you anything you want to know and teach you anything that you want to learn from me,'" Klein recalled him saying. "And I remember thinking about it and thinking, 'You know, why not?'" From that day on and until the day his grandfather died, the two talked on the phone for at least an hour every day, and his grandfather would take Klein along on his business travels. "Just the act of seeing . . . what enthused him about being a businessman, sort of set the ball in motion for me in terms of my desire to learn what made it possible for him to do those things," Klein said.

Indeed, for anyone seeking eminence, a teacher is always part of the equation. And of all the ingredients of expert performance, instruction might seem both the most relevant and the most familiar to leadership in organizations. After all, businesses spend billions of dollars annually on leadership training alone.[24] However, on closer examination, instruction of the sort depicted by the literature on expert performance turns out to be pretty rare in business. Skilled coaches capable of the kind of assessment, dialogue, and on-the-spot feedback that promising musicians or baseball players need are rarely allocated to business managers early in their careers. Executive coaches are familiar and growing rapidly in number, but they are an expensive commodity usually reserved for the upper rungs of the hierarchy. Classroom-based and electronic training have increased in both quality and availability in recent years, though they remain incredibly sensitive to business cycles; but who would ask a budding Derek Jeter or Mikhail Baryshnikov to learn their trade from a DVD?

The obstacles to effective instruction for young leaders are not simply ones of cost, exclusivity, or shortfalls in supply. The challenge has as much to do with the antagonism between "learning" and "leading" in most organizations. That is, as Ed Schein has noted, one of the core weaknesses of leadership (in the American context especially) is the importance attached to avoiding situations where you have to admit publicly that you don't know something.[25] Worse yet would be for a leader to publicly admit that he or she doesn't know something *about leading*.

Feedback

Feedback, especially immediate feedback, is vital to anyone who ventures into the world of performance. Sometimes the feedback is obvious: fidgety silence can mean as much as, if not more than, thunderous applause. But more often, the message is nuanced; cellist Yo-Yo Ma is highly regarded by the musicians with whom he plays, as well as by audiences, because of his ability to read their moods and to adjust on the fly to inspire them both. Feedback enables a performer to adjust, perhaps even to change her style quickly, and so to improve both the result and the audience's experience.

But feedback can be expensive too. For example, a baseball batter only gets a few chances to work on his batting stance during three or maybe four appearances at the plate, and it can be risky, to say the least, for a novice to try something new in real time. That's why performers like Boston Red Sox slugger David Ortiz are so special: their ability to experiment and adjust in the midst of performance enables them to take advantage of every opportunity for learning.

Feedback is vital to organizational leaders, too, and they are often as hungry as performers (and politicians like former New York City mayor Ed Koch) to know "how am I doing?" But even with a broader and more routine use of 360-degree assessments, employee surveys, balanced scorecards, and the enormous potential of enterprise software packages to pump out performance numbers, there is no effective substitute for immediate feedback, whether the leader in question is a frontline supervisor or the CEO. Indeed, for a CEO like Nestlé's Peter Brabeck-Letmathe, a campaign to revitalize an ailing giant won't generate meaningful results for months or even years. Yet, getting that feedback is critical to the learning process. That's why Brabeck-Letmathe, like other leaders such as UPS's Mike Eskew, mentioned earlier in the chapter, is constantly in contact with the people most likely to see results first: frontline employees and customers.

So what does all of this add up to? It would be a huge mistake to conclude that research on expert performance has arrived at a formula for eminence: a do-it-yourself cocktail where one combines a modicum of talent, a grasp of method, ambition, instruction, and feedback, and stirs. The journey to eminence is never simple or linear. The closer you get to the pinnacle of your field, the more you realize how little you really know. Or as Picasso remarked in his eighties, "It has taken me a whole lifetime to learn to draw like children."[26]

What's missing is a vital and catalytic ingredient in the evolution of an expert performer: the discovery, application, and refinement of a Personal Learning Strategy (PLS).

TOWARD EMINENCE: ADOPTING A PERSONAL LEARNING STRATEGY

Many performers and many leaders are unconsciously competent. They can do the things that warrant the label adept or eminent, but they are hard pressed to explain what it is they do or how they learned to do it.[27] The few who are consciously competent may not call their approach a PLS, but they recognize that their style, combined with their vision, is something they own, that's driven by their ambition, that's tailored to how they learn best, and that borrows from sources of inspiration they prefer (or find handy) to keep adapting and creating—whether they are personal experience, crucible events, or the works and lives of others.

A Personal Learning Strategy lives in both the head and the heart. For anyone aspiring to eminence, it's essential to investigate both.

In the Head

The cognitive side of a PLS consists of lessons about how one learns and learns best. Revelations about learning cumulate over time—sometimes in isolation and other times with the assistance of coaches and critics.

Take the case of Pinchas Zukerman, noted Israeli violinist, winner of two Grammy Awards, and music director of Canada's National Arts Centre.[28] As an adolescent violin prodigy touring the world playing to overflow audiences, Zukerman recalled being struck one evening by a profound "aha." He realized that although he was good—very good—he suddenly understood that he had made it thus far because of simple talent. If he wanted to progress further, he'd have to change. "I would have to embrace a form of discipline that I had only flirted with up till then," he recalled. "I had to dedicate myself to disciplined play." For Zukerman, a Personal Learning Strategy grew out of two powerful insights: that there were borders to be crossed, and that crossing them would require him to learn new things in a new way.

Or consider the case of Dee Hock, who developed, in 1968, the concept of a global system for the electronic exchange of value and a new form of organization for that purpose: a decentralized, nonstock, for-profit membership institution to be owned by financial institutions throughout the world. That organization, Visa International, is now a $1.5 trillion enterprise jointly owned by more than twenty thousand financial institutions in more than two hundred countries and territories.

Hock believes that the concept of the organization derived from a deeply personal dissatisfaction with existing models of the business enterprise and the behaviors they induce on the part of leaders. He pointed to one experience in particular that triggered his search for an alternative form of organization, when he was just a young manager in a remote branch of a consumer finance company with three direct reports. "Our average age was about 19½, and we just trashed the company manual and started doing things as common sense and circumstances seemed to indicate," he said. "Within two years, this little office was leading the company in every measurable category. Growth, percentage of profit, we met a credit and loss recovery. We collected more bad debt than we charged off. And I thought 'Wow, this is great. Here I am 21 years old.'"

But as Hock put it, "We couldn't hide any more. The anonymity was gone. And that great fist of corporate power just came down and crushed us for not following company policy." Hock went on to describe how that led him to evolve his own working definition of a Personal Learning Strategy, as a "living process" of reading, thinking, comparing, analyzing, puzzling, and constantly questioning himself. "And worrying about why I felt so oppressed by and often abused by organizational structures," he added. "And why I found myself becoming oppressive and abusive in the process."

Recognizing that there are boundaries that define any form of expression, and that they as individuals can learn what's necessary to go beyond them, is what prods performers like Zukerman and leaders like Hock to go further, to see what else they can discover or, better yet, invent. They are apt to devise pathways for themselves that, of necessity, pass through periods of severe testing, via *crucibles*—whether it's submitting themselves to the authority of another in order to learn or stumbling through unknown materials and dynamics—because they know (or sense) that that is how they will continue to grow and how their art, whatever form it takes, will continue to evolve.

In the Heart

The emotional side of a Personal Learning Strategy is no less important than the cognitive: it is in the heart that most eminent performing artists and outstanding leaders believe that inspiration lives. There is no reason to doubt what they say. The intensity with which Tiger Woods approaches tournament play suggests that winning is not just an intellectual exercise. The same can be said for how a musician like Paul Simon sets about assimilating aboriginal rhythms into rock and roll, or for how Starbucks founder Howard Schultz talks about his vision of building a compassionate company. It is a force that will not be denied. Embedded within that surging energy is a desire to accomplish something grand: to make a mark on the world, to leave a lasting memory or legacy, to be recognized, to have one's meaning understood.

But the heart is not just a repository. It is a lens through which feelings and experience are clarified, magnified, interpreted, and reproduced. Not surprisingly, performing artists frequently (though not exclusively) point to significant objects and events in their lives and in the lives of those they observe as a source of inspiration. Bill Russell, remembered best for his central role in the Boston Celtics basketball dynasty that won eleven championships in thirteen seasons, found inspiration at an early age from an unlikely source: the library. His mother made sure he had a library card, and Russell spent a lot of time with, of all things, books on Renaissance art. At home, he'd practice drawing some of the paintings he'd seen. "Most of the lines and the dimensions were correct," he said, "but I somehow missed the paintings completely. I realized—as a kid—that what these artists had that I didn't was a distinctive quality, a kind of signature statement . . . The way I took to Leonardo and Michelangelo was eventually how I took to the game of basketball."[29]

Sometimes it's a phrase or a sentiment that serves as the source of inspiration that guides both the heart and the mind. For example, Frances Hesselbein refuses to call herself a leader—despite having held formal leadership roles in the Girl Scouts, starting with thirty ten-year-old girls in the basement of the Second Presbyterian Church in Johnstown, Pennsylvania, through to her retirement as executive director of the Girl Scouts of America, an organization comprising nearly eight hundred thousand members. For Hesselbein, the word that best summarizes her objectives and her style is *opportunity*—because she has so often found herself surrounded by it. But she tries to remember what management guru Peter Drucker once told her: "'Frances, remember your job is not to provide energy, it is to release energy.' So I keep saying to myself, How do I release the energy of other people, not think I have to do it?" she said. "But I release the energy . . . You and I have loads of opportunities. How do we disperse them? How do we open up opportunities to a lot of people who aren't as fortunate as we are? . . . It's all part of a larger philosophy. You can't just have a passion for your work. You have to have passion for living. It doesn't stop when you open the door of your office or begin when you open it."

Should a Personal Learning Strategy—the catalytic ingredient that does so much to distinguish eminent figures in the performing arts—have a place in leader development? Although my answer would be a resounding yes, I think the real question is, *Does a PLS have an analog in practice?* That's not so clear.

Certainly, students of leadership have devised many useful developmental models that strive to take into account what roles the head and the heart play in becoming a leader, how those roles change over time, and how organizations ought to take each into account.[30] Most important among them have been the extensions into the realm of emotional intelligence, with the incumbent focus on self-awareness or, as Ellen Langer has suggested, mindfulness.[31]

Yet while experts on leadership often draw comparisons between business and performance, many of their models of leadership development don't include the need for a Personal Learning Strategy—something that expert performance stresses so clearly. I have come to believe that three aspects of the PLS are vital: (1) A method for extracting insight from experience. Without it, aspiring leaders will miss the rich and frequent opportunities to learn from the challenges that life continually dishes up, including crucible experiences that can define them as leaders. (2) A powerful aspiration that encourages one to grow and adapt. This is something quite private and yet profoundly public in its consequences. It is individual and idiosyncratic and therefore difficult to shape into classroom lessons, and yet, as we will see, it is the glue that holds a Personal Learning Strategy together. (3) A concept—and a regimen—of deliberate practice that connects learning and performance. Practice may not make perfect, but unless practice occupies a central and honored role in leadership, it's hard to imagine how novices will ever become adept or eminent—that is, something most aspiring leaders truly desire.

In the next three chapters, which compose part II, Crafting a Personal Learning Strategy, I offer a very practical, hands-on approach to exploring the intersection of experience, aspiration, and deliberate practice.

PART TWO

CRAFTING A PERSONAL LEARNING STRATEGY

THE CORE OF A PERSONAL LEARNING STRATEGY

Recognizing and Transforming Crucible Experiences

*Learning is not attained by chance, it must be sought
for with ardor and attended to with diligence.*

—Abigail Adams

*Many eyes go through the meadow,
but few see the flowers in it.*

—Ralph Waldo Emerson

WE'VE BEEN LOOKING at the work of expert performers and how that can translate to the highest levels of leadership. But what do eminent performers' experiences have to do with your own crucibles, and what you learn from them? Everything. Leaders in industry, government, and the social sector need all the things that athletes and performing artists do in order to reach top form. They need a deep and thoroughgoing grasp of method. They need ambition to fuel them over time and setbacks. They need instruction and coaching, whether it comes from a teacher, a mentor or a coach, a team, subordinates, or a spouse. And they need feedback over time—from all of the year's business quarters, not just the most recent.

But even that's not enough.

For leaders in business, government, and the social sector, the stage shifts constantly. The demands on leaders' attention are growing exponentially, and they have to assimilate new information daily. Meantime, the rules often change midgame as the cast of collaborators and competitors turns over continuously. For leaders to prosper in such an environment, not just to survive, my interviews suggest that individuals need a playbook that helps them decide how and when to adapt, to distinguish what's urgent and strategic from what's transient yet annoying, and to guide their own process of learning and growing.

This chapter will translate my research findings about crucible experiences into a systematic and replicable process for creating a Personal Learning Strategy. I will show how a PLS can take what science has learned about the path to expert performance and shape it to fit the reality of contemporary business and to the diversity of individual attributes and aspirations. Although a PLS draws from the wealth of competency-based courses and workshops organized by human resource departments and business schools, it is much more than a checklist or a menu of potential assignments.[1] Rather, it is something to be owned and enacted by an *individual*, driven by his or her *personal vision*, tailored to his or her *learning style*, aimed to *extract insight* from the broadest possible range of *experiences* (off-the-job, especially in crucible situations, as well as on-the-job), and dedicated to achieving *meaningful results*.

This process begins by exploring the internal beliefs and motivations and the conscious competence that can make one an adept or even, ultimately, an outstanding leader. The real work begins with deep reflection on *why* you want to lead and to what end? This requires you to be honest with yourself about your aspirations, beliefs, and desires. From there, we'll address the sources of motivation. By shutting out the din of other people's expectations, you can get a glimpse of your most energetic and ambitious self—and this, in turn, will help sustain you in the face of fatigue, setback, and all the thousands of small cuts that will discourage you from learning and growing.[2] Finally, you'll reflect on the contexts and the ways in which you have learned the most important lessons of your life. In other words, what does it take for you to learn important things? How do you learn best? We'll take an excursion through the most prominent learning theories to help assess your learning style.

Let's begin now with the critical question of why you want to lead in the first place.

WHY LEAD?

As a young man, John W. Gardner had no ambition to lead, much less to manage. Yet when he passed away in 2006, his accomplishments included serving as secretary of health, education, and welfare under President Lyndon B. Johnson (despite being a registered Republican), presiding over the creation of the Public Broadcasting System, founding two successful public action lobbies (Common Cause and the Independent Sector), presiding over the Carnegie Corporation, and serving as a Marine Corps officer in World War II. What kindled his desire to lead?

Finding himself in a small management job at the Federal Communications Commission during World War II, he recalled, "I began to get quite impressive praise for my management skills. And it wasn't even on my map! I mean I didn't even respect managers. But apparently some qualities were there waiting for life to pull those things out of me." Gardner deeply believed that life was a tug-of-war between what "was" and what "was possible" and that the principle human challenge—his challenge—was one of continuous renewal even in the face of what might seem to be implacable opposition and constraint. As he put it, "The need for endless learning and trying is a way of living, a way of thinking, a way of being awake and ready. Life isn't a train ride where you choose your destination, pay your fare and settle back for a nap. It's a cycle ride over uncertain terrain, with you in the driver's seat, constantly correcting your balance and determining the direction of progress. It's difficult, sometimes profoundly painful. But it's better than napping through life."

There is no point in trying to assess people's abilities without first finding out what they care about. The same goes for trying to assess things such as "leadership potential" or "creativity" out of context. One has always to ask, in relation to what? Thus, before we address motives and skills, we start by asking, Why do you lead? Why does a person seek out, or accept, the burden of leadership? A Personal Learning Strategy begins and ends with *why* as the central question and with you as the central character. You alone can answer these questions. The vessel you are creating will hold your aspirations and your passions and provide a shield that defends you from the fears and inhibitions that learning inevitably summons up. (See the box, "Why Lead?")

Why Lead?

ROB MCKENNA AND PAUL YOST, two of the early designers of Boeing's Waypoint program for leader development, recently turned their attention to the leadership challenges that pastors and preachers encounter at the level of neighborhood congregations.[a] Perhaps not surprisingly, they've found that church pastors face challenges that many line managers in business would find very familiar: like how to deal with absenteeism, how to get resources to keep the organization afloat, and how to exercise influence without formal authority.

Yet they have also discovered a marked contrast in the way pastors and business managers talk about their leadership challenges. When asked *how* they lead, many pastors struggle to answer; they point to their lack of formal training in leadership, in the technical elements of managing, and the like. Asked *why* they lead, however, they overflow with reasons: service to humanity, inspiration by a higher source, doing God's work, living a spiritual life, fulfilling a profound desire to be closer to God, and so on. *Why* never stumps a man or woman in the clergy.

It's just the opposite for many managers. Ask *how* they lead, and managers cite chapter and verse from the canons of the leadership literature, sprinkled liberally with pearls of personal experience. But asking, Why do you lead? or Why did you seek out the responsibilities of being a leader? can (and often does) kill the conversation. It's not that they are stumped—indeed, many eventually rally back and cite a plethora of motives individual and institutional; it's that the connection between job descriptions and personal aspirations tend to be indirect, at best. There are the money and the status and the perks, of course, but in business, where the bottom line seems to justify itself, you don't often hear about a feeling of moral uplift or a greater good or service to humanity or creating beauty that motivates someone to lead.

a. Rob McKenna and Paul Yost, personal communication with author, June 2006; see also Robert B. McKenna and Paul R. Yost, "The Differentiated Leader: Specific Strategies for Handling Today's Adverse Situations," *Organizational Dynamics* 33, no. 3 (2004): 292–306.

Let me illustrate the importance of *why* for both leading and learning with a story someone once told me. A disciple asked his teacher, "Guru, why do I not see and feel god the way you do?" The guru had no instant answer for him. But the next day, as they were going for a dip in the holy water of the Ganges, the guru found a strange way to answer his disciple's question. As the disciple bent toward the water, the guru forced his head down and did not let him up, leaving him to struggle and gasp for breath. When he finally let him up, the guru asked his disciple, "Do you want god the way you wanted to breathe under the water?" The disciple had his answer.[3]

How many of us want to lead or to learn as badly as we want to breathe? What follows are three exercises designed to help you understand why you want to lead.

EXERCISE 1:

Getting Clear About What You Want

HERE IS AN EXERCISE intended to give greater depth and texture to your own answer to the *why* question.[a] It will get you to clarify your aspirations and begin crafting your own personal vision. Perhaps more importantly, it will help you start identifying something attractive enough to serve as an anchor to keep you rooted during the trying times that accompany active efforts at learning. In chapter 6, Exploring Your Capabilities, you will see how this ties in directly to your Personal Learning Strategy.

Begin by getting a pen and pad of paper and finding a relaxing place to sit. Close your eyes if that helps you set aside the distractions around you, and slowly take a few deep breaths just to get you focused a bit on the exercise. Start by visualizing yourself the way you'd like to be a year from today—not how you are now, although that might be a very comfortable place to be, but how you'd imagine yourself in peak form in twelve months' time. Project that image on your mind like a movie on a screen. Take some time to explore that image: How do you look? How do you feel? What's distinctive about how you look and feel?

After a close look at yourself, shift your focus to what you're doing as you operate at peak form. Imagine yourself at work, interacting with colleagues. Where are you? How do you feel about your interactions? What are people saying to you? What are they saying about you? Again, explore the scene. Look at it from a variety of angles. What's distinctive about what you're doing and feeling? Note a few words or images that stick with you.

Consider now the work that you're doing with these other people. What sort of results are you producing? What do important people, whether they are people you report to, your customers, your peers, or others with a stake in you and your team's performance, have to say about your performance? How do they describe working with you? Look as well at the environment you and your team are working in: Where are you working? How does it feel as a workplace?

Now, gradually widen your focus to include other aspects of your life—for example, your life at home. Who is there with you? How do they appear? What are you saying to them, and what are they saying to you? Explore the feelings associated with the image of you and your family and/or friends enjoying each other's company. Linger awhile there, and notice where you are, how you're living, what it feels like to be at that peak of your life. Commit a few images and words to memory.

Finally, let your mind drift a bit while you start to think of yourself leading. What are you doing? What's the context in which you're leading: is it at work or someplace else? What results are you helping create? What's your contribution to those results? What are the feelings you associate with leading? Is it pleasurable, scary, exciting, uncomfortable, all of those things? Where are you feeling these things? In what part of you are you feeling those feelings? In what place or context are you leading (and feeling those things)? Again, recalling that you are operating in a peak state, what is distinctive about you when you lead? Commit those images and feelings to memory.

Slowly withdraw yourself from your reflective state and write down some of the key things you saw and felt, either on your pad or in the space provided. Write them down as you saw, heard, and felt them, without any regard to what it took to get there. Write them down in the present tense.

What you want

Images, feelings, words

Myself in peak form

Myself in peak form at work

Myself in peak form with family and friends

Myself in peak form as a leader

(continued)

a. I am grateful to Charlie Keifer, Steve Ober, Bryan Smith, Joel Yanowitz, Carol Morse, and Julia Seger, former colleagues at Innovation Associates, for introducing me to this exercise that is built from their and Peter Senge's work on "personal mastery." For greater detail on this and similar exercises, consult Peter M. Senge et al., *The Fifth Discipline Fieldbook: Strategies and Tools for Building a Learning Organization* (New York: Currency, Doubleday, 1994); and John Whitmore, *Coaching for Performance* (London and Santa Rosa, CA: Nicholas Brealey Publishing, 1996).

EXERCISE 2:

Getting Clear About Where You Are

A S ANY GOLF INSTRUCTOR or drama coach will tell you, it's essential to take stock of where you are in order to judge the distance to where you want to be and to select the kinds of practice that will accelerate you to where you want to go. Peter Senge refers to it as "creative tension," and like a stretched rubber band that illustrates the idea of potential energy, no tension exists without a candid, honest assessment of one's current reality to serve as a counterweight to lofty aspiration.[a]

So, the next step in this exercise is to repeat the visualization, but this time with an unblinking, all-seeing, painfully honest eye (closed or open) focused on your current performance. The intent is not to find fault. Indeed, you'll likely find many things to be quite pleased with. But you should also avoid embellishing. Note and record what you see, starting with your current state. What do you look like? How do you feel? How would you characterize your performance? As before, linger a while, take notes, and record images.

Shift once more to yourself at work. Picture yourself interacting with your colleagues: peers, superiors, and subordinates. How do you feel about those interactions? What are people saying to you? What are they saying about you? Again, explore the scene. Look at it from a variety of angles. What's distinctive about what you're doing and feeling? Note the words and images that stick with you.

Consider now the work that you're doing with these other people. What sort of results are you producing? What do important people, whether they are people you report to, your customers, your peers, or others with a stake in you and your team's performance, have to say about your performance? How do they describe working with you? Look as well at the environment you and your team are working in: Where are you working? How does it feel as a workplace?

Focus again on your home life. Who is there with you? How do they appear? What are you saying to them, and they to you? Explore the feelings associated with the image of you and your family and/or friends enjoying each other's company. Linger a while there, and notice where you are, how you're living, what it feels like to be at this point in your life. Commit a few images and words to memory.

Finally, let your mind drift a bit while you start to think of yourself as a leader. It doesn't matter what context you have in mind; just summon up an image of yourself leading. What are you doing? What are the feelings you associate with leading? Is it pleasurable, scary, exciting, uncomfortable, all of those things? Where are you feeling these things? In what part of you are you feeling those feelings? In what place or context are you leading (and feeling those things)? Again, recalling that you are looking at yourself today, what is distinctive about you when you lead? Commit those images and feelings to memory.

Once again and on a separate sheet of paper or in the blanks provided, jot down the images, feelings, and words that characterize your current reality. When you're done, set the two pages side by side: one with the depictions of you operating at peak performance at work, with your family and friends, and as a leader; and the other with the parallel description of your current reality. You might try a split screen image in your mind: on one side is you at peak performance, and on the other is your current reality.[b] See the difference? Feel the tension?

Where you are

Images, feelings, words

Myself today

Myself today at work

(continued)

Myself today with family and friends

Myself today as a leader

Like potential energy, that tension wants to be resolved. It won't be resolved on its own, however. Moving from current reality to peak performance takes deliberate action that requires tapping motivational factors and learning styles that can accelerate or inhibit progress in the direction of your aspirations.

a. See Peter Senge, "The Leader's New Work: Building the Learning Organization," *Sloan Management Review* 31, no. 1 (Fall 1990).

b. You might also want to set up an encounter with your "future self" as a way to assess how much progress you've made against your aspirations. As an avid reader at ten years old, I noticed that many of my favorite fictional heroes chronicled their adventures in diaries. The idea of a personal history intrigued me, but I was the kind of kid who'd much prefer a glimpse into the future to a rehash of the past. While reading Isaac Asimov's *Foundation* trilogy, I came upon the idea of seeding an encounter with my "future" self by writing a note on a slip of paper and secreting it deep in the pages of a book I loved and knew I would someday pick up again. In this note I quizzed myself: Who was I now? What did I look like? What was I doing and why? Did I remember what it was like to be ten years old? As the years have passed, I've found my note, and I've had the inner dialogues I'd hoped to engender. Each time I put the note back (usually in a different book), feeling a little bit more whole, connected with my past, and, for reasons I've never truly understood, optimistic about the future.

EXERCISE 3:

Obstacles to Overcome

BEFORE WE TURN TO MOTIVATION and learning, it makes sense to take a few moments and simply catalog from memory the kinds of things you know you've done in the past to circumvent or undermine prior efforts at self-improvement. The intent here is not to depress you or to marshal evidence as to why you're not going to be successful this time. Instead, you do this because no one knows better than you the ways you can divert your attention (or be diverted) from a goal you care about. Once you write down these diversion tactics, you ought to consider them no longer available. Either you will have to invent new excuses or diversions or you may find yourself seeing openings in what might otherwise appear to be an iron curtain separating you from your aspirations.

Legendary basketball coach Bobby Knight once remarked, quite aptly, "Everyone wants to be on a winning team, but no one wants to come to practice."[a] The same could easily be said for dieting, daily exercise, or in the case of aspiring leaders, effective communication, creating a vision, or soliciting meaningful feedback from peers and subordinates. So, the question is, What are the things you already know of that you will allow to get in the way of practice and, therefore, improvement?

The solution to these obstacles will not come from simply swearing to not fall prey to them. The challenge is admittedly not so simple. However, having described them, you are at least putting yourself on notice that you know they are there.[b]

Finally, you might want to try simply doing some of the things you envision yourself doing in twelve months' time—within reason, of course. Don't just lace up and head out on a marathon because getting in shape is part of your personal vision. Instead, take the advice of choreographer Twyla Tharp when I asked how she creates a dance: "I just start to move." Or in the words of sociologist Howard S. Becker in his admonition to students beginning their doctoral dissertations, "Just start writing . . . anything will do to get you started."[c]

a. "Charlie Rose with Bobby Knight," Public Broadcasting System, March 15, 2001.

b. In chapters 6 and 7 we take up ways to enlist others in drawing attention to your real or impending lapse into unproductive and/or stalling behaviors. For a more thorough discussion of the way we try to fool ourselves, see The Arbinger Institute, *Leadership and Self-Deception: Getting out of the Box* (San Francisco: Berrett-Koehler, 2002).

c. Howard S. Becker, *Writing for Social Scientists* (Chicago: University of Chicago Press, 1986).

THE MOTIVATION TO LEAD

Now that you've begun to answer questions about *why* you want to lead, let's examine your more fundamental, perhaps even unconscious, motivators.

Outstanding leaders acquire their qualities through practice, but a leader's aspirations—his or her vision of what could be, despite what is—are fueled by intense personal motivation. Talent is important, without a doubt, but as we've seen, raw talent is not enough. Motivation is an enduring factor that can accelerate or inhibit your improvement as a leader. Thus, understanding what motivates you—what influences the way you think and behave in the most fundamental ways—will make it easier to identify and exploit the right learning opportunities for yourself, particularly crucible experiences. Likewise, understanding how and when you learn best helps *sustain* your motivation to grow and learn as a leader.

Motivation is not the same as aspiration. Aspirations, such as those we explored in the preceding exercise, are images of the way things ought to be and, if we apply ourselves, how they will be. Although these images provide data that is valuable in exploring your motives, they are not the same as motives.[4] Motives are predispositions or background desires—often opaque because they are not routinely examined—that lead us to act in particular ways. Needless to say, furious debates in the field of psychology have flourished for decades as to whether we can ever truly understand individual motives, much less change them. However, I come down on the side of using all available means to explore one's motives for insight into why we behave the way we do. Thus, rather than argue that we are slaves to passions we cannot discern, I argue that our motives are very real and analyzable, that they do indeed influence the way we think and behave (and thus we ought to examine them closely), and that they quite often temper the aspirations we set for ourselves.

Indeed, many psychologists who study individual motivation, most notable among them being David McClelland, his students, and his colleagues, believe that what distinguishes leaders is not their behavior but their inner motivation—in particular, the way they think about leadership.[5] In other words, statements about aspirations provide valuable detail and a clearer sense of context, but similar aspirations can be arrived at by different paths. For example, a personal aspiration may prominently feature you as an admired leader, a perennial face on the cover of *Business Week*. You can, however, get there any of a number of ways: building a company through hard work and dedication, unleashing extraordinary efforts from ordinary people, or finding uncharted accounting techniques with which to pump up your company's share price.

Likewise, a statement of aspirations may give only a modicum of insight as to whether an individual can realistically achieve them. This caution is important on two levels. First, even when you take the time to create tension between where you want to be and where you are, there is no guarantee that you aren't coloring your aspirations in such a way as to reflect what's socially acceptable or desirable versus what you really want. For example, although MBA students love to quote from articles that venerate participative, group-oriented leadership styles, I've often seen those same students after hours reading dog-eared copies of such bibles of individualism as *The Fountainhead* and *Atlas Shrugged*.

Second, you may envision yourself behaving in a way in which you are really not disposed to behave. Though one of the central premises of this book is that human beings are mutable—they can change their behaviors and even the way they think—never would I argue that change is easy or straightforward. If you find great pleasure or comfort or reduced anxiety by staying in the background, working in isolation on something you understand, then it's going to be difficult to step into the limelight, point in the direction of unknown territory (no matter how attractive it might appear), and link arms with people you don't really know.

That's why it's important to give serious thought to what truly motivates you to perform. Unfortunately, the most effective tools for exploring your motives demand textbooks' worth of explanation and skill in interpreting individual results that are well beyond a book focused on learning from experience. But as I'll show in the upcoming section on learning styles, there are many useful assessments and inventories available through human resource departments, management development consultancies, college textbooks, and even online that you can tap into for more detailed insight. Even the popular personality profiles like the Myers-Briggs Type Indicator (MBTI) or the Fundamental Interpersonal Relations Orientation-Behavior (FIRO-B) can provide a wealth of insight into thought styles, values, and motivations.[6]

Here's an exercise that I have found to be a useful starting point when assessing your underlying motivations.

Exercise 4: Finding Your Passion

IMAGINE THAT YOU SUDDENLY HAVE an extra day each week and you alone are responsible for deciding what to do with that day. Consider this question: what two alternative pursuits would you choose— even if one of those pursuits involved staying in bed asleep all day? Then, having satisfied yourself that those answers really portray what you would do, answer this question: what do those choices share in common?

Exploring your answers gives you an opportunity to better understand the pursuits you gravitate to and away from. The options you actively choose are indicators of something you deeply value and/or find missing in your life—things you may, in fact, find yourself straining to realize at work or in the "rest of your life." By digging beneath the surface of the pair of options—using them as clues rather than answers— you may actually illuminate an easier or a more likely path to follow in growing as a leader. An example can clarify what I mean.

Glenn was a prominent executive in his midforties and well regarded as a manager in a Silicon Valley software company. He and I had been talking about a challenge he'd recently received from his bosses: to bring more products to market at a faster pace. Glenn was responsible for a department composed largely of software developers, many of whom were creative individuals who, in Glenn's words, "don't respond well to heavy-handed management" and who "tend to be suspicious of people who assert themselves as leaders." Glenn was proud that he'd created an environment that fostered innovation and that he'd done it without heavy-handed management; but now he sensed that he'd have to crack the whip in order to speedily commercialize ideas that had been languishing on the shelf. He questioned whether he had the skill to lead such a change. He wondered whether he could adjust.

Glenn's was, in many respects, a classic leadership challenge: could he alter his style in response to an external demand? Sensing that Glenn was asking a question about authenticity—his own authenticity as a person and as a leader—rather than about leadership style or technique, I initiated a brief exploration of what was at the core of his definition of himself as a person and as a leader. What was making him uncomfortable about what he felt he was being asked to do and to be?

I asked what he would do with an extra day a week. After a minute, he offered up sailing with his friends and camping with his wife and eight-year-old son. I pressed him to explain why those pursuits. As he did, he began to talk about how, for him at least, those two activities combined freedom and connectedness in the right measure. "I can point the boat in whatever direction I want—sail to an island in the distance if I choose—or we can just chase the wind. It's up to me and to my ability. I am free to choose." Yet he also cherished the feeling of being deeply in concert with his friends, his boat, and with nature: "It's almost like we are one entity: me, the crew, the boat, the water, and the wind. It's like being a flock of birds moving in unison." Unobstructed yet intimately connected. Camping with his family produced a similar sensation: "We are out in nature, away from the constraints of the city, free to roam wherever we want. But we do it as a family, as a team, as an intimate group."

What does that tell him (or us) about his motivations? Sailing and camping are obviously pleasurable pursuits, but at a deeper level they provide the opportunity to experience both freedom and connectedness. He valued being able to strive and to explore and to do so with people he cared about. To see things through his own eyes, at the helm of his own ship, but also to have others along to enjoy the view. These things mattered to him.

(continued)

Is this a complete assessment of his motivations? By no means. It doesn't provide the depth of insight that psychological testing or psychiatric analysis might. (And as an assessment, it didn't jump out immediately either; we spent several hours over several days teasing it out). But at the same time, a simple question provided him with insight about what really matters. As we talked, we both got a clearer sense of at least one path he could follow in addressing the challenge he was posed. He volunteered that he could put much more emphasis on the destination than he had before; up to now, he conceded, he and his team had reveled in the process of creating software, but had downplayed the arrival point that also represented an important part of the journey. In his broader philosophy of life, he subscribed to the notion that "the journey is as important as the destination," but now, he concluded, it was essential to highlight the *destination*. It wouldn't be too great a stretch or too much a departure from how he'd behaved or how he perceived himself. This was something of which he was capable, in much the same way that he was capable of being very directive with his crew when the boat encountered dangerous waters or a sudden storm, and in much the same way that he was capable of coaxing his family to the end of a long and arduous hike.

In other words, he concluded, the challenge he faced did not really demand a dramatic shift in style or a betrayal of values in which he believed deeply. Rather, what was required was a shift in emphasis, a shift to a leadership style with which he was already familiar (in another part of his life) but which he did not routinely employ at work. Pondering what he'd do if he had a stretch of "free" time led him to reflect on what he really liked to do (or didn't do enough of); from there it was a short hop to concluding that maybe he could surmount the challenge in a way that wouldn't make him feel inauthentic or heavy-handed.

Now consider this: Why did *you* select those pursuits ahead of all the other things you could be doing on that free day? What do you find attractive about them? What do they enable you to do, or feel, or be that you don't have enough time for in your current week?

How You Think Influences How You Behave

One of the most widely used and, from my perspective, the most usable assessments of individual motivation was developed by McClelland and his team to shed light on the connection between the way people think and the way they behave. Behaviors, like any outcome measure, may be relatively easy to document and observe, but the real leverage for change comes from examining the patterns of thought that lead to behavior, even when those patterns are not immediately obvious or easy to articulate. Through systematic analysis of stories collected from thousands of people around the world, McClelland's team concluded that some 80 percent of the stories consisted of some combination of three social motives:[7]

- *Achievement*—a concern with excellence or doing things well and efficiently, expressed in stories by competing with the self or with the performance of others, by doing something unique, or by advancing one's career. Common characteristics among those motivated by achievement include preference for individual work, responsiveness to individual goals and incentives, willingness to undertake moderate risks in tasks/goals, difficulty in dealing with people (low emotional intelligence), and a tendency to seek and need hard, quantitative feedback.

- *Affiliation*—a concern with friendship, expressed in stories by wanting to be liked or accepted or to participate in social situations. Common characteristics among those motivated by affiliation include preference for working in groups, responsiveness to group goals and incentives, low willingness to undertake risks in tasks and goals, many friends and high levels of emotional intelligence, discomfort in leadership roles, and a tendency to see feedback as personal—an evaluation of liking or disliking.

- *Power*—a concern with influence and influence relationships, expressed in stories by powerful actions, arousing strong emotions in others, or being concerned about one's reputation, prestige, or position. A person's orientation for power can be one of three types: personal, institutional, and interactive.[8] Those who are oriented toward personal power want to direct others, and this need often is perceived as undesirable. Persons oriented toward institutional power want to organize the efforts of others to further the goals of an organization; they are not, however, likely to share power with subordinates. People oriented toward interactive power derive their influence from others—for example, the team or organization they lead. Common characteristics among those motivated by power include very high emotional intelligence, willingness to take moderate risks in influence situations and either high or low risks in task situations, verbal facileness, a preference for qualitative feedback, and ability to persist in a goal for lengthy periods without feedback or with negative feedback.

McClelland's prescription is simple: if you desire to be a leader, you have to think like one. To the extent that you are motivated by a need for affiliation or achievement, you won't think the way power-oriented leaders do.

Of course, changing the way you think is no easy chore, but David Burnham prescribes a very distinctive pattern of thinking and a systematic process for shaping thought patterns that, according to his published research, lead not only to desired actions but also to results predicted by the theory. At the heart of that process is a form of deliberate practice that would look familiar to students and teachers of music, chess, or any of a number of complex, highly intentional pursuits—most emphatically in terms of approaches like the Suzuki Method. In this case, deliberate practice revolves around crafting stories that contain statements and directions that are consistent with the core ideas about interactive leadership.

The most important thing to notice about this description of Burnham's approach is its attention to conscious documentation and articulation of thought in the drive to change behavior. In crafting stories—writing and rewriting one's own as well as deciphering others'—you are compelled to render visible (if only in the minds' eye) how you think. As Michelene Chi and others have found in research that asks experts to verbalize their thoughts and their associations, and as Donald Schon found in his transcripts of experts' interchanges with apprentices and students, speaking one's thoughts is not an easy thing to do, particularly when so much of the activity of leading (or architecting) is conveyed through gestures.[9] Nonetheless, it can be inordinately productive when one tries to uncover the assumptions and symbols that influence the conclusions we reach—and, often, the actions we take.

Verbalization and documentation help us get help, too. Psychiatrists encourage patients to externalize their thoughts and fantasies in order to uncover logic and associations that could lead to deeper insight. Professionals of all sorts, including automotive designers, conduct design reviews that generally involve talking about pictures and assigning to inanimate objects the desires and intentions of their designers. Many is the time, in my capacity as a consultant, I have sat in on a design review and heard an engineer talk about "what the car wants to be," when, in fact, he is describing what *he* wants the car to be.[10]

The benefit of verbalization and documentation is what it contributes to achieving conscious competence—that is, the ability to notice what you are doing as you do it and, if you desire, to alter it, experiment with it, and assess whether it fits what you are trying to achieve.

DISCOVERING HOW YOU LEARN BEST

Throughout this book I have argued that learning is a critical part of leading, particularly leading for a lifetime. Adaptive capacity is all about learning, and each time I have mentioned it, I have been careful to draw the link between an individual's ability to adapt and his or her ability and willingness to learn. Moreover, the ability to engage others in shared meaning rests heavily on understanding how others learn.

Most people have a sense of how they learn. Some learn by hands-on experience, others by trial and error, reading, observation, or some combination of these.[11] Most of us are at least aware that another person's learning style may differ from ours—and that those differences require us to exercise some flexibility in the way we teach or attempt to impart information and technique. Seems obvious, but ask yourself seriously, How much do I understand about how I learn or about the differences between my most familiar or comfortable mode of learning and the ones others rely on?

I personally learned the answer to that question after trying to teach my daughter to ride a bike when she was six. I began by wheeling her to a nearby playground with a big empty basketball court. My explanation, from my perspective at least, was simple and straightforward: "Hold on to the handlebars, keep your feet on the pedals, keep the pedals going at a nice, even speed, and pick out something like that bush off in the distance to ride toward. Just focus on that bush. Don't worry about anything in-between." Ever the dutiful child, my daughter nodded in understanding, gritted her teeth, and focused on the bush. Clutching the back of her seat, I gave her a gentle shove. Off she went—for about ten feet. She stopped pedaling, the front wheel wobbled furiously, and down she went, scraping her knee in the process. Once the tears subsided and I convinced her that she really ought to get on and try again, I repeated my instructions, with even more emphasis on the pedaling part.

Another shove and . . . twenty feet later, crash: another scrape, more tears, and a kick to the seat for good measure. My wife, who up to this point had been watching quietly from the sidelines, asked whether she could give it a try. "Sure," I said, not convinced in the least that she'd do any better. Looking our daughter in the eyes, she said simply, "Look, I am going to run alongside you, holding on to you and to the bike, and when you feel like you're ready to ride by yourself, you tell me and I'll let go." Off they went, slowly crossing the basketball court. Periodically my wife would ask, "Do you feel it?" For the first minute or two, she shook her head no. Then, inexplicably, on the fifth or sixth try, my daughter declared, tentatively, "I think I've got it, Mommy." My wife let go and off our daughter went, a little wobbly and hardly straight, but riding by herself.

The moral of the story? I have a keen professional interest in learning, yet I still missed three very basic principles: first, my daughter doesn't learn the way I do; second, unlike my wife, I didn't vary my teaching style to match my daughter's learning style; and third (something I didn't realize until after this episode), I don't actually learn the way I teach. This last point might seem obscure, but it's important to formulating your Personal Learning Strategy.

It turns out, I'm not alone in the misperceptions I had about learning. Espoused theories of learning, to borrow Chris Argyris's term, frequently give lip service to the importance of matching learning environments and technologies to differences in learning styles. Theory in practice, on the other hand, operates on what philosopher Paulo Freire characterized as the *banking model* of education: deposit facts and methods in a student's head, and she will store them there until she needs them.[12] To this day, most primary, secondary, and even postsecondary educational institutions subscribe in practice to the banking model. When I taught at several major universities in the first fifteen years of my postdoctoral career, I routinely lectured to students, assigned them hundreds of pages of reading on a weekly basis, and expected them to repeat back to me the things that I had said or some other sage had written. Yet, in my heart of hearts, I knew that I didn't like to read hundreds of pages; I even remembered, with no small amount of chagrin, the dozens of reading assignments I'd skimmed while in college myself because I couldn't help but doze off after a few pages of turgid academic prose. Yet here I was, adhering to convention, depositing facts and methods in the heads of my students with the assumption that if they listened, read, and took copious notes, they would learn. I *knew* that that wasn't the way I learned. But it was the way I taught—at least up to that point!

The point is that when it comes to developing a Personal Learning Strategy, being clear about how you learn and how you learn best is essential. Such clarity will allow you to leverage the resources available to you, whether they are structured classes and workshops, on-the-job training, or crucible experiences. One thing you can do immediately is to reflect a bit on how you learned something recently.

EXERCISE 5:

Something You Recently Learned

THINK ABOUT SOMETHING you learned recently. Not a fact, like the capital of Azerbaijan (Baku), but something along the lines of either a new skill or technique or a new insight. Relevant examples might involve learning a new cooking technique, a language, something your organization does that you'd never really understood; or discovering that you weren't especially good at teaching your child to ride a bike. Think for a moment about what you actually learned that was new to you. It might not be the activity so much as it is the way you perceive what you're doing. Then think about what enabled you to learn. That is, what circumstances or resources made it possible for you to learn something you didn't previously know? Explore those factors at the individual level (e.g., what drove you to learn?) Who else was involved in your learning, and what role did they play? As I noted earlier, learning is often a lonely process, but rarely do people learn by themselves alone.

Fortunately, most organizations subscribe to one or another popular assessment of learning styles. As in the case of motivational assessments, I strongly encourage you to take advantage of what employers already offer. But, again, even if they do not offer an assessment (or if you worry about sharing the results of your assessment), there are many tools available in the market and on the Web. David Kolb's Learning Style Inventory is one of the most widely used and accessible diagnostics around and at modest cost provides a wealth of material that can be used in filling out your PLS.

Kolb's research on how people use experience in learning builds from distinctions along the lines of the VARK model and adds to them the dimension of "efficacy"—that is, how effectively people translate something they see, hear, or feel into a new understanding.[13] According to Kolb, most of us develop a strength in, or orientation to, one of four basic learning styles (see table 5-1):

TABLE 5-1

Kolb's four basic learning styles

Learning style	Attributes	Preferred learning situations
Converging	• Solving problems • Making decisions • Reasoning deductively • Defining problems • Being logical	• Finding practical uses for theories and ideas • Dealing with technical tasks, rather than social and interpersonal issues • Simulations, lab experiments, practical applications
Assimilating	• Planning • Creating models • Defining problems • Developing theories • Being patient	• Understanding a wide range of information and putting it into concise, logical form • Developing theory that has logical soundness, even more so than practical value • Lectures, readings, time for reflection
Diverging	• Being imaginative • Understanding people • Recognizing problems • Brainstorming • Being open-minded	• Observing, rather than taking action • Situations that call for a wide range of ideas and information • Working in groups • Listening with an open mind • Receiving personalized feedback
Accommodating	• Getting things done • Leading • Taking risks • Initiating • Being adaptable and practical	• Learning from hands-on experience • Being involved in new and challenging experiences • Situations that call for "gut" decisions versus logical analysis • Working with others to define problems and solutions

Source: Adapted from David A. Kolb, *The Learning Style Inventory: Technical Manual* (Boston: McBer and Company, 1976); David A. Kolb, "Learning Styles and Disciplinary Differences," in *The Modern American College,* ed. A. W. Chickering (San Francisco: Jossey-Bass, 1981); and David A. Kolb and Ronald E. Fry, "Toward an Applied Theory of Experiential Learning," in *Theories of Group Process,* ed. Cary L. Cooper (London: Wiley, 1975).

converging, assimilating, diverging, or accommodating. Each learning style is an ideal type, and, as was the case with McClelland's motivational types, people rarely operate from just one. For purposes of this discussion, however, let's consider what differences in learning style mean.

Someone with a diverging style, for example, is much more comfortable learning from dealing with open-ended problems and situations that call for creative responses, compared with, say, someone with a converging style who learns by chopping problems into smaller, more rational and manageable pieces. Thus, the fuzzy front end of a product development process, when it's not at all clear what will ultimately emerge, is a place where someone with a diverging learning style would claim he learns best. On the other hand, someone with a converging learning style would say she learns best when she has things under control and where there is a new but logical method for solving problems to be learned.

Try the following exercise for yourself to see where you come out in this kind of inventory.

EXERCISE 6:

Kolb's Learning Style Inventory

USING TABLE 5-1 as your guide, determine which of the learning styles (and situations) most closely approximates your own.[a] Then take a look at the "opposing" style to see how it differs from your own: converging and diverging are, not surprisingly, on opposite ends of a continuum, as are assimilating and accommodating. The "adjacent" learning styles (e.g., assimilating and accommodating for someone with a predominantly converging learning style) share some aspects in common with your dominant style. As I'll note in chapter 6, adjacent learning styles and situations represent a place where you can extend your dominant or native learning style. Opposing learning styles and situations will present you with significant learning challenges.

a. Better yet, seek out an opportunity to fill in Kolb's inventory or something similar.

Not Just Style, But Stance, Too

Your Personal Learning Strategy needs to address not only your learning style, but your learning "stance," as well. By stance I mean how open you are to learning new things, particularly under high-stress conditions. In chapter 3 I took up the question of how some people learn from crucible experiences, and in chapter 4 I dove into the research on expert performance; in both cases I drew attention to the barriers to learning that can crop up during periods of stress, when new or disconfirming evidence can appear without warning. Thus, it's not enough to gain insight into how you learn when things are going smoothly; you must also have a clue as to how you react to learning opportunities that present themselves as stressful, uncomfortable, perhaps even unnerving events. Not surprisingly, your reactions will be of signal importance when it comes to crucible events on the job and off.

Although we take up the connection between your learning style and crucible experiences explicitly in the next chapter, you might consider the following thought experiment to begin assessing your own learning style under stress.

EXERCISE 7:

The Alien Test

THIS THOUGHT EXPERIMENT draws on a theme encountered in two movies made nearly a half century apart. Both movies depicted a similar set of events and illustrated remarkably similar reactions to unprecedented, arguably crucible-like, events: *Independence Day* (1996) and *The Day the Earth Stood Still* (1951).[a] In both films, extraterrestrial beings arrive on Earth with unclear intent. People of all sorts, from presidents to private citizens, exhibit one of three basic behaviors. Some run in horror; the very idea of alien life forms scares them to death. Some rush forward with open arms; alien life is a reason for joyous celebration. And then there are the others who do nothing; alien life is so far out of the realm of reason that it is easier to just ignore it than to try to comprehend.

Think or write about which of those three ways you might respond to such an invasion from outer space. What do you think your reaction tells you about your ability to process new information in stressful situations? The purpose of this exercise isn't to judge any particular reaction; rather, you'll ideally gain valuable insight about yourself that can help you understand your default learning style. In conjunction with the two preceding exercises, it will also help you define where your learning edge is—that is, where and under what conditions you are most likely to challenge the long-held assumptions that give you comfort but that might also keep you from adapting to change.

a. *Independence Day* was directed by Roland Emmerich and written by Dean Devlin and Roland Emmerich. *The Day the Earth Stood Still* was directed by Robert Wise and written by Harry Bates (story) and Edmund H. North (screenplay).

YOUR CRUCIBLE EXPERIENCES

So far in this chapter we have walked through three steps to help you begin exploring your internal beliefs and motivations. At this juncture it makes sense to address directly what all these ideas have to do with how you learn from your own crucible experiences.

As you've thought about your own experiences, compared them with those of the people I've quoted, and pondered questions about why you lead and what your own personal aspirations and motivations are, as well as how you lead, you've been processing in the background your most influential leadership experiences. Now is the time to bring them to the forefront.

The following exercise involves recollecting and analyzing several of your crucible experiences. The exercise is structured to enable you to quickly surface key insights and assumptions and then to document them so they can be used in subsequent chapters as "data" and points of reference. Completing the exercise will be extraordinarily helpful in crafting your own Personal Learning Strategy in chapters 6 and 7.

EXERCISE 8:

Your Learning Lifeline

FOR OUR BOOK *Geeks and Geezers*, Warren Bennis and I asked the people we interviewed to draw out a lifeline from birth to their current age, indicating critical events or relationships along the way that shaped them as a leader. Try doing the same thing now. Leave a lot of room on a big piece of paper because you may be surprised how many events or relationships you will recall.

Looking over your lifeline, pick out three or four points that you would think of as turning points. These should be events or relationships in which you learned something really important about yourself that affected the way you behave as a leader. Next to the ones you choose, or on a separate sheet of paper, answer the following questions for each crucible:

- What was the insight you got about yourself or the lesson you learned?

- What kind of crucible was this? (new territory, reversal, suspension, or some combination?)

- What resources (people, institutions, ideas, finances, etc.) helped you get through this time and/or helped you learn what you learned?

(continued)

- What did you learn about how you learn?

Then, looking across the three or four crucibles you chose, search for commonalities and contrasts among them. Were they, for example, similar in type (i.e., all involving new territory)? Were there differences in the kinds of resources you used to get through these times?

As a result of your comparison of these crucibles, what would you conclude about how you learn important things? What would you conclude about what resources help you learn important things? How do these conclusions compare with your experience in other learning settings, such as classroom-based training, off-sites, or training programs?

As you complete this exercise, document your insights someplace where they will be accessible to you later on, for chapters 6 and 7. Again, the intent is to heighten your ability to articulate your observations so that you can grow into conscious competence.

In the two chapters that follow, you will be guided toward creating your own Personal Learning Strategy. Chapter 6 gives you the opportunity to assess yourself along the core leadership dimensions—adaptive capacity, ability to engage others through shared meaning, and integrity—and suggests exercises to help limber your mind along each dimension. Chapter 7 will help you design more concretely a Personal Learning Strategy.

$$\begin{bmatrix} 6 \end{bmatrix}$$

EXPLORING YOUR CAPABILITIES

Begin with a Candid Self-Assessment

I am learning all the time. The tombstone will be my diploma.

—Eartha Kitt

I am always ready to learn although
I do not always like being taught.

—Winston Churchill

RECALL THE AMAZEMENT with which you first watched a glassblower draw a delicately fluted champagne glass out of a glowing blob of liquid crystal or a gifted orator achieve rapport with an audience of strangers. The effects these people created seemed magical, even mystical. Even though you knew that nothing ethereal was going on, you could not help but feel awestruck.

How did they get there?

Practice, practice, practice. No one skill defines an eminent glassblower, a public speaker, or a leader. But mastering many skills and combining them with greater and greater ease can produce the kind of effect that an adept performer creates. (See the box, "Practicing While You Perform.")

Looking back on the leaders' stories recounted so far in this book, recall that crucible experiences taught two lessons, not just one. There are the lessons about leading—and each lesson is profound and consequential in its own way. But then there are also the lessons about learning, about the importance of preparedness, about the need to recognize, reframe, and resolve the tension between what is and what could be, and ultimately about the process of adapting and growing. The very skills that crucibles enhance (perhaps even teach) turn out to be the skills that individuals come to practice on an everyday basis: skills like observing and communicating, questioning and comparing, acting and reflecting on action, being in the maelstrom but being able to step out or above to see oneself and the context more clearly. In other words, everyday practice holds the key to surviving extraordinary events—and extraordinary events can teach a person what to practice every day.

In this chapter I'll pose questions that will help you assess your mastery of the skill sets or moves that effective leaders practice. The chapter consists of three self-assessments—one each for adaptive capacity, ability to engage others, and personal integrity. Following each self-assessment is a series of exercises that feature skills that underlie each leadership practice.[1] If you assess yourself deeply and honestly and fully engage with the exercises, you will be in the position to start honing the same qualities that the men and women have who've made the most of their crucible experiences. You will be ready to design your own Personal Learning Strategy, beginning in chapter 7.

Practicing While You Perform

EXPERT PERFORMERS DON'T PRACTICE the way novices do, and they don't think about practice the same way, either. In fact, interviews that I have done with golf, music, acting, and flying instructors suggest that practice occurs at several distinctly different levels. For example, there's what a flight instructor referred to as *technical practice*: alert and concentrated enactment of the technical skills involved in keeping an aircraft stable and properly oriented to the horizon. Akin to the repertoire of techniques found in music (e.g., fingering, reading music, and achieving harmony) or the moves that underlie the performance of magic (e.g., palm, switch, drop, and misdirection) these are very specific skills that need to be mastered—often in isolation—so that they can later be combined to produce desired effects.

Then there's *rehearsal*. Tom Stein, professor at the renowned Berklee College of Music in Boston, advises students to work on improving their technical skills no more than fifteen minutes a day. They should, however, perform for between two and five hours a day "in real places with real audiences—either musicians, or on the street for an audience, or in front of teachers."[a] His point is clear: spend your time doing the thing that you most want to be and enjoy doing. In the process, you'll improve your performance and expand your repertoire.

Background practice is a third form of practice. It's something you can do that addresses aspects of what you're trying to accomplish or become without occupying center stage in your attention. Nothing illustrates this better than something I observed at a social gathering I attended recently. At the party, I couldn't help but notice a young, very athletic couple who stood out for two reasons: their bohemian dress and the fact that they were constantly moving. Not dashing about, but bending and stretching and flowing smoothly from one position to the next, even as they stood in place and talked with other people. They didn't touch—in fact, their clothes and their movements were the only thing that seemed to connect them—but it was clear that they were doing something more like one another than like anyone around them. I commented to a friend on what I saw. "Oh," he announced after glancing in their direction, "they're dancers." "Hmm, do dancers always move around like that?" I asked. "No," he repeated this time with an arched eyebrow, "they're *dancers*. They're just trying to get comfortable with a new ballet." In other words, they were practicing offline at a level of background consciousness—not fully engaged mentally, but mindful at some level that they had to pull and knead themselves into new shapes.

(continued)

Finally, there's the real-time form of practice we first discussed in chapter 1: *practicing while you perform*. This is self-aware, attentive practice that takes place in the midst of performance, whether the performance is for a huge audience or a single individual. The key is that a portion of consciousness is reserved for observing yourself, the people with whom you are interacting, and the situation that encompasses you both at the same time that you go about performing—whether that's speaking, listening, writing, or working. That portion of consciousness that's reserved for practicing while you perform enables the expert to see his action and the reaction he gets, to vary the action on the basis of a hunch or a hypothesis about what the reaction will be, and to compare the reaction with what he expected.

As an illustration, consider storytelling. Storytelling can be a powerful way in which to communicate a vision or illustrate a key value or lesson—both of which are central to the ability to engage people through shared meaning. Effective storytelling takes practice, not just in telling a story, but in gauging an audience's reception of the story, the level of energy or emotion that's being created by the story and the telling, and the course of a story itself (should it be shortened or lengthened to maximize the effect?).

What are the levels of practice in storytelling? Technical practice would most likely involve a course or a workshop, replete with trained instructors, an introduction to the theory, history, and lore of storytelling and to different storytelling methods, structured exercises with immediate feedback, and a set of lessons on what to do on completion of the workshop. Rehearsal would involve identifying a situation in which you'd like to tell a story, perhaps to enliven a speech or a presentation or to illustrate a particular point to a specific group of people you're trying to influence, and practicing the telling in front of a mirror or a coach or family members so that you can vary your delivery, your inflection or posture, and assess the different effects you create. Background practice would involve finding places and times in which you can exercise elements of storytelling skill without necessarily telling a complete story—for example, explaining something complicated or frightening to a child by finding an illustration that is neither complex nor frightening.

Practicing while you perform would involve telling your story in a real situation—a situation where it matters—and watching people's reactions and then repeating the situation but varying your delivery to see whether the response differs in ways you might have hypothesized.[b]

Each form of practice—technical, rehearsal, background, and real-time—needs to be made part of a Personal Learning Strategy. Technical practice helps you master underlying moves so that later they can be combined with what appears to be effortless ease. Rehearsal directs you to grab large blocks of time to practice under conditions that approximate performance. Background practice insinuates simulated performance into times and places where it can be made to fit. And practicing while you perform helps time-starved individuals learn while they are doing.

a. Tom Stein, personal communication with author, July 2006.

b. Leaders often have to give the same speech or presentation to multiple audiences. This makes it easier to practice while you perform.

ADAPTIVE CAPACITY: YOUR ABILITY TO OBSERVE AND BE OPEN TO LEARNING

Adaptive capacity includes such critical skills as the ability to understand context and to recognize and seize opportunities. It may be the essential competence of leaders. People with ample adaptive capacity learn important lessons and new skills that allow them to move on to new levels of achievement and new levels of learning. This ongoing process of challenge, adaptation, and learning prepares you for the next crucible, where the process is repeated. Whenever you encounter significant new problems and deal with them adaptively, you achieve new levels of competence, which better prepares you for the next challenge.

Daunting, perhaps, but worth striving for. The question is, How adaptive are you? In the assessment exercise that follows, I've identified several dimensions of adaptive capacity, based on my interviews with lifelong leaders and a review of the research on adaptability and resilience.

Self-Assessment A: Adaptive Capacity

Think back to a recent experience that either illustrates how, for example, you explored something out of your comfort zone or, alternatively, how you avoided doing so. Then carefully consider each question below and respond accordingly. Your responses will be important in allocating your time, energy, and attention in the Personal Learning Strategy you'll develop in the next chapter.

Self-assessment A: adaptive capacity

1 = Never, 2 = Seldom, 3 = Sometimes, 4 = Usually, 5 = Always

1. Are you constantly on the lookout   1   2   3   4   5
   for ways to improve your performance
   as a leader?

   Recent example:

   _____

   _____

2. Do you set stretch goals for yourself?   1   2   3   4   5

   Recent example:

   _____

   _____

3. Do you think it's interesting to learn   1   2   3   4   5
   and develop new hobbies?

   Recent example:

   _____

   _____

4. At work, do you want to learn about   1   2   3   4   5
   different aspects of your organization?

Recent example:

_____

_____

5. Do you stay current on new technologies   1   2   3   4   5
    or other potential disruptions to your
    organization?

Recent example:

_____

_____

6. Are you intrigued by the patterns   1   2   3   4   5
    you find in art and nature?

Recent example:

_____

_____

7. Do you enjoy concentrating on a fantasy   1   2   3   4   5
    or daydream and exploring all its
    possibilities?

Recent example:

_____

_____

8. Are you a good judge of character?   1   2   3   4   5

Recent example:

_____

_____

9. Do you persevere through difficulties?   1   2   3   4   5

Recent example:

_____

_____

(continued)

10. Do you volunteer for difficult   1   2   3   4   5
    assignments?

Recent example:

_____

_____

Now add up the numbers you circled in the assessment. In the next chapter you will use this assessment to identify specific actions you can take to enhance or to sustain your adaptive capacity. A score of 10–25 suggests that adaptive capacity is a dimension you ought to focus attention on; a score of 26–40 suggests that you have some skill in this space but ought to work on aspects on which you score lower; and a score of 41–50 suggests that adaptive capacity is already a strength of yours. But because capacities, like muscles, tend to atrophy without regular exercise, in the following section I offer some exercises for you to try.

Do You See?

Adaptive capacity rests heavily on your ability to see, to observe, and to comprehend the world from different angles so that you can quickly and accurately increase the information that's available to you. We start with this dimension because it is a cornerstone to building conscious competence as a leader. John Berger, the art critic, painter, and novelist, characterizes "seeing" as an underappreciated skill: "Seeing comes before words," he writes. "The child looks and recognizes before it can speak. It is seeing which establishes our place in the surrounding world; we explain that world with words, but words can never undo the fact that we are surrounded by it. The relation between what we see and what we know is never settled. Each evening we *see* the sun set. We *know* that the earth is turning away from it. Yet the knowledge, the explanation, never quite fits the sight."[2]

To be an effective observer, you need to hone your awareness, to use every available sense organ to collect inputs. You need to see without supposition and inference. You can do that best, paradoxically, by increasing your sensitivity of the biases, distortions, and shorthand devices (e.g., stereotypes) you routinely bring to make sense of the things you see and hear.

The following set of exercises will test your own perceptions.[3] Two are best pursued outside work; but three others ought to be undertaken at work.

EXERCISE 1:

Go to an Art Museum or Gallery

NOTHING QUITE EXCITES THE SENSES or polarizes a crowd like a piece of art. Visit an art museum or gallery and roam around until you spot a piece of work that you find either really pleasing or really repulsive. Mild reactions won't do; it's got to be something you feel deeply, even physically. (Don't worry if you start with something that disgusts you; you'll repeat the exercise with something you love.) Stand in front of the work and take it in. If it's repulsive, don't back away or rush off after a cursory look. The point of this exercise is not for you to try to figure out what the artist is "saying" with the piece; that's immaterial.

What is material is what *you* are seeing or hearing from the piece. As you scrutinize it, take note of the impressions you're experiencing: does it make you feel happy or sad or calm or jittery or hungry? Once you've begun to center in on a central or dominant impression, ask yourself, Why is that impression so strong? What is it about the image you're taking in that ignites those impressions?

Don't stop there. Press deeper: Why do I find that attractive or repulsive? Where or when have I felt a similar feeling? What set of images or events makes me feel this way? When was the last time I felt this way?

Repeat the exercise with a piece of art that creates the opposite impression.

This exercise may confound you a bit initially because it's easy to look at something and proclaim that "it is what it is." But once you open yourself to associations—neuroscientists theorize that memory is a network of associations—you'll find yourself flooded with feelings and images. The point is not to suggest that you should block associations in order to improve your observational powers but, instead, to alert you to the way in which images often carry with them feelings—some attractive and pleasant, others repulsive and discomforting—and to get you to notice that you may linger with some images and rush away from others. What you see, in other words, may be determined by what you feel about what you see.

My interviews with accomplished leaders alerted me to the way that acuity in observation was often linked to the ability to sense a crucible occurring. Occasionally, as noted in chapter 2, someone would refer to a sensation bordering on a premonition that preceded an important event. What was being described was not a premonition; instead, it was much more likely to have been an association with a situation or an event that had already occurred but that had not been consciously surfaced—yet.

For practical purposes, one way to increase your skill at seeing is to give yourself time to do a mini after-action review at the end of each day. Build a ritual around a full sensory review of events of the day: what really pleased you, what really troubled you, what felt incomplete, as well as what associations preceded, accompanied, and followed particularly memorable events. Doing this kind of review not only will get you accustomed to parsing the difference between what you saw and what you may have missed, but it will also more deeply embed in your consciousness the ability to calibrate your observations in real time (when it often matters the most).

EXERCISE 2:

Shopping Cart

IMAGINE YOU ARE IN THE SUPERMARKET you usually frequent, and you've wheeled your cart into the express lane (ten items or less). As luck would have it, someone has left their cart in the lane unattended. Feeling generous, you decide to leave it where it is. While you wait your turn, you take a look into the unattended cart and this is what you see: a quart of skim milk, a head of broccoli, a flashlight in a package, a quart of motor oil, a large package of disposable baby diapers, a copy of the *Wall Street Journal*, and three dozen eggs.

To pass the time, you decide to imagine who this cart belongs to. Who is this person?

Don't take more than a few seconds to arrive at an image. On a piece of paper jot down in rapid succession your answers to these questions: Is this person male or female? Does this person have children at home and, if so, how many? Does this person work outside the home and, if so, what does he or she do? What sort of education does this person have? Is he or she married and, if so, for how long? What does the spouse do for a living? Where does this person live—for example, in a house, a condo, a rental apartment? Does this person drive a car and, if so, what kind? What year? What color? Finally, what color shoes will this person be wearing when he or she shows up to claim the cart?

Having completed your list, notice two things. First, note how much detail you are able to drag out of so little information. Even though the exercise asked you to engage your imagination, it probably was not difficult to fill in the blanks.

Second, if you compare notes with other people on the same assignment, you will quickly notice just how different your associations are from theirs. In the dozens of times I've asked groups to complete the assignment, I have found that women routinely associate a woman with the cart; men most frequently see a man with the cart, but they often complain that the mixed "gender identity" of the objects (diapers and a quart of motor oil in the same basket?) complicates the task. The point here is that stereotypes run deep. Not that stereotypes are necessarily bad; indeed, they are, as decision theorists remind us, powerful shorthand devices for assimilating and making sense of information under the pressure of time or other constraints.[a] The key is that you are more likely to see things you have already seen.

For practical purposes, you might want to start asking questions before you attribute meaning to events or comments. Chris Argyris and Donald Schon pioneered a distinction worth considering in this regard.

They distinguished between conversations—internal dialogues as well as interchanges between people—that revolved around assertions and conversations that revolved around hypotheses.[b] The former are studded with beliefs parading as facts—for example, "Everyone knows that men are more aggressive than women." The latter are composed of hypotheses in search of facts—for example, "I have seen many more situations in which men dominate business meetings than women have."

Another illustration, drawn from my own observation, shows how it is possible to alert yourself to situations in which your attributions may derail the performance of others. Frank was a highly successful government official who had engineered the turnaround of a troubled agency but who was, by his own admission, feared by many of the people who worked for him. He knew that because it came across with trumpets blaring in the 360-degree performance review he had initiated after his first year in office. Though not unaware of his reputation for such things as "crucifying and publicly humiliating people whom he deemed unprepared" in formal presentations (a quote from his performance review), Frank was nonetheless stumped as to how he could prevent himself from being demonized for his comments in the conference room.

With Frank's permission, I set up a video camera in the corner of his conference room and taped several staff meetings. In the course of those tapings, there were three separate occasions on which Frank made comments that signaled annoyance, impatience, or both. I watched the presenters cringe in each instance. But I also noticed in each instance preceding his comments that Frank appeared to be contorting his mouth and fingering the gap between two of his top teeth as if trying to dislodge a piece of food. Abruptly, he'd stop and then fire off an acerbic comment.

Later on, I showed Frank the videotape and asked him what was going on. Scratching his head, he started to speak and then paused. "You know what," he said, "I think I see what you're saying. There's no food there, but it's a funny place that starts to itch when I start getting upset. I know what's coming just by feeling it. I just don't stop myself." Seizing the opportunity, I asked Frank whether he would mind if I intervened the next time I saw him start picking his teeth like that. He agreed.

Several meetings later (all of which went smoothly, without an out-burst from Frank), I noticed Frank starting to squirm in his seat and go for his incisor during a presentation from one of his employees named Sarah. Quietly, from across the table, I asked Frank whether he was going to say something. He looked at me as if I'd caught his hand in the cookie jar, and smiled. "Yeah," he said, "I was just going to ask if maybe Sarah wouldn't mind it if we picked up the pace in her presentation a little. We're covering ground that most everyone is familiar with." He held his tongue, and the meeting went on without incident. Over time, Frank's meetings came to be regarded as helpful and productive, no longer nicknamed the "star chamber."

The key here is that the more alert you are to these kinds of triggers, the more likely it is you can intercept them before they have negative consequences, or at least consequences you'd prefer not to experience.

a. See Max Bazerman, *Judgment in Managerial Decision Making* (New York: Wiley, 1986); and Malcolm Gladwell, *Blink: The Power of Thinking Without Thinking* (New York: Little, Brown, 2005).

b. Argyris and Schon referred to these as Model 1 and Model 2 conversations. See Chris Argyris and Donald A. Schon, *Theory in Practice: Increasing Professional Effectiveness* (San Francisco: Jossey-Bass, 1974).

EXERCISE 3:

Record a Meeting

GO TO A MEETING (best if it's not one you're chairing) and try to record as much as you can about what you observe. Take notes if you like, but once you're away from the meeting, write down all you can remember. Don't limit yourself to the traditional minutes of the meeting; try to re-create the words, gestures, ambiance, intimations, body language, and history that enable you to understand what was going on. (It might be easier to write out your notes in the manner of a movie script.)

(continued)

Ask yourself, If the meeting were a multilateral tennis match, who did most of the serving? Who was most likely to return a serve? How long or sustained were the volleys or interchanges among participants? Did you notice any patterns in the interactions you observed?

The goal here is not to get you to remember everything, but to gain insight into what you remember and why. For example, you might want to notice how you recorded your observations. Quite often, people come equipped with pad and pen but limit note taking to what they decide are the "important" things that get said or concluded. But how do you know what's important ahead of time? What if you mistakenly classified something as unimportant but it turned out to be important later on? How would you know? Equally important, people often don't notice that their physical location influences what they can see. If you elect to sit in a corner, in order, for example, to be less conspicuous in your observation and note taking, does that prevent you from seeing the faces of people with their backs to you? Are you inclined to infer whether they are smiling (e.g., making a signal of encouragement to a speaker facing you) or frowning (and signaling disagreement or displeasure)? Or do you ignore them altogether?

Don't despair if you find this exercise difficult to carry through to completion. The key here is to recognize how everyday events in organizations quite often carry with them a great deal of information that we routinely miss, overlook, or ignore. Many times, we engage in censoring activities without even being aware of it. For example, did you find this task stressful or irritating? Most people do, and only a few can sustain the intensity of attention required to document their observations for more than a few minutes. They "tune out," even when they deem the task relevant and important, because it is just plain hard to attend to all the information that's available.

Or they begin almost immediately to categorize and prioritize information as if they knew with confidence in advance that they could capture "the important things." The problem is that although those schemes— like stereotypes—may make it easier to condense and process information, they also prevent you from seeing and hearing things you don't anticipate. They make it hard to learn.

By this point, you may be wondering whether it is physically or mentally possible to take everything in, much less to maintain an inner dialogue prompted by questions like "What am I *really* seeing?" Two things matter here. First, you are improving the quality and the quantity of the information you have at your disposal. Repeating this exercise (or variations of it) will pay off in better decision making and a greater likelihood that your decisions will get implemented.[a] Second, the more you practice, the better you'll get at reading situations and people. This will increase the speed and the accuracy of your assessments.

"Noticers" are trend spotters and pattern recognizers. They tend to see or sense an emergent phenomenon before others do. Trends can reside in markets, in large group behavior, in meetings, and even in conversations.[b] Noticers are not only more likely to spot a trend in its infancy, but they are also more likely to recall from past observation other events that belong in a similar class. In other words, by not categorically dismissing observations as unimportant, they keep them available for use later on.

a. Decision theorists like Vroom and Yetton have long argued that decision quality—a product of information quality and the implementability of a decision—is strongly influenced by a manager's skill in selecting whom to include in decision making and how to listen to them. See Victor H. Vroom and P. W. Yetton, *Leadership and Decision Making* (Pittsburgh, PA: University of Pittsburgh Press, 1973).

b. Steve Ober and David Kantor theorize that when a group's members become better observers of their behaviors (e.g., in meetings), they can operate more effectively, prevent delays, and keep moving in a common direction. They break organized interactions into four underlying actions: a move, which is a statement that initiates action ("Let's buy that company"); a follow, which supports or confirms a move ("I agree, let's make an offer"); an oppose, which either contradicts a move or calls for a redirection ("That undermines our strategy"); and a bystand, which most often comments on the group's process ("I thought we said we weren't going to make a decision today"). These actions cluster into interaction patterns that are either productive or unproductive (the latter they refer to as "structural traps"). The key, according to Ober and Kantor, is that by recognizing patterns, groups can pull themselves out of traps. See Steven P. Ober and David Kantor, "Achieving Breakthroughs in Executive Team Performance," *Prism*, Summer 1996, 84–95.

EXERCISE 4:

Videotape Yourself at Work

VIRTUALLY ANYONE WHO PURSUES serious instruction in golf will find themselves being videotaped by an instructor. There's no way to hide the flaws in your swing or the overall body image that somehow doesn't quite jibe with the way you see yourself in the mirror. Yet golf instructors use video not to embarrass, but to instruct.

In this exercise, ask someone you know reasonably well to videotape you as you make a presentation or speech. Firmly instruct them that you want them to shoot you as they normally see you. No staging or props. Resist the temptation to stop and restart in order to get the best take. Keep the camera going for twenty minutes or so. Ask your videographer to capture other people's reactions to you, as well.

Now for the tough part: rewind the tape and watch yourself in action. What do you see that surprises or distresses you? What do you like or dislike about your performance, and why? As you watch the tape, note on paper some of the impressions that strike you. Recognizing that we are usually our own worst critics, it's important to also note the positive as well as the negative or unpleasant impressions. Notice how people react when you speak. Are they engaged? What does their body language tell you? How much of that information did you get while you were "performing"? Again, along the lines of the earlier visit to the art museum, take a few minutes to explore why you feel the way you do about specific moments in the tape.

The greatest benefit of this exercise derives from the fact that it gives you the opportunity to literally get out of your skin and use what you see as the raw data for your own analysis. Practicing this makes it easier to follow Heifetz and Linsky's advice: go up to an imaginary "balcony" in your mind, and watch yourself in action.[a] It also serves as valuable preparation for real-time self-observation—that is, practicing while you perform.

Outstanding leaders demonstrate remarkable adaptive capacity in large measure because they leave themselves open to experience, open to surprise, and open to learning. They do that not by making themselves an open book or starting always with a clean slate, but rather by being attentive to themselves as observational instruments.

They may or may not be happy with the stereotypes, predispositions, or associations that they carry around, but they are mindful of them and make a point of registering how they are coloring what they see and hear and, on occasion, subjecting what may seem to be the most mundane and obvious observations to close questioning.[b]

It is important to recognize that adaptive capacity is *not* only about looking inward. Inward-looking exercises are intended to aid you in a process of self-calibration: to wit, how good an observational instrument am I? Astronomers routinely factor in imperfections in the curvature of the reflecting mirror—and so should leaders.

That said, the strength of a leader's adaptive capacity also depends on her ability to discern patterns before they become obvious to everyone else. Pattern recognition—the ability to extract meaning from a mass of data (observations, interactions)—takes a variety of forms. Bird-watchers like globe-trotting McCormick & Company director Hank Kaestner excel at distinguishing a bird from a thicket of multicolored leaves. Kaestner is also extremely good at picking out a good crop in a warehouse of seemingly identical bundles of spice. Sailors like Bob Crandall, former CEO of American Airlines, read the contours of a body of water in search of shifting winds. Often, the distinction between adept and novice resides in the ability not only to sort out the information quickly but also to then infer what to do next on the basis of partial information. For example, chess players look for patterns and signature moves: one look at a board and they have a pretty good sense of what has happened and what could happen.

Another form of pattern recognition involves finding similarities among otherwise incomparable examples. For example, I had the opportunity to observe this at work with the senior vice president of R&D for a major consumer products manufacturer who was struggling with how to consolidate three labs without weakening the company's legendary record as an innovator. One day he stopped in midsentence while we were discussing his dilemma and started waving his arms as if he were conducting an orchestra. Laughing at my befuddlement, he told me of a newspaper article he'd recently read about the business director of a major European opera company who'd been tasked to collapse five state-sponsored orchestras into two—also without weakening their musical performance. A few days later, out of a meeting with the opera director came a powerful insight into the role of the "first chairs," the pivotal players who could make or break the orchestra and who, it turned out, had been instrumental in making the consolidation work. Therein lay what turned out to be a successful strategy for the R&D leader.

The key in both examples of pattern recognition is the ability to leverage observations—yours and others'—to extend your eyesight. In the case of bird-watching and sailing, it takes the form of indirect information that tells you where something you want is. In the case of the R&D director, it takes the form of finding a class of events or phenomena that your problem (and, therefore, your solution) belongs to. Not unlike Jack Welch's injunction to "manage the white spaces"—that is, the places not touched by the formal rules of the organization—adaptive capacity relies on pattern recognition to identify opportunities in what might otherwise appear to be a very crowded space.

a. Ronald A. Heifetz and Marty Linsky, *Leadership on the Line: Staying Alive Through the Dangers of Leading* (Boston: Harvard Business School Press, 2002).

b. Readers interested in further exercises to sharpen their observational skills, as well as fascinating research-based insights on the challenges of perception, will find it useful to consult one or more of the following sources: John Berger, *Ways of Seeing* (London: British Broadcasting Corporation and Penguin Books, 1972); Ian I. Mitroff and Harold A. Linstone, *The Unbounded Mind: Breaking the Chains of Traditional Business Thinking* (New York: Oxford University Press, 1993); and Todd Siler, *Think Like a Genius: Use Your Creativity in Ways That Will Enrich Your Life* (New York: Bantam Books, 1996).

EXERCISE 5:

Kill Your Company

SENIOR EXECUTIVES FROM A WELL-KNOWN CANDY and confectionary company were assembled in the conference room of a research group with whom I am affiliated, and their objective was to scan the environment for threats to their market position. The team came armed to the teeth with the latest business intelligence, analyst reports, company profiles, and the like. But less than an hour into the exercise, one member leaned back and took a deep breath; to no one in particular, he said, "I don't think there's anything in these reports we don't already know. And there's stuff here that we know we don't know enough about. But I bet what's going to kill us is what we don't know that we don't know." He was referring to what in the aerospace and defense community has traditionally been called the "unk-unk": the unknown unknown.

With his declaration still hanging in the air, this executive offered a different assignment to the group: "Let's figure out how to kill our company. We know what our weaknesses are better than anyone else. What's the product or the process or the whatever that could do us in? Not a catastrophe or a stupid mistake or a moral lapse. Let's figure out how to kill our company and then," he added with eyes afire, "let's figure out what it will take to become the thing that could put us out of business before it does!"

Your challenge, in this exercise, is to do the same. Even if you lead a small department or a not-for-profit organization, the exercise remains the same. For example, many not-for-profits found themselves starving for financial support and teetering on the brink of collapse in the wake of Hurricane Katrina in the autumn of 2005. They had weathered the cycles of fund-raising but were completely unprepared for a catastrophic event that might result in funds being diverted for an extended period of time to other causes.

You can complete this exercise by yourself, but it will be much more valuable if you undertake it as a collaborative effort. That way, you can practice listening to others, getting their input rather than telling them the answers, and identifying who among your team has the most to contribute to solving unconventional problems.

ENGAGING OTHERS THROUGH SHARED MEANING: TELLING YOUR STORY

Stories are how we remember important things. Bulleted lists and diagrams may communicate a logic chain, but stories weave images, emotions, and events into a portable tapestry of meaning.

Don Novello, a comedian who played the role of Father Guido Sarducci in the early days of television's *Saturday Night Live*, made this point with a hilarious monologue about what he referred to as the "Five-Minute University." Five years after you graduate from college, he argued, you only remember about five minutes' worth of material from all the classes you took. And most of that consists of memorable stories told by a few good professors (most of whose names you no longer remember). His plan was to sell you that five minutes of learning at a fraction of the cost of four years' tuition.

Screenwriting coach Robert McKee makes a parallel point, but also suggests that storytelling appeals to something distinctly human, as well: "Stories fulfill a profound human need to grasp the patterns of living—not merely as an intellectual exercise, but within a very personal, emotional experience."[4] Stories help us make sense out of confusion. They reassure us by telling us that someone, somewhere has been where we are now. And in this regard, the telling of a story completes what "seeing" begins: a process of engagement. According to psychologist Robert Kegan, "What the eye sees better the heart feels more deeply."[5]

Effective leaders are often consummate storytellers, and among the most influential stories they tell are their own. These stories are rarely self-adulatory, but each is a variant on the hero's journey, a tale in which the individual is tested—sometimes sorely tested—and ultimately triumphs. As we saw in chapter 2, leaders unanimously agree that the insights they had won justified whatever hardships they had endured. In every case, they learned, and they grew. Their stories explained, amused, engaged, and often enrolled others in the narrator's vision.

The following assessment is designed to help you probe your skill at engaging others. Just because you don't feel yourself to be extraverted or outgoing by nature, it does not mean you cannot engage people. Small voices can silence a room if used at the right time. And engagement is not about conversation, although good conversationalists and engaging leaders often enjoy a similar re-action from their audiences: rapt attention.

Self-Assessment B: Engaging Others

Consider the following questions and rate yourself accordingly.

Self-assessment B: engaging others

	1 = Never, 2 = Seldom, 3 = Sometimes, 4 = Usually, 5 = Always					

1. Do you encourage (and actively listen to and consider) dissenting opinions?   1   2   3   4   5

   Recent example:
   _____

   _____

2. Do you maintain relationships with people in other lines of business and walks of life?   1   2   3   4   5

   Recent example:
   _____

   _____

3. Do you make a point of communicating your goals to the people who work with you, and then checking to see whether you're understood?   1   2   3   4   5

   Recent example:
   _____

   _____

4. Do you attempt to get "buy-in" before implementing your ideas?   1   2   3   4   5

   Recent example:
   _____

   _____

(continued)

5. Do you communicate to others a strong   1   2   3   4   5
   sense of your purpose in life?

Recent example:

6. Do you take an active role in career   1   2   3   4   5
   development efforts of the people
   who work for you?

Recent example:

7. Do you seek out others for career   1   2   3   4   5
   advice?

Recent example:

8. Do you find it easy to empathize—   1   2   3   4   5
   to feel what others are feeling?

Recent example:

9. Do you tell stories to illustrate your ideas?   1   2   3   4   5

Recent example:

10. Are you able to detach yourself from your   1   2   3   4   5
    emotions in conflict-filled situations?

Recent example:

As in the earlier assessment, sum the numbers you circled above. In the next chapter, you will use this assessment to identify specific actions you can take to enhance or to sustain your ability to engage others through shared meaning. A score of 10–25 suggests that engaging others is a dimension on which you ought to focus more attention; a score of 26–40 suggests that you have some skill in this space but ought to work on aspects on which you score lower; and a score of 41–50 suggests that engaging others is already a strength. Note again that capacities, like muscles, tend to atrophy without regular exercise—and thus in the following section, I provide some opportunities to flex those muscles.

Your Crucible Story

According to Robert McKee, a good story expresses how and why life changes: "It begins with a situation in which life is relatively in balance," he writes. "You come to work day after day, week after week, and everything is fine . . . But then there is an event . . . that throws life out of balance. You get a new job, or the boss dies of a heart attack, or a big customer threatens to leave. The story goes on to describe how, in an effort to restore balance, the protagonist's subjective expectations crash into an uncooperative objective reality. A good storyteller describes what it's like to deal with these opposing forces, calling on the protagonist to dig deeper . . . take action despite risks, and ultimately discover the truth."[6]

Earlier, in chapter 5, I asked you to populate a lifeline with critical events and relationships that shaped you as a leader and then to examine closely a few of the most memorable of those crucibles. In the next exercise, I ask you to revisit that exercise— or complete it if you didn't earlier—but this time with an eye to telling it as a story in several different ways.[7] Leaders need to be able to communicate the same information to different audiences and to become adept at understanding (often rapidly) what styles of communication work best with a given audience.

EXERCISE 6:

Telling Your Story

T HINK ABOUT YOUR CRUCIBLE STORY, and reframe it in your mind or on paper as an incident that threw your life out of balance, setting the stage with a brief introduction that describes life in balance. Describe how your crucible experience put you at odds with your expectations, and do so in a way that lets the listener in on the feelings associated with being caught in the middle of opposing forces. Recognizing that a good story resolves the tension, but does so in a realistic way, explain how you survived and what you learned in the process. (See "Almost Climbing to the Top of Mt. Kilimanjaro" for a short example of a well-told crucible story.[a])

Almost Climbing to the Top of Mt. Kilimanjaro
by Jan Houbolt

I went to climb to the rooftop of Africa—Mt. Kilimanjaro—and descended into the depths of my soul.

I never have had the desire to do serious mountaineering, but Brian (the expedition organizer) asked me to join him, and some friends agreed, so I said yes. Why? Because Brian is special and he asked me. Also, it appeared as an opportunity to push the limits a little further than I was used to—and who knew what forms of growth could come out of this experience?

Day 1: Even before we left, I was faced with a challenge. After a minihike, I became aware that an old foot injury was going to be a serious and painful challenge. After several months of time spent with podiatrists dealing with the foot injury, the advice of doctors and common sense told me to call off the trip. Somehow, one last minijaunt with some of the guys, and I reversed positions and found myself recommitted to the climb against the doctors' advice.

Day 2: The climb was sometimes steep, with some rock scrambling and slowly moving into a more barren state. Everyone was in a good mood although some talked a bit about headaches from the altitude as we are now close to thirteen thousand feet. I'm amazed. No headaches, nausea—not even a hint of altitude symptoms. A good sign, I think to myself. I am the oldest and in the poorest physical shape, and I am doing just fine.

Day 3: We wake up in the morning and the camp is buzzing. Ahead of us there has been a tragic avalanche. Three Americans are dead and a number of porters are seriously injured. Everyone is very concerned about their relatives back in the USA, and a couple of folks with international cell phones get calls back to the U.S. letting everyone know we are all right. I feel sobered by the fact that this is dangerous business. I am clearly the slowest of the group of eleven, but I have my excuses: bad foot, I am the oldest, everyone else is in better shape, and the one person close to me in age being only about four years younger is an endurance athlete who biked across the USA two years ago. Anyway, I tell myself, slow is good: it allows for acclimatization and this isn't a race.

Day 4: I spent the whole night up with diarrhea and start the day 100 percent dehydrated with forty-five minutes of sleep and an inability to eat. Hours in the freezing cold, squatting over a makeshift latrine. Everyone is eating breakfast. Food looks truly revolting to me. Someone finds a rehydration mix and puts it in a cup of hot water. It tastes awful and I almost gag it right back up. I finally get one piece of bread down, nibble by nibble. No opportunity to gather myself together—it is time to go forward or quit.

I choose to go forward, although I also notice a feverish feeling settling in.

The next several hours are spent traversing up and down the slopes of valleys that have carved their way into the mountain's face. As we approach each new cliff top, I think it's the last—only to see another valley to descend and then a new cliff to climb.

I apologize profusely to the group for slowing them down and being a burden. Finally Brian tells me that if I apologize again they will all have to beat me up. I love them all.

I move upward, taking steps of two or three inches at a time whenever there is no new rock to step up on. I will never forget the

*feeling of support of several of the guys who patiently are follow-
ing me. We reach the top. I am borderline hallucinating and beyond any exhaustion I have ever felt in my almost sixty years on this
planet. I know I have a fever, but think maybe if I lay down for a
while it will go away.*

*Cliff takes my temperature. Initially says 104.8—I can see by the
shock on his face that something is awry, and request the truth.
When he tells me what the thermometer reads, I casually think,
"Well, I am dead." He leaves the tent for a minute and then comes
back and says, let's take your temperature again—this time it reads
101. It feels like a reprieve.*

*Cliff tells me that tomorrow morning I am going down and that
he is going with me. I agree that I should go back, but start to say,
"Oh Cliff, not you . . ." Cliff cuts me off, letting there be no doubt
that he is escorting me along with a guide. I choke up and tell him
that I love him.*

*Day 5: Tonight everyone will be climbing at midnight to the final
summit, and I find myself choked up that I am going down. I have
breakfast with the group and am able to eat a little porridge. I say
a few words from the heart and read Mary Oliver's poem "The
Journey." I feel that they will all make it.*

*The bottom line is, I did not make the final summit with the rest
of the group. This initially burned with painful intensity.*

*The real bottom line: my true self is not summit achievement at
Mt. Kilimanjaro or what others may think of it. My lifelong fixation
with achievement is a false god in comparison to being in a state of
grace and self-acceptance. The real journey is one of personal and
spiritual development and not meeting the expectations I perceive
others have of me or even my own false personal expectations. This
is my true essence project. This is the summit I am still climbing.*

To a Child

Tell your crucible story to a child. As a parent or grandparent, you
would have a wonderful opportunity to share an important incident
from your life that those children may not have heard or may not have
heard framed this way.

To Coworkers

It's not easy to manufacture the perfect venue or time to tell a crucible story to coworkers, certainly if you're nervous about drawing attention to yourself. But as a leader, you have many opportunities to invite people to talk about difficult times—whether on the job or off it—especially when there's a positive ending to celebrate.

Presentations I've made about the findings from the research on which this book is built have almost invariably resulted in discussions of individual crucible experiences. Indeed, the most frequent response I've received has been the unsolicited crucible story. People want to have their stories heard. So if you're concerned about drawing attention to yourself, it may make the most sense for you to invite others to tell their crucible stories before you share yours. But share your story you must.

In the telling, pay close attention to whether or not your listeners show signs of engagement. Are they searching out your eyes? Are you looking to make contact with theirs? Can you draw people closer by lowering your voice? Have you spotted the person in the audience whose head bobs in accord with key points you make? Are you acknowledging their attentiveness, without focusing overly much on them? In other words, are you addressing everyone or just the people who appear to you in the moment as if they are engaged? Having told your story, test for meaning—that is, ask someone then (or afterward) what the moral or punch line of your story was. Did you get your point across?

a. Jan Houbolt graciously allowed me to reprint this version of an e-mail he sent out to friends and supporters who wanted to learn more about his first mountain-climbing experience (at the age of fifty-plus).

Telling the Stories Around You

Telling a story—or your story—is only half the job. You must also pay much closer attention to the stories told around you—for example, the stories that epitomize things like family lore and workplace culture. Great leaders are often great storytellers, but more important than the story is its effect. That is, stories have the ability to give identity to a group, to draw boundaries that tell who's in and who's out, and to call members to action.[8]

Here is an example of what I mean: during an interview with the head of human resources for a major hotel chain, I asked how the company maintained a common culture as it grew globally. "Let me tell you a story about that," the manager replied.

> *I arrived at Kuala Lumpur about three years ago, probably about noon. I got into a cab and immediately walked into a meeting at our Kuala Lumpur hotel. I didn't interrupt, but at a break I said, "What are you getting out of these two-day meetings? What subject are you learning about?" And they could have said something about the payroll system or whatever. But they said, "The discussions on culture." When I asked them what their greatest concern was, they said, "To ensure that the culture is maintained." So here are people in Malaysia and the number one issue on their minds is the culture! Now that in itself is worth billions of dollars, that they even put it at the top of the agenda.*
>
> *Then, two days later I'm in mainland China, up the Po River several hours out of Beijing. I'm getting a tour of a hotel and the guy who's leading me doesn't speak English, but he's a local general in the Red Army. The government owns the hotel and he's showing me the executive suite and this and that. The HR person is there. And I said, "Now what I'd like to see is the employee cafeteria, the employee locker room." In that one moment I conveyed to everybody that I want to see where the workers sleep, where they eat, what they eat, where they shower, their sense of privacy when they go to the bathroom and everything like that. Here he is, a communist who looks like Chairman Mao, who couldn't give a hoot about the worker, and I'm the capitalist coming in wearing a pinstripe suit, and I'm saying, "This is what's important."*

The following two exercises may help you find and use some of the stories around you, just as the manager did in Kuala Lumpur.

EXERCISE 7:

Find Someone's Passion

STRIKE UP A CONVERSATION with a coworker about passion. Inquire about something they do at work or through work that they care deeply about.[a] Passion at work or for work is generally less obvious; it requires digging and careful thought about how to frame questions that will get a conversation—or a monologue—started.[b]

The result, for a leader especially, will be greater insight into the emotional attachments that people have made to their work, often to the moral overtones of excellence at work, and therefore to motives and aspirations that leaders need to discern. Listen to what they say, and, more importantly, listen to how they say it. What happens when someone talks about something they feel passionate about? What happens to you, the listener? What's different about the interchange that takes place between two people when one is describing his or her passion?

Here's an illustration of my point; I call this "the mysterious case of the cookie jar collector." While studying technological change in unionized workplaces, I entered the lunchroom of a weathered old sheet metal–stamping plant and sat down next to a veteran operator named Rusty.[c] We struck up a conversation after I noticed that he was reading a newsletter on whose cover was a cookie jar in the shape of a popular cartoon character. I asked what that was about, and Rusty cracked a crooked smile through the stubble of a three-day beard. "Oh, that," he said. "That's a little hobby of mine. I collect cookie jars." Intrigued, I asked whether there were a lot of people who collected cookie jars. Rusty lit up as he told me, by degrees, that not only was there a big network of collectors, but he was the president of an association. He maintained a database of recent sales and prices. He wrote and distributed the newsletter. And with eyes twinkling, he told me he just received a "five-figure check" from a major auction house for having appraised the value of Andy Warhol's collection of cookie jars.

The story gets even more interesting. After mentioning to the plant manager that I'd met "the cookie jar collector," I was told that Rusty was something of a legend in the plant—not for his cookie jars, but for his outright refusal to cooperate with management in bringing on board a new generation of computer-controlled presses. Rusty, it seemed, had rebuffed every entreaty by management to aid the production engineers responsible for implementing the new technology. His direct supervisor had concluded that Rusty was either a modern-day Luddite— someone who resisted new technology on principal—or he was too old to learn something new.

Yet, as it turned out when I tracked Rusty down for another conversation, his reluctance derived from the experience of having been "consulted" about past equipment and process changes, with no apparent effect. His memory, longer than any manager's, trumped his fascination with technology. But no one knew.

a. People are often eager to talk about their children or a hobby, but this task is intended to be harder than that.

b. You might consider asking a leading question, such as "Have you ever lost track of time doing something you really enjoy at work? What were you doing?"

c. Robert J. Thomas, *What Machines Can't Do: Politics and Technological Change in the Industrial Enterprise* (Berkeley: University of California Press, 1994).

EXERCISE 8:

Build a Community

IN AN AVERAGE WEEK, working adults spend the largest fraction of their waking time at work, usually confined to eight hundred square feet of office or factory space. In the 1800s, if you spent that much time in one place, you called it home, or at least community. How much of a community is the place you work? Or, better yet, how could you make your workplace more of a community? That's the challenge.

Students of architecture and urban planning have long been fascinated by what makes for a community, as have sociologists and anthropologists. In a pathbreaking work, *A Pattern Language*, architects Christopher Alexander, Sara Ishikawa, and Murray Silverstein (and their collaborators) identified five features shared in common by successful communities across the sweep of time: a crossroads, or a place where people might meet in the normal course of life; a heart, or a central space where people congregated to meet others or to be seen; a founder's tale, or something that gave an account of the community's origin; a conversation piece—for example, a bell tower or a signature building; and finally, a mystery, or some part of the community's history that was the subject of dispute and intrigue.

Suppose you had the opportunity to build a community at work—out of your existing office space or in a new building. What could you do to create a crossroads, a heart, a founder's tale, a conversation piece, and a mystery? The exercise may not be so theoretical. Consider how often companies reorganize, change dwellings, or build new spaces. Each represents an opportunity to build community.

INTEGRITY: WORKING WITH VALUES

Leadership is always about integrity. Why? Because what people around leaders respond to is the leaders' conviction, character, sense of justice, and passionate desire to do the right thing. Whatever they believe, outstanding leaders behave in ways that reflect their awareness of the value and rights of other people. The outstanding leaders interviewed in this study—irrespective of where they plied their trade or what belief systems they identified with (Jew, Christian, Muslim, Mormon, Scientologist, Conservative, Liberal, Libertarian)—each demonstrated a remarkable clarity about what they believed in, and each could easily identify decisions of significance they'd made in their lives vis-à-vis the values they held.

Integrity meant not simply being possessed of values or a moral code, but feeling somehow *completed* or made whole by those values.

Since they strive to understand the role that values play in their own perceptions of the world, outstanding leaders are comfortable working with values. They understand and act on their own values, help others articulate what they value, deal straightforwardly with value conflicts, and make value-based decisions. They don't shy away from conversations about values, and they don't limit their convictions about values to the drafting of corporate value statements; they live them.

They also seek out feedback from the people they respect as to whether they are living the values they espouse. This is by no means an easy chore, in part because (in Western societies especially, but not exclusively) friends often find it difficult to combine conviviality with honesty. Walter Sondheim, a Baltimore civic leader and businessman, made the front page of the *Wall Street Journal* when, on the cusp of his ninetieth birthday, he sent out this note to ten of his friends: "The older one gets, the more reluctant one's friends and associates are to suggest to him that the time has come to 'hang up the spikes.' In recent years I have had two very good friends who have served in extremely important roles, long beyond their days of competence. I am frank to tell you that I am haunted by the fear that this might happen to me, or indeed might already have happened."[9]

The response he received convinced him to keep at it, but more impressive to him was the way his colleagues responded: each in a different way explained to Walter that the way he phrased his request forced them to set aside the affection and admiration they felt for him—feelings that might very well have caused them to tell white lies—and, instead, to offer a truly candid assessment.

Use the following self-assessment to help you look at your own sense of integrity as a leader.

Self-Assessment C: Integrity

Carefully consider the questions below and answer accordingly.

Self-assessment C: integrity

1 = Never, 2 = Seldom, 3 = Sometimes, 4 = Usually, 5 = Always

1. Have you acted out of conscience where   1   2   3   4   5
   you disagreed with the majority (at work
   or in your personal life)?

Recent example:

2. Are you consistent with your   1   2   3   4   5
   opinions/principles?

Recent example:

3. When you make a commitment, can you   1   2   3   4   5
   be counted on to follow through?

Recent example:

4. Do people come to you for advice on   1   2   3   4   5
   nonwork issues?

Recent example:

5. Do you sometimes experience a deep   1   2   3   4   5
   sense of guilt?

Recent example:

6. Do you believe in yourself?   1   2   3   4   5

(continued)

Recent example:

_____

_____

7. Do people consider you honest?   1   2   3   4   5

Recent example:

_____

_____

8. Are you willing to give up the lead, even   1   2   3   4   5
   when there are significant rewards to be
   had for being the leader?

Recent example:

_____

_____

9. Do you know when people are agreeing   1   2   3   4   5
   with you just because of the formal
   position you occupy?

Recent example:

_____

_____

10. Are you comfortable with being proved   1   2   3   4   5
    wrong?

Recent example:

_____

_____

As in the earlier assessments, sum the numbers you circled. In the next chapter, you will use this assessment to identify specific actions you can take to enhance or sustain your sense of integrity. A score of 10–25 suggests that this is a dimension on which you ought to focus more attention; a score of 26–40 suggests that you have some skill in this space but ought to work on aspects on which you score lower; and a score of 41–50 suggests that integrity is already a strength. Note again that capacities, like muscles, tend to atrophy without regular exercise.

Here are four exercises to start with. They can be undertaken at work or outside of work. They are only useful if you are ruthlessly honest with yourself.

EXERCISE 9:

Summing Up Your Commitments

A T THE END OF AN ESPECIALLY BUSY WEEK, stop for a moment and think about all the agreements, commitments, obligations, and promises you made. List them on a piece of paper. The list should include not only the items that might be on your to-do list, but also the more subtle agreements that you enter into. For example, when someone buys you lunch or just a cup of coffee, is an implicit obligation incurred? How many commitments did you make? How many of them do you plan to keep? What is the cost of not fulfilling them or of having them made to you but left unfulfilled?

This exercise is more difficult than it might seem at first. As we noted earlier, recall is a tricky thing, especially when we're not aware of the blinders and filters we impose. For example, we might make offers to do things completely out of courtesy or habit, with no clear expectation (on either side) that the offer or commitment will be fulfilled. It's just the polite thing to do. But suppose the other person took you at your word—for example, that you would read his report and respond in a timely way? Suppose further that he teed up a set of commitments of his own based on the expectation that you would fulfill yours? What would be the consequence of your failure to perform?

Convinced that accountability for commitments was a logical companion to his company's efforts at Total Quality Management (TQM),

(continued)

Ray Stata, founder of Analog Devices, challenged his management team a few years back to achieve 100 percent compliance with all their commitments. The team discovered two important things: (1) roughly half the commitments managers made were left unfulfilled; and (2) managers started being far more selective about the commitments they made.[a]

a. This simple example underscores something that advocates of TQM and Six Sigma approaches to quality have been arguing for years: quality is personal. See, for example, Harry V. Roberts and Bernard F. Sergesketter, *Quality Is Personal: A Foundation for Total Quality Management* (New York: Free Press, 1993); Shoji Shiba, Alan Graham, and David Walden, *A New American TQM: Four Practical Revolutions in Management* (University Park, IL: Productivity Press, 1993); and Steven J. Spear, "Learning to Lead at Toyota," *Harvard Business Review*, May 2004.

EXERCISE 10:
A Value Statement from the Outside In

A COLLEAGUE WHO HAD BEEN INTIMATELY INVOLVED in the start-up of a new division of an established automobile company told me a story about how the divisional president asked him to draft and circulate a values statement for the new entity. On reflection, my colleague demurred and suggested instead that the president and his leadership team ought to conclude among themselves what values they wanted to communicate and then to let their actions, not words on paper, do the talking.

Inspired by that example, this exercise asks you to do two things. First, on a sheet of paper, write down the values—in statements rather than one-word bullets—that you believe you enact on a daily basis. Then, enlist a friend or family member to put down on paper what *they believe* are your core values according to what they've observed of your behavior. Recognize that there is risk involved for both of you; and if this exercise is to have a benefit, you need to be prepared to hear things you may not agree with, and you need to ensure that the person you enlist is not going to regret volunteering. Much as is the case with "active listening," what's often forgotten is that you may not hear what you want to hear; listening without defensiveness is essential.

With your value statement in front of you, gently and politely inquire about the specific behaviors and instances that led your friend or family member to conclude that those are your values. Then have a conversation in which you share with your partner the value statements you wrote about yourself, and see whether the two of you can find the points of greatest overlap and separation in the respective lists.

EXERCISE 11:

Forming a Personal Board of Directors

"FORUM" IS A VERY IMPORTANT FACET of the Young Presidents' Organization (YPO), a global organization dedicated to mutual support for young entrepreneurs facing the challenges of starting and sustaining businesses in their most fragile stages. Forum is both a place and a process. In Forum, members can talk about anything they need to in privacy and confidence, whether it's about business, partnership, or family life. Besides confidentiality, what makes Forum so powerful is that it provides participants with resources, most important among them being information, in moments when people are under greatest stress and in danger of doing things they might later regret. The formation of a peer cohort makes it possible for people to find others not only whom they can trust to respect their confidence but to whom they can turn for honest, constructive advice.[a]

So the assignment here is to create your own personal board of directors. Like a corporate board, directors are selected for their experience, their knowledge in areas in which you may not feel qualified, and their integrity. In particular, these should be people who care enough about you to tell you the truth. Your challenge, besides identifying them, is to devise a workable model for how you will interact with your board (e.g., singly or all at once), a schedule for interacting (e.g., if it's periodic and/or unscheduled, how will you ensure their availability?),

(continued)

and a value proposition (i.e., why they should agree to serve—for example, offer them a pledge to serve in a similar role for someone they nominate).

a. Indeed, an important but as-yet-unverified advantage of groups like Forum is the insurance they may provide against moral or ethical lapses. An admittedly unsystematic review of both corporate scandals and whistle-blower cases suggests that people are more likely to make decisions they later regret (or go to jail for) when they are under great time pressure and political pressure (often by bosses or peers) to do something iffy, when they are feeling particularly vulnerable (e.g., before a promotion opportunity or during economic recession), and when they do not have a rich network of friends or colleagues to whom they can turn for advice.

EXERCISE 12:

Values in a Crisis

IN THE IMMEDIATE AFTERMATH of a product recall (occasioned by the detection of E. coli bacteria in a shipment of produce), a former student called me to describe to me proudly his company's "Tylenol moment."[a] When routine tests of its irrigation water revealed the presence of the deadly bacteria, his company had immediately contacted the FDA and the Department of Agriculture and initiated a recall of potentially contaminated produce. Remembering what Johnson & Johnson had done in 1982, he'd assembled the management team, and, within minutes, they concluded that the company's value statement would demand nothing less than immediate action—no matter the cost.

Imagine that you received a call from a credible source that a product or service that your organization, business unit, or department produced was believed to have been responsible for harm to one or more of your clients. Would you be prepared for your Tylenol moment? What would you do to hold your group accountable to your values?

a. In 1982, Johnson & Johnson experienced a major crisis when it was discovered that numerous bottles of its Extra-Strength Tylenol capsules had been laced with cyanide. By the end of the crisis, seven people had died. How Johnson & Johnson dealt with this situation set a new precedent for crisis management. The company was lauded for its quick decisions and sincere concern for its consumers.

If you completed the assessments and exercises in this chapter, you have likely broadened and deepened your awareness of the opportunities for growth that coincide with a dedication to learning from experience. In the next chapter, we turn to crafting a Personal Learning Strategy that will help you address the challenges of leveraging insight from experience and, more pragmatically, of learning in the midst of a crucible experience.

[7]

CREATING YOUR OWN
PERSONAL LEARNING
STRATEGY

A Step-by-Step Approach

The man who carries a cat by the tail learns
something that can be learned in no other way.

—Mark Twain

WE HAVE ARRIVED now at the critical moment, the point toward which this book has been leading. It is time to develop your own Personal Learning Strategy—to carry the cat by the tail, as Twain put it so vividly, and see what emerges from the experience. Developing a Personal Learning Strategy means crafting a systematic approach to practice—and to practicing while you perform—tailored to your talents and your aspirations. Your PLS will do two things: it will aid you in the process of learning from experience—especially, though not exclusively, crucible experiences—and it will enhance your ability to adapt to change as a leader.

Some, perhaps many, of the resources that you need to develop as a leader are available from sources within your reach—for example, your employer. However, the responsibility for creating and enacting a PLS falls squarely on your shoulders. No one but you can know what you want to accomplish with your life. No one but you can know the obstacles in your way (and who, including you, put them there). Ultimately, no one but you can get you up at 4 a.m. to lace up your skates, hit the ice, and practice.

The logic behind a PLS is straightforward: leadership, like other performing arts, is distinguished by levels of accomplishment (i.e., novice, adept, eminent) and by constituent ingredients that are essential for progressing between levels of accomplishment. Four ingredients are important to becoming adept—thorough grasp of method, ambition, instruction, and feedback—and the fifth, your Personal Learning Strategy, holds the key to eminence.

On the basis of the exercises in the preceding two chapters and the examples throughout this book, you should be in a good position to create version 1.0 of your Personal Learning Strategy. There are three parts:

- Part 1 builds from the discussion of aspirations, motivation, and learning styles in chapter 5. The goal is to capture here, in one place, the driving forces behind your effort to grow and learn as a leader. In effect, part 1 will be a touchstone to which you will refer frequently—perhaps even on a daily basis—to keep yourself on track.

- Part 2 encourages you to rate yourself along three leadership dimensions discussed in chapter 6: adaptive capacity, engaging others through shared meaning, and integrity.[1] Included in part 2 are example activities and potential crucible experiences tailored to specific aspects of each leadership dimension; consider them to be exercises for specific muscle groups.

- Part 3 guides you in cementing a plan for improving your leadership capabilities by creating intermediate goals to support their attainment.

You should include as inputs to your Personal Learning Strategy any and all results you can gather from leadership, learning, and personality assessments that your employer makes available (e.g., the Myers-Briggs Type Indicator [MBTI], the Fundamental Interpersonal Relations Orientation-Behavior [FIRO-B], or Kolb's Learning Style Inventory, as well as results from 360-degree leadership assessments and annual performance reports). Take full advantage of the opportunities for technical training and technical practice that your organization provides. If your organization's human resource group has detailed a set of leadership competencies, you should become intimately familiar with them and avail yourself of the assessment centers they have likely created (insisting, as you do, on receiving detailed feedback on their results).

Use your Personal Learning Strategy to set priorities when it comes to the training you invest in and the assignments you are offered. Since your career will likely span multiple organizations, only you will have the truly long-term view.

So let's begin. In the following sections of this chapter, you will consider questions in the three broad areas I just outlined—and ultimately build your own Personal Learning Strategy. We begin with aspirations, motivation, and learning style.

PART 1: ASPIRATIONS, MOTIVATION, AND LEARNING STYLE

Leadership may be actively sought or reluctantly accepted, but it is a behavior deeply rooted in, even inspired by, personal values.

Why I Lead

"Why I lead" may be the most difficult place to start if you have not thought long and hard about it. If you are writing longhand rather than typing on your computer, I encourage you to use pencil (this is, after all, version 1.0) to jot down in the space provided a few key words that sum up your personal anthem. If you get stuck, that's perfectly fine. Move on to the next step in part 1 and return later.

Why I lead

Why I lead:

_____

_____

_____

_____

_____

If you have something to say, document it. Then, sit back for a moment so you can explore this more. Borrowing a familiar device from Total Quality Management, pursue the "5 Whys" for each item or statement that describes why you lead.[2] That is, if you put down something like "I lead to make life richer and more rewarding for the people who work in my department," then ask yourself, Why do I do *that*? One answer might be, "Because I believe that they deserve richer and more rewarding lives." Again, why is *that* important? "Because I believe these people are capable of great things—more self-expression, more creativity, and more things that they and our customers value—than they are likely to experience if I don't lead them."

Only two *whys*, and already there's much more grit, detail, and insight to the response than when we began. Now we can say, "I lead because I want to help people express themselves, realize their creativity, and produce things that they and our customers value."

Changing the question to "Why *you*?" leads to a deeper exploration of what qualifies you to lead, and so on: "I feel a personal obligation to take responsibility, to make things happen, to create the conditions under which people can do and be things that really matter to them." Fine, but again, why *you* (and not someone else)? And so on.

Two important notes here: first, don't obsess. This is just an exercise—a glimpse at something you will muse about (and probably have mused about) for a long time. There's no reason to believe that you will or must get the answer complete the first time through. Second, it's a worthwhile exercise for you to evolve a shorthand version of your personal vision to serve as a goal, as well as a talisman, that reminds you of why you are on this journey to eminence as a leader. Use it the same way a taxi driver uses a photograph of his children taped to the dashboard of his cab (and if you have children yourself, no doubt they are also why you lead).

Myself at Peak Performance

In chapter 5 I recommended a split screen visualization exercise that began, as I do here, with your projecting ahead in time (to a certain date) images of yourself operating at peak performance. Now for this piece of your PLS, you get the opportunity to document, in as much detail as you can, the texture of that image. To aid you in making it graspable, we encourage you to use the present tense to describe what you see—not "I will" but "I am." And don't describe what you had to do or stop doing or give up in order to get there. Describe instead who you are as a result of some, as-yet-unexplored, intervening process.

Myself at peak performance

(future date:)

1. As a person:

_____

_____

_____

(continued)

2. At work:

_____

_____

_____

3. As a leader:

_____

_____

_____

4. At home:

_____

_____

_____

It is important to be as explicit as you can be when describing yourself at peak performance. Don't stop when, for example, you say that as a person, you are "athletic and trim." Give it detail so you can measure it: "I weigh 175 pounds and play tennis three times a week." Ask yourself each time you describe an attribute, How would I know whether I'd achieved that?

Once you complete this segment of the PLS, review it and see whether what you have written here extends, amends, or contradicts what you might have written earlier about "why I lead."

My Current Reality

Now it is time to focus on the other half of your split screen: your current reality. By the very naming, *current reality*, you might feel inclined to be self-critical, dour, and disappointed. After all, once you have envisioned yourself at peak performance, it can't help but be a letdown to look in the mirror. Recall, however, Bill Russell's self-assessment: I have the pieces, but I don't yet have the whole. There are likely to be many things that you will want to preserve and add to, as well as things that you'll want to grow or discard, in pursuit of your aspirations.

So, describe in as much detail as you can the facts of your current reality. Again, be explicit; unless you have a meaningful baseline, you'll have trouble discerning when you've gained ground on your aspirations.

My current reality

(today's date:)

1. As a person:

_____

_____

_____

2. At work:

_____

_____

_____

3. As a leader:

_____

_____

_____

4. At home:

_____

_____

_____

Managing Creative Tension

If you've taken the last two steps seriously, you are likely to be feeling a little tension. Perhaps more than a little. That's actually a positive because most of us need both a push and a pull to get change started. Waiting for what Richard Boyatzis and Annie McKee term a "wake-up call" is both inefficient and risky.[3] Discovering your most powerful and meaningful aspirations right after you've had a heart attack or some other near-death experience may not leave you able to do much about them.

So, use the creative tension between your current reality and yourself at peak performance to get "unstuck" and start to move. Begin with the supply side of the equation: what are the things you could do—the high-impact moves—that could give you the energy you need to overcome the inertial forces of your current reality? High-impact moves are actions you can take that will have a disproportionately positive effect on your development as a leader.

How can you know what those are? Interestingly, intuition is not a bad place to start, because, to paraphrase Ed Schein, most leaders know what they need to do and what they are doing wrong.[4] They just need a reason to think it through and commit to doing something about it.

Of course, intuition and self-reflection are generally not enough, and there's real benefit to be had from external, even clinical, judgment. That's why, in chapter 6, I provided assessments of three core dimensions of outstanding leadership as a foundation to build on. It's also why I encourage you to take advantage of assessments and coaching that may be provided by your organization. Recall the vital role played by coaches, mentors, and counselors in many of the crucible stories analyzed in chapters 2 and 3.

Finally, there are the obstacles that we encounter and often allow, consciously or not, to divert ourselves from accomplishing things we value, or things that we at least say we value. Stop for a moment and consider what some of your favorite diversions, time wasters, and "suddenly important" chores are. For example, when it came to writing, I used to find it impossible to start an article unless I had twenty pencils sharpened to a needle point and arrayed in my favorite pencil holder. Diversions are different from rituals; rituals are a valuable way to ingrain desired actions into an automatic routine. Diversions are ruses: they appear to move us forward but generally sidetrack us because they find partners, and together they create lengthy diversionary chains—for example, needing writing pads of paper of a specific color and style to go along with the sharp pencils, a clean desk that requires a can of furniture polish, a trip to the sock drawer for a worn sock to use as a polishing rag, an excursion to the mall to replace several pairs of worn socks, and a side visit to look at ties that might match a newly purchased sport coat. Sound familiar? (I will have more to say about the value of rituals and renewal in part 3).

Managing creative tension

1. How I manage the creative tension between the two visions:

2. High-impact moves I can take to accelerate progress:

3. Obstacles I routinely set for myself, and how I prevent them:

Motivations

Motivation is obviously an important aspect of your PLS, but it is likely to be the one about which you have the least insight unless you have taken a motivational assessment and have the results to work with. As noted earlier, many organizations do use these assessments. If you can get access to one, be sure to insist on a complete analysis of the results and their implications for your personal and career development.

Motivations

1. What motivates me most? (e.g., power, achievement, or affiliation):

_____

_____

_____

2. I know this is important to me because:

_____

_____

_____

3. These are the implications for my career goals:

_____

_____

_____

The results of a motivational assessment are only as useful as they are believable *to you* and actionable *by you*. In the space provided, see whether you can cite examples of critical choices you have made in your career or, more generally, in your life that reflect the underlying motivation. Test yourself and see whether you cannot document equally compelling evidence for the influence of other motivations. Though it may be quite valid, the conclusion that you are motivated by the opportunity, say, to exercise power does not imply that you should abandon any activity or avocation that deviates from that motivation. No one is a pure type, motivations can change across different stages in adult development, and personality tests can be suborned by conscious or semiconscious gaming (e.g., "What would I like to think or have said about myself?"). The intent of any assessment is to help you deepen your self-understanding and to bring your aspirations into greater alignment with your more enduring traits.

Since career objectives will likely form a big part of your individual aspirations, it makes sense to give some thought to what the implications of your core motivations are for how you think about a career. Ed Schein's concept of "career anchors" may be a useful one to consider as you think through the implications of underlying personality traits and lifelong work pursuits.[5] According to Schein's research, there are eight themes for which people will have a prioritized preference. These themes are not necessarily predictive of what careers people will end up in; however, people often find themselves understanding better the dissatisfaction they're feeling with a current career when they review the results of their career anchors assessment.

Learning Style

There are two levels of learning to address here: how you learn under conditions of stress and challenge—as might be the case in a crucible—and how you extend your ability to learn from experience. Let's consider each in turn.

As you will recall from the discussion of learning in crucible situations in chapter 2, research suggests that conditions of stress and challenge occasion dramatically different learning behaviors: often either we "snap back" to behaviors that are well ingrained (conceivably even comforting) but that make it difficult to learn new things in the moment, or we "lean forward" to behaviors characterized by an openness to learning. Begin this part of your PLS by reviewing the lifeline and the crucible stories you documented in chapter 5. What did you conclude about the conditions and the behaviors associated with learning something important about leading or about yourself as a leader? Did you tend to lean forward or snap back?

If you tended to snap back or assumed a defensive posture (that still did not prevent you from learning), it might help to jot down what you can recall about the way you came to recognize that you'd learned something important. For example, how long did it take, and what prompted you to recognize that something important had happened? Was a friend or adviser or coach involved? Did you notice something about an experience someone else had that led you to an "aha?" Did that insight come even more obliquely—for example, while watching a movie or reading a novel? The intent here is to render explicit—and therefore repeatable—the conditions under which you gain insight into something complicated, even difficult.[6] If you can more easily recognize the conditions under which learning occurred—no matter how distant in time they may have been from the triggering events—then you increase the odds of learning again.

Learning style

1. How I learn best (according to experience):

2. Using the Kolb model, my preferred learning style is:

3. This means I am most likely to learn important things in these kinds of situations:

_____

_____

_____

4. My opposing and adjacent learning styles are:

Opposing: _____

Adjacent: _____

Extending your ability to learn from experience is the objective of completing a learning styles assessment on the order of the Kolb inventory. You can gain insight into your default learning style, *and* you can identify situations where it will be possible to experiment with other approaches. The key, however, is to force yourself out of your learning comfort zone: not just what you know, but *how* you know.

PART 2: MY LEADERSHIP CAPABILITIES

Before you begin to look more closely at enhancing your capabilities as a leader, think again about what you're trying to accomplish here. If your goal is to become the CEO of your company, there is a definable set of assignments, competencies, relationships, and outcomes that will enhance your chances of achieving that goal. No guarantees, obviously, but a lot of hard work and a couple of well-placed internal coaches, and you are on your way.

But if your goal is to carry out your answer to "why I lead" and to fulfill the aspirations you've laid out earlier, then you need a plan that is far more robust. Allow me to offer a personal illustration here. When my daughter took up piano lessons, I suddenly got interested in learning to play too. I envisioned myself playing a Thelonious Monk tune that I especially loved. I saw people drifting into our living room while I played. They were obviously enjoying my playing, and I was absolutely perfect in my rendition. I stopped there. I knew my current reality: I couldn't play piano. I knew what I had to do: get lessons. But when I talked with my daughter's piano teacher the first day he arrived, I boldly cut to the chase:

> "I see myself playing this Monk tune and everyone is enthralled. So I don't need all the handholding my daughter's going to need; I just want to learn that song— as a starter."
>
> Smiling, he said, "I can teach you to play that song. But there's a catch: you'll only be able to play that one song. Nothing more."
>
> I thought about it for a minute. "Hmm . . . ," I started to say. But he cut me off.
>
> "On the other hand," he said, "how would you like to play any song? Any song you wanted to?"
>
> I thought about it again. "Okay!" I exclaimed.
>
> "Good," he replied. "Then sit down next to your daughter."

The outstanding leaders I've studied—men and women who have proved able to lead for a lifetime—have opted, metaphorically speaking, to sit down at the piano for the full range of lessons. Hence, I focus this part of the PLS on the three core capabilities: adaptive capacity, engaging others through shared meaning, and integrity.

Adaptive Capacity

Review your responses to the adaptive capacity self-assessment, and complete the following segments of your PLS. Note that on the next set of pages provided for each of the facets of the assessment, you'll find both an example activity in which you could engage and a potential crucible experience that could enhance your ability in that area (see table 7-1). If your firm has identified organizational assignments or roles that provide learning opportunities paralleling any of those facets, by all means sample them as well. (I'll take up the issue of timing and pacing of activities in part 3 of the PLS.)

Adaptive capacity

1. My score in the adaptive capacity self-assessment was _____

2. The facets of adaptive capacity where I scored myself most in need of work were (lowest-ranking three) and activities that I can begin in the next three months to enhance each:

Facet: Activity:

_____   _____

_____   _____

_____   _____

3. The facets of adaptive capacity where I scored myself in need of work were (middle-ranking three or four) and activities that I can begin in the next six months to enhance each:

Facet: Activity:

_____   _____

_____   _____

_____   _____

(continued)

4. The facets of adaptive capacity where I scored myself highest (top-ranking three or four) and activities I can engage in to sustain them:

Facet: Activity:

_____   _____

_____   _____

_____   _____

_____

Engaging Others Through Shared Meaning

Review your responses to the engaging others through shared meaning self-assessment, and complete the following segments of your PLS. Again, note that in table 7-2 we have provided for each of the facets of the assessment both an example activity in which you could engage and a potential crucible experience that could substantially enhance your ability in that area.

Engaging others through shared meaning

1. My score in the engaging others self-assessment was _____

2. The facets of engaging others where I scored myself most in need of work were (lowest-ranking three) and activities that I can begin in the next three months to enhance each:

Facet: Activity:

_____   _____

_____   _____

_____   _____

3. The facets of engaging others where I scored myself in need of work were (middle-ranking three or four) and activities that I can begin in the next six months to enhance each:

Facet: Activity:

_____   _____

_____   _____

_____   _____

4. The facets of engaging others where I scored myself highest (top-ranking three or four) and activities I can engage in to sustain them:

Facet: Activity:

_____   _____

_____   _____

_____   _____

5. My crucible story:

_____

_____

_____

_____

_____

_____

_____

_____

_____

_____

_____

_____

TABLE 7-1

Enhancing adaptive capacity: example activities and potential crucible experiences

	Example activity to begin with	Potential crucible experience
1. Seek ways to improve as a leader	Solicit feedback on your performance in a particular leadership skill—e.g., communication or goal setting—from a sample of peers and direct reports	Volunteer to lead a youth group—e.g., Boy Scouts or Girl Scouts—or become an active member of an organization where you cannot be a leader
2. Set stretch goals	Achieve a significant, difficult-to-obtain outcome, directly related to your statement of personal aspirations—e.g., run in a 5k road race within six months	Pursue a significant, difficult-to-obtain outcome, directly related to your statement of personal aspirations, that requires you to change your life routine in fundamental ways
3. Develop a new hobby	Attend an "appreciation" event or course that introduces you to a new avocation—e.g., a lecture at an art museum or a gallery opening, or purchase a pit pass to a NASCAR race	Take up karate, sailing, or sewing (especially quilting since its traditions are as critical as its techniques), or learn a new language
4. Learn about different aspects of my organization	Identify a part of your organization that is totally unfamiliar to you (best if it is a part that you are not interested in), and find out why some people think it is the most interesting part of the organization	Volunteer to take a rotation assignment in a part of the organization that you are unfamiliar with—particularly if it has the reputation for being an organizational Siberia—and make it a showcase
5. Stay current on potential industry disruptions	Read industry reports to identify a major threat to the status quo for your industry and/or company, and then research, including attending professional conferences, so that you can write a one-page position paper and a plan of action to share with your peers and superiors	Organize an event that brings together leading thinkers and practitioners in the area of disruption in question, and lead them to develop a set of action alternatives—with no budget and outside your formal job description
6. Find patterns	Spend an afternoon bird-watching (if you are not already a bird-watcher), and come up with your own rules for effective bird-watching	Figure out who your organization's most dissatisfied customers are, and spend enough time with them that you can argue convincingly that they are right

(continued)

TABLE 7-1 (continued)

Enhancing adaptive capacity: example activities and potential crucible experiences

	Example activity to begin with	Potential crucible experience
7. Concentrate on a fantasy	Take a recurring daydream or fantasy and treat it as if it were a work project: scope it, develop a budget for allocating scarce resources to it, and generate a timetable with major milestones	Assemble a team of people who live at the margins of your organization, and, with them, devise a vision of the ideal place to work
8. Become a good judge of character	Volunteer to serve in a fund-raising capacity for a not-for-profit organization since that role demands the ability to discern who will pledge and who will make good on a pledge	Volunteer to serve as a review panel member for a philanthropic organization
9. Persevere through difficulties	Teach a child how to ride a bicycle, or help a stroke victim regain his or her speech	Volunteer to take a leadership role in a turnaround, organizational downsizing, postmerger integration situation, or large-scale technological change
10. Volunteer for a difficult assignment	Agree to serve on a citizen-review panel for your local police department	Volunteer to serve on a cross-functional task force in your organization

TABLE 7-2

Enhancing capacity to engage others through shared meaning: example activities and potential crucible experiences

	Example activity to begin with	Potential crucible experience
1. Encourage dissenting opinions	Set aside time in routine meetings for people to actively consider dissenting views on topics where there may be hidden disagreement	Identify a topic that is causing unproductive conflict in your work group, and organize a meeting that leads to honest dialogue and action; take responsibility for managing conflict, identifying actions that can be taken to mitigate the problem, and commit yourself publicly to seeing those actions through to completion and review
2. Develop relationships with people in other lines of business and walks of life	Attend a social gathering where you make it your private but dedicated purpose to learn something about each person you meet that makes them special and interesting	Join a group that is just starting out, and help it refine its vision, mission, and objectives . . . and then stay with that group long enough to see the consequences of your work; e.g., a neighborhood crime watch, an after-school tutoring program, or a local disaster-relief group
3. Send a clear message, clearly understood	Systematically assess whether the people who report to you clearly understand your position on a policy that is important to you and/or your organization—one that you think you have been extremely clear and consistent about	Run for elective office
4. Get "buy-in" before implementing ideas	Condense your case for making change in your organization—work or otherwise—into a ninety-second elevator pitch, and present it to key stakeholders; assess their level of agreement and points of resistance; refine your pitch and try again	Run for elective office
5. Hone a strong sense of purpose to my life and communicate that to others	Write and submit your own entry to National Public Radio's program titled *This I Believe*	Volunteer to give a sermon or a speech at your church or synagogue in which you discuss a value that is central to your life

(continued)

TABLE 7-2 (continued)

Enhancing capacity to engage others through shared meaning: example activities and potential crucible experiences

	Example activity to begin with	Potential crucible experience
6. Take an active role in subordinate career development	Set aside time with each of your direct reports and with at least three others who don't report to you to find out what they are passionate about in their lives—and then suggest ways for them to pursue those passions at work	Volunteer as a tutor in a public school, coach a sports team if you have never done so, or work as a Big Brother or Sister
7. Seek out others for career advice	Find someone at work who can serve as your personal coach	Form your own personal board of directors
8. Practice empathy	Identify the stakeholder in a change effort you are leading who most scares or concerns you, and seek him or her out for advice on how to be successful in your change effort	Volunteer to serve as a tutor at a prison or correctional facility
9. Tell stories to illustrate my ideas	Take a workshop or a course in storytelling, and use it to hone your own crucible story	Write a short story about a critical event in a character's life and submit it for publication
10. Become able to detach myself from my emotions	The next time you find yourself in the middle of an intense debate, notice the circumstances, notice your physical state, especially your breathing—and relax	On a topic about which you care passionately, search out and compile evidence that suggests that you are completely wrong

Integrity

Review your responses to the integrity self-assessment, and complete the following segments of your PLS. Again, note that in table 7-3 we have provided for each of the facets of the assessment both an example activity in which you could engage and a potential crucible experience that could substantially enhance your ability in that area.

Integrity

1. My score in the integrity self-assessment was _____

2. The facets of integrity where I scored myself most in need of work were (lowest-ranking three) and activities that I can begin in the next three months to enhance each:

   Facet: Activity:

   _____   _____

   _____   _____

   _____   _____

3. The facets of integrity where I scored myself in need of work were (middle-ranking three or four) and activities that I can begin in the next six months to enhance each:

   Facet: Activity:

   _____   _____

   _____   _____

   _____   _____

4. The facets of integrity where I scored myself highest (top-ranking three or four) and activities I can engage in to sustain them:

Facet: Activity:

_____   _____

_____   _____

_____   _____

_____

PART 3: SETTING MY AGENDA

Each of these new behaviors is intended to have a start date and an end date, to be built on every three to six months, and to be replaced with additional new behaviors. The purpose is to give yourself ample opportunity to practice while you perform. The key is to look for behaviors you can consciously practice at work *and* at home. (See the box, "Recovery and Renewal for [Corporate] Athletes.")

Likewise, since we tend to play to our preferred learning style, there is substantial opportunity for personal and professional growth if you seek out experiences and situations in your adjacent and opposing learning styles. Scan your landscape at work and at home, and identify those instances and roles out of your comfort zone that will allow you to stretch into new behaviors, perspectives, and leadership capabilities.

Recovery and Renewal for (Corporate) Athletes

IN A MARKED PARALLEL to studies of expert performance, researchers (and former sports coaches) Jack Groppel as well as Jim Loehr and Tony Schwartz have developed approaches to individual development that focus on the interdependencies between physical, emotional,

TABLE 7-3

Enhancing integrity: example activities and potential crucible experiences

	Example activity to begin with	Potential crucible experience
1. Disagree with the majority out of conscience	Don't go looking to pick a fight, but the next time you find yourself in a situation where you strongly disagree with the majority opinion, speak up	Campaign publicly for a cause you hold dear
2. Test the consistency of public and private views	On a single sheet of paper, write down the values, in statements rather than one-word bullets, that you believe you enact on a daily basis; next to each value, list an example of how that value influenced a recent decision you made	Expand the circle of people whom you routinely turn to for feedback, and include at least one person who has publicly opposed you; let them know that you seek their counsel because you respect their integrity, and ask them to provide you with their insights on a matter of great importance to you
3. Follow through on commitments	For a week, as a routine part of every meeting you attend, whether or not you call or chair the meeting, do not allow the meeting to conclude without summing up the commitments that each individual has made, and make sure that each knows that you will hold them accountable for fulfilling the commitments they have made	Instead of contributing money to a cause you support, give your time, energy, and ideas
4. Make myself available to others	Offer to mentor or coach someone in your organization; be sure that you are prepared to do so, however; that may mean attending a workshop or seeking instruction on how to mentor or coach	Offer to join the board of directors of a small, underresourced not-for-profit that is committed to a cause you support but is not visible and popular in the social circles you inhabit
5. Explore guilt-inducing situations	Identify at least two situations at work that cause you to feel guilt—e.g., where you could have done something to right a wrong but didn't, or an act you committed that now causes you to feel shame; for each situation, write down in detail in one column of a page why you feel guilt, and then in the opposite column write down what you should have done or will do should a similar situation arise, again in detail	Do or participate in something you can be incredibly proud of

(continued)

TABLE 7-3 (*continued*)

Enhancing integrity: example activities and potential crucible experiences

	Example activity to begin with	Potential crucible experience
6. Believe in myself	Schedule time each day to review the positive things you accomplished, and congratulate yourself for accomplishing them	Start your own business
7. Find out whether people think I am honest	Incorporate into your 360-degree leadership assessment explicit questions about your perceived honesty	Make honesty and transparency central to your organization's mission
8. Give up the lead	Prepare someone else to take your place as a leader in an activity that you deeply enjoy and value	Agree to take responsibility for the success of an important undertaking—preferably something you care about—but do so under the condition that you will not be visibly assigned to it and that you will never get credit if it succeeds
9. Know the power of my position	At a social gathering among friends, offer a prize to the person who, by consensus opinion, does the best job of imitating you in voice and body language	At the outset of a new assignment, ask the members of the team you work with to write out (and seal away) one or two paragraphs that describe their positive and negative expectations of you as a leader; then, at the conclusion of your time in that assignment, hand back their statements (unopened), and ask them to comment, anonymously and on the same page, on which expectations you mirrored and which you contradicted
10. Be open to being wrong	Institutionalize the role of devil's advocate in your team so that each time you propose an action, there is a protected position from which contrary views can be launched	Publicly apologize and take responsibility for a mistake you or your staff made

intellectual, and spiritual dimensions of performance.[a] Most important for our purposes are the points they make about the significance of recovery/renewal and ritual in support of long-term improvement.

Recovery/Renewal

Simply put, any system, whether it's physical or cerebral, needs rest after it's worked hard. Work and rest support one another. So do work and play. For example, in describing how weightlifting tones and shapes muscles, Loehr and Schwartz note that muscle tissue needs time to recover and heal from the stress of the lifting activity before it strengthens.

Recovery can take many forms. Limiting the time devoted to technical practice gives you an opportunity to relax and reflect. While a hectic schedule may require "bursts" or concentrated periods of rehearsal, a great deal can also be accomplished through background practice, where your mind is free to indirectly and independently sift and sort through the work of leadership—for example, while weeding a garden, watching a ballet, listening to a symphony, or hiking in the woods.

Ritual

Many of the things humans do are unconscious or at least semiconscious.[b] In a fast-paced, information-rich environment, it's not surprising to discover that attention is, as Tom Davenport and John Beck put it, "rapidly becoming the scarcest commodity in the marketplace."[c] Adding another thing to do is difficult, and when that other thing or things are not inherently enjoyable—or may be predefined as "hard work," like not eating donuts or getting up early to go to the gym— backsliding may not be excusable, but it sure is understandable. Finding ways to ritualize—and therefore render subconscious—the key physical and intellectual exercises is essential.

Like a string tied around your finger that, when noticed, reminds you of something you must do, rituals are intended to both soothe and irritate. Little rituals provide an opportunity to rest, to regroup, and to prepare. For example, scheduling a regular appointment with yourself is a way to set aside time to review your aspirations—similar in intent to what we described earlier as the process of decomposing motives. Acting and speaking coaches as well as golf instructors advise their clients to get into a rhythm that's distinctly their own in order to force out distractions and to set in motion a process that, once initiated, seems almost automatic. Loehr and Schwartz describe tennis player Ivan Lendl's ritual between serves: "Each time Ivan Lendl stepped up to the line to serve during a tennis match, he predictably wiped his brow with his wristband, knocked the head of his racquet against his heels, took sawdust from his packet, bounced the ball four times and visualized where he intended to hit the ball. In the process, Lendl was recalibrating his energy: pushing away distraction, calming his physiology, focusing his attention, triggering reengagement and preparing his body to perform at its best."[d]

A business leader renowned for his ability to "connect" or establish rapport and common ground with widely divergent groups once described to me a ritual he believed helped him connect. "Every night before an important meeting or encounter," he said, "I sit and think it through. I always ask myself two questions: What are the three things that need to happen in this meeting? And what is the one thing that cannot happen in this meeting? The first question gets me clear on why I'm there and forces me to keep focused. The second question gets me thinking about what I need to do to make sure we achieve our goals. When I do that well, I often get a sense of déjà vu in the midst of the meeting."

Rituals, whether big or small, activate a level of conscious rededication to the goal while, at the same time, lowering the amount of attention paid to the activity—often the uncomfortable activity—that will get you to the goal. In that respect, rituals are also a critical part of keeping "why I lead" close to the foreground.

a. Jack Groppel, *The Corporate Athlete: How to Achieve Maximal Performance in Business and Life* (New York: Wiley, 2000); and Jim Loehr and Tony Schwartz, *The Power of Full Engagement: Managing Energy, Not Time, Is the Key to High Performance and Personal Renewal* (New York: Free Press, 2003).

b. Some researchers estimate that upward of 95 percent of behavior is semiconscious. See, for example, Loehr and Schwartz, *The Power of Full Engagement*, 168.

c. Thomas H. Davenport and John C. Beck, *The Attention Economy: Understanding the New Currency of Business* (Boston: Harvard Business School Press, 2003).

d. Loehr and Schwartz, *The Power of Full Engagement*, 172.

Use table 7-4 to set a list of tasks in key areas of practice, a start date for each, and a schedule for how often you need to practice. Don't try to start everything at once, but also don't be shy about giving yourself a weekly regimen to pursue. Think, again, about instances in which you have actually stuck to a plan for yourself: what were the circumstances, how did you keep yourself focused and your energy consistent, what support did you need in order to keep going? That experience could have involved a sport, a discipline you imposed on yourself to take and pass a test, how you quit smoking or lost weight, or how you acclimated yourself to a new job or a new city.

TABLE 7-4

Setting my agenda

	Task	Start date	Frequency
Part 1			
Why I lead	Review and refine	Immediately	Daily
Myself at peak performance; my current reality; managing creative tension	Review and refine	Immediately	Weekly
Motivations	Complete formal assessment; receive and review findings; incorporate into PLS	Within the first three months	
Learning styles	Complete formal assessment; receive and review findings; incorporate into PLS	Within the first three months	
Part 2			
Adaptive capacity	Identify intersections with training in leadership competencies offered by my organization, and enroll in relevant courses	Within the first three months	At least one course or training event per year
	Undertake exercises that address areas of greatest development opportunity	First three months	One exercise per month
	Pursue a crucible opportunity in an area where I feel most in need of development	Second six months	One per year

(continued)

TABLE 7-4 (continued)

Setting my agenda

	Task	Start date	Frequency
Part 2 (continued)			
Engaging others through shared meaning	Identify intersections with training in leadership competencies offered by my organization, and enroll in relevant courses	First three months	At least one course or training event per year
	Undertake exercises that address areas of greatest development opportunity	First three months	One exercise per month
	Pursue a crucible opportunity in an area where I feel most in need of development	Second six months	One per year
Integrity	Identify intersections with training in leadership competencies offered by my organization, and enroll in relevant courses	Second three months	At least one course or training event per year
	Undertake exercises that address areas of greatest development opportunity	Second three months	One exercise per month
	Pursue a crucible opportunity in an area where I feel most in need of development	Second year	One per year
Part 3			
Resetting my agenda	Review and amend self-assessments in each leadership area		Every six months
	Review and amend PLS		Once each year

The idea in the opening paragraph of this chapter bears repeating: developing a Personal Learning Strategy means crafting a systematic approach to practice—and to practicing while you perform—tailored to your talents and your aspirations. In other words, only you can craft a PLS that both captures your imagination and contains within it the motivations that will help you adhere to it. If you discover that your most effective PLS need not take as structured or as regimented a form as the one I've suggested here, then so be it. The test, in the end, is the power and the durability of your answer to the question, "Why lead?"

Parts I and II of this book have focused heavily on the individual's journey to eminence as a leader, inspired in part by Benjamin Franklin's sage advice that "being ignorant is not so much a shame as being unwilling to learn." In part III, however, we helicopter up to the level of organizations in order to see better what they have to offer individual leaders in their quest to learn. We'll find that organizations have a great deal to offer, but not in conventional ways. In fact, it may be the unconventional organization that shows us the most creative ways in which crucibles can be harnessed to develop leaders.

PART THREE

THE BIG PICTURE

EXPERIENCE-BASED LEADER DEVELOPMENT

The Organizational Dimension

Experience is not so much what happens to you
as what you make of what happens to you.

—Aldous Huxley

WHERE DO THE MOST IMPORTANT formative events for leaders occur? If you've read to this point in the book, you already know what the answer *isn't*: it isn't in the classroom, the assessment center, the company off-site, or the annual performance review. It isn't in the conventional domain of leader development, and it isn't within the purview of most performance management systems. Rather, the richest and most memorable events are leaders' personal crucible experiences.

So, do organizations take full advantage of these rich development opportunities? Not really. In fact, my research suggests that implementing a process through which to leverage experience poses fundamental challenges for organizations. Crucibles are hard to schedule. It can be difficult to tell when they are occurring—for individuals or for organizations. There's a good chance crucibles won't occur on the job. And if they do occur on the job, they don't stop with the closing bell and restart the following morning. Finally, crucibles are idiosyncratic; they won't be the same for everyone in either their origin or their impact.

There is, however, an upside: crucibles are frequent and free.

Organizations can tap into the power of crucibles by adopting an *experience-based approach* to leader development. An experience-based approach represents a comprehensive new way of developing leaders because it weaves together life experience, on-the-job experience, and specific skill development. In other words, employees need more than a laundry list of classes and programs tenuously linked to career development. And organizations need to find ways to draw personal experience and aspirations into the development process, instead of treating these facts of life as if they were out of bounds. What I propose is an approach that can be adapted to the needs and opportunities of people at *all* stages of their careers and that can help them on their journey from novice to adept to eminent leadership. It is an approach that can also adapt to the changing needs of organizations operating in complex and uncertain environments.

This chapter will examine the efforts of several organizations that have sought explicitly to incorporate experience into leader development. We will also take a closer look at a pair of organizations that have fully embraced an experience-based approach to leader development and have benefited enormously as a result.

WHAT EXPERIENCE-BASED LEADER DEVELOPMENT CAN DO

The goal of experience-based leader development is to equip employees so that they can mine their experiences—continuously and intensively—for insight into what it takes to lead, what it takes to grow as a leader, and what it takes to cultivate the leader in others (peers and superiors as well as subordinates). The experience-based approach builds from the research reported in the preceding six chapters and from the classic works on learning, especially the writings of John Dewey, Kurt Lewin, Paulo Freire, and David Kolb and their specific applications to leadership by Warren Bennis, Ed Schein, Chris Argyris, Donald Schon, and Morgan McCall.[1] (See the box, "The Learning Cycle.") Their inspiration will be obvious in what I describe as the core "moments" in experience-based leader development: *preparing*, *deploying*, and *renewing*.

The Learning Cycle

THEORIES OF LEARNING—such as Lewin's model (see figure 8-1)—treat learning as a continuous and contingent process, not as an outcome.[a] Learning can produce outcomes in the form of knowledge and predictive statements. But knowledge—for example, that an inflated balloon will explode if pierced by a pin—must always be treated as conditional. That is, you need to know not only that cause and effect are related but also that the relationship may be contingent on certain conditions. Will a balloon inflated with sand burst when stuck with a pin, or will it simply leak?

FIGURE 8-1

Lewin's model of learning

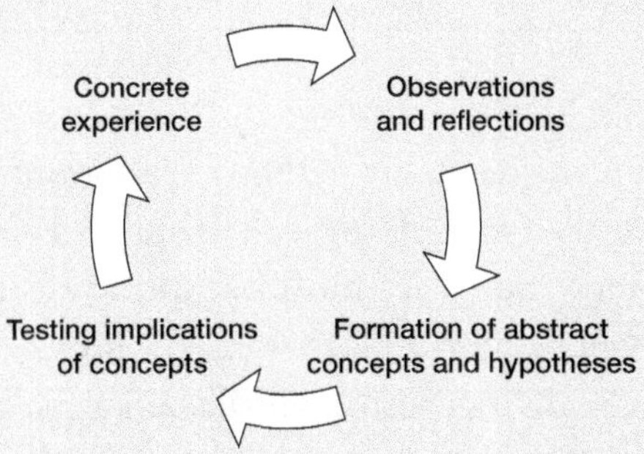

Source: Adapted from Kurt Lewin, *Field Theory in Social Science: Selected Theoretical Papers*, reprinted edition (Washington, DC: American Psychological Association, 1997), chapter 4.

(continued)

Paulo Freire portrayed learning as a tactile and active process of inquiry: "Knowledge emerges only through invention and reinvention, through the restless, impatient, continuing, hopeful inquiry men pursue in the world, with the world, and with each other."[b]

Anyone who tries to influence the course of human affairs, whether in small groups or large organizations, knows intimately that knowledge is conditional and that knowledge of conditions is critical to effective action. A deep understanding of theories of motivation or group dynamics is great, but if you don't have a grasp of surrounding conditions, of history, of dominant values, it's remarkably easy to fail. The challenge for leaders is enormous because conditions rarely remain static for very long. Today's opportunity can quickly become tomorrow's obstacle.

For these reasons, there is a natural alignment between acuity at learning and development as a leader. Leaders need deep skill in observation, in reading and interpreting situations and people (*preparing*), in devising and carrying out experiments to test what they know (*deploying*), and in adjusting in response to initial results (*renewing*). The same logic applies whether the playing field is a big experiment, like turning around an ailing business and a flagging culture, or a little one, like testing for agreement among the members of an executive team; or whether the time frame is months or moments.

a. Kurt Lewin, *Field Theory in Social Science: Selected Theoretical Papers*, reprinted edition (Washington, DC: American Psychological Association, 1997).

b. Paulo Freire, *Pedagogy of the Oppressed* (New York: Continuum, 1974), 58.

However, I want to do more than create yet another interesting but difficult-to-assemble model. Instead, I hope to link the leader development activities most organizations already have in place—assessment centers, classroom training, career development, succession planning, performance management, and the like—with real work assignments, innovative uses of technology, and, most importantly, individual Personal Learning Strategies to grow more leaders at all levels faster than ever before.

Ambitious though this undertaking may appear, the logic is simple: we know that concrete experiences—in particular, crucible experiences—are not only a vital part of the learning process; they are often the best teacher too. But we also know that experience by itself is not enough. Individuals must *prepare* to make the most of experience. They need observational skills, comfort with techniques of experimentation, and more than a modicum of self-understanding in order to extract insight from experience. The burden or responsibility for acquiring requisite skills, perspectives, and self-understanding—the elements of a PLS—falls squarely on the shoulders of the individual, not the human resource department. Only an individual can understand her own aspirations; only she can be truly aware of the prism of past experiences, personal values, and preconceptions that shape what she sees; only she can honestly assess how she learns (and why she learns that way); and only she can choose the level of risk she is willing to take in order to learn.

We know that organizations have at their disposal resources that individuals need, like self-assessment tools, classrooms, coaches, and experiences—stretch assignments, foreign postings, or mentoring relationships—that can enable them to *deploy* or apply valuable skills and teach valuable lessons about leading. And we know that organizations can create processes, like assessment and tracking and personal development planning, that can guide the selection and grooming of leadership candidates. But if those developmental experiences and processes do not align with individuals' aspirations, motivations, and learning styles—their Personal Learning Strategies—there is little reason to believe that they will have the effect that organizations hope for. And if the results of personality assessments and learning diagnostics are not shared with individuals in a way that educates them as to their abilities and options, then the value of testing and tracking will be limited by more than half. In other words, organizations routinely deploy people into assignments, but often development is only loosely coupled with deployment. Managers either don't ask what a candidate should learn from an assignment, or they do but don't follow up to see whether what was intended was actually achieved. Filling the leadership pipeline is not just a supply chain problem.

Finally, we know that the ability to *renew* and enhance oneself by learning from experience is not something that we should automatically expect from incumbent leaders or from candidates for leadership positions. In many organizations, individuals have advanced up the hierarchy in the early part of their careers by outperforming their peers (what researchers refer to as a tournament model of career mobility).[2] This can easily lead them to the conclusion that continued success—especially movement into the executive suite—will come about as a result of honing and refining *what they already know*, not from experimenting and learning new things.

An experience-based approach does not abandon the time and money already invested in assessment centers and training programs. It leverages those investments. But it does call for a reorientation on the part of top management—the men and women ultimately responsible for identifying and developing the next generations of leaders—and on the part of the professionals formally charged with recruitment, training, and succession planning.

Organizations, in short, must commit themselves to providing robust resources and durable processes that will *prepare, deploy*, and *renew* existing and prospective leaders by means of a more active and creative use of experience. That commitment must be visibly enacted and supported by top management if an organization truly hopes to make learning from experience a central value.

EXPERIENCE-BASED LEADER DEVELOPMENT IN ACTION

Fortunately, both the profit and the not-for-profit sectors can provide examples that can give us an inkling of the shape and the potential benefits of experience-based leader development. Companies like Toyota, Boeing, and General Electric and organizations like MIT's Leaders for Manufacturing program have undertaken initiatives that leverage experiential learning.

Yet as we will see, few organizations successfully integrate crucible experiences into leader development, even when those most responsible for leader development recognize—indeed, testify—that experience is the best teacher. Indeed, when it comes to looking for ways to integrate experience into leader development, most tend to stay comfortably within their own boundaries. They restrict their search to allied industries and settings, leaving aside the possibility that someone in a nonindustrial or nonbusiness setting may have already solved their problem. They enact what I described in chapter 5 as the banking model of learning: a semi-industrial process in which cost per unit is the key performance measure and knowledge is something deposited in students' heads for later use. They encourage aspiring leaders to "get experience," take on stretch assignments, take risks, and the like, but provide precious little guidance in how to mine experience for insight.

Even when organizations recognize the influence of crucible events, they find it difficult to engage leaders and leadership candidates in dialogue about them. The chief leadership officer at a major pharmaceutical company put it simply: "Incorporating life experiences into work experiences is taboo, even if it would give more insight into individuals and what shapes them as leaders," he said. "So, it's taken us a long time to get to the point where we are now: experimenting with a developmental process that actually understands [very senior executives] as individuals."

The irony, he went on to say, was that those executives have proved very open in talking about what has shaped them as leaders. My experience in talking with hundreds of business and governmental executives echoes this point: given the opportunity, leaders want to talk about their developmental experiences; they practically gush with exuberance. The limiting factor, therefore, may not be individual privacy but organizational ability to make use of that very valuable data. It's almost as if organizations—and especially the people responsible for leader development—are residents of a high-rise, witnessing a mugging ten floors below: they very much want to help but don't know what to do.

Toward the end of this chapter, I present as a partial remedy two examples that illustrate the real potential of crucibles for leader development—in two organizations on opposite ends of virtually any spectrum: the Church of Jesus Christ of Latter-day Saints (the Mormons) and the Hells Angels (an outlaw motorcycle gang).[3] Aside from their appeal as exotic stories, these two cases demonstrate experience-based leader development in action.

But first, let's examine more closely the three core moments in experience-based leader development: preparing, deploying, and renewing.

Preparing

Huxley made the point beautifully: experience is not so much what happens to you as what you make of what happens to you. Preparation, like the stance a tennis player takes while waiting to receive a serve, is about being in motion, observing and adjusting, anticipating whatever comes. Motorola's Bob Galvin underscored that point when he told me, "You have to have a disposition to being in motion, anticipating what's coming."

Organizations often do an excellent job of teaching analytical skills—how to diagnose problems and fix them—but many struggle with helping leaders hone their skills at sensing and observing. They might benefit from a closer look at what's been going on at Boeing.

The Boeing Company

A comprehensive program of preparing leaders to learn from experience has been under way for several years now at Boeing—and the company has linked the effort directly to business strategy. Best known for its eponymous commercial aircraft, Boeing has grown by leaps and bounds over the past decade, acquiring rival McDonnell Douglas, the space and defense business of Rockwell International, and Hughes Space and Communications. The technical integration tasks by themselves were monumental, but of equal concern to Boeing's leadership has been its ability to prepare the next generation of executives to lead the network of businesses as a coherent whole. Leader development and training became a central initiative in achieving integration, in two distinct ways.[4]

The first prong of Boeing's strategy was to create a leadership center that would serve as both a training ground and a crossroads for all of the company's leaders. Collaborative learning features prominently at the center, particularly experiences that familiarize leaders from disparate corners of the company with the organization's products and technologies and that help form shared mindsets among the next generation of leaders. At center stage is an elaborate computer-based simulation that offers leaders an opportunity to work together in high-pressure situations.

Consider Boeing's simulation of an as-yet-infant underwater transportation industry. The simulation centers on a company it calls AquaTek and two other fictional competitors. Participants in the simulation are assigned to all the major functional roles one might find in a small but growing business and are given realistic budgets and constraints. They draft learning contracts based on their experiences during the simulation, and these, in turn, become a vital guide for the coaches responsible for follow-through. Even during the simulation, coaches review the experience with participants as individuals and in their teams.

The simulation experience is like spring training for major league business. According to Ron Marcotte, deputy general manager of Air Force Systems for Boeing, "It gets people out of their comfort zones and stirs them up to learn about everybody else's business. On the last day, you end up presenting to the real CEO, and nerves go to a fevered pitch." The whole process is ideal preparation for future leaders and has the added benefits of providing a crossroads for the company's far-flung leadership and giving peers the opportunity to witness one another's business strengths directly.

The second prong of Boeing's strategy for preparing leaders to make the most of experiential opportunities involved a pilot effort called Waypoint. The brainchild of a vice president of human resources and a small cadre of researchers, Waypoint sought to leverage the findings of Morgan McCall's research (and subsequent development at the Center for Creative Leadership) to create a database of leadership lessons learned from a variety of assignments that Boeing managers had described in interviews.[5] The objective was to generate a resource that managers and their career coaches could consult once they had identified developmental needs by mapping out "the invisible markers, the key turning points in managers' careers."[6]

After five years of intensive interviews and systematic tracking of a cross section of Boeing managers (121 in total), the Waypoint project accumulated enough data and insights to create a series of career-planning tools, including a growing catalog of assignments classified by the developmental opportunities, and a companion Web site on the company portal that allows individuals and their career counselors to link to resources that Boeing managers recommended on the basis of their experience.

Learning from experience, interestingly enough, has become the hallmark of an innovative approach pioneered at an educational institution best known for its research labs, the Massachusetts Institute of Technology.

MIT's Leaders for Manufacturing Program

In the mid-1980s, when the United States was in the midst of a debilitating recession and the international outsourcing of manufacturing employment was just in its infancy, a group of faculty, government, and industry representatives convened at the Massachusetts Institute of Technology and launched a no-holds-barred investigation into the roots of America's industrial malaise. The result was the provocative 1989 book *Made in America*, which pointed to a vacuum in the leadership ranks of major manufacturing firms.[7] Not only were U.S. companies shortsighted when it came to product development and unwilling to learn from the best global competitors, but also the best leadership talent was assiduously avoiding manufacturing companies and the manufacturing function, in particular. Intent on addressing those shortcomings, a group of companies banded together to underwrite the creation of a program of education and research called the Leaders for Manufacturing program, or LFM.

LFM fosters leadership in both technology and organization, and nowhere is this emphasis greater than in the education of the Leaders Fellows. From the moment of their arrival on campus, Fellows are immersed in discussions about, and practice in, leadership. Throughout the two years of the program, leadership occupies center stage as an organizational problem, a technical challenge, and a personal goal. And with an alumni network of well over seven hundred members, it has also become a focus for continuing education and dialogue among cohorts of graduates.

The LFM starts from the assumption that the most important lessons about leadership cannot be taught in traditional ways. LFM director Donald Rosenfeld described it this way: "Experience is critical to the learning process. So, too, are opportunities to reflect on practice . . . to connect the analytical side of leadership training with personal experience." The program accomplishes this in several ways. For example, in the first week, students—who average eight years of work experience in diverse backgrounds—are immersed in a unique program titled "The Universe Within," devoted to opening students' eyes to how they learn, how mental models shape their perceptions and constrain their ability to talk across cultural and disciplinary boundaries, and how they, as a cohort, can achieve a measure of collective intelligence based on teamwork and competition. This focus on observation and inference provides a valuable foundation for student internships, the crown jewel of the program.

At the end of the first year of core courses in management and engineering, students are dispatched to six-month internships at sponsoring companies, where they are tasked to work with (and in some instances to lead) a team in resolving a significant manufacturing problem. The internship represents a unique laboratory for applying and evaluating ideas about world-class manufacturing and supply chain management, but it also provides practice fields for students to gain experience in leading organizational change. Subsequent classes on leadership and change draw explicitly on students' experiences and challenge them to make sense of what they learned on the factory floor.

Learning does not end with graduation. In fact, one of the most distinctive features of the LFM program is the size and vitality of its alumni network. The network holds annual meetings to discuss and debate new developments in manufacturing practice and business strategy and to counsel the program's administrators about how to keep the educational process and content in sync with industry developments. Moreover, the trust and mutual respect forged in the common, crucible-like experience of classes, team working, and internships has made the network a valuable source of advice for its members, akin to what I described earlier as the YPO Forum.

Of course, all the preparation in the world won't help if you tense up and revert to old habits in the face of a crucible. That's why it is essential for organizations to find ways to support leaders so that they deploy newly acquired skills.

Deploying

Most organizations do not manage their leadership assets as carefully or as systematically as they do their capital assets. They treat succession as a queuing problem and discover too late (and too often) that the people currently in the pipeline lack some of the skills or the perspectives that the CEO and the board now realize are essential for success in a changing competitive landscape.[8] Fact is, they know very little about the people ten or fifteen years removed from the top leadership slots: how they think, what they've learned from the assignments they've had, what they care about, or how they define success for themselves and for the organization.

While there is no denying that demographic shifts are part of the root explanation for the troubles facing industry, equal weight needs to be given to the failure of many organizations to grow leaders *through* work.[9] However, several organizations renowned for their financial prowess and their accumulated intellectual capital may hold promise for how effective deployment of experience can lead to more effective leader development.

General Electric

Although this leadership powerhouse has been examined many times, there are still some foundational lessons to learn from General Electric. Most important is the way in which learning and doing are woven into the very fabric of its process and culture.

General Electric, particularly under Jack Welch, is legendary for the attention it gives to selecting and developing leaders at all levels. Welch assiduously tracked potential leaders throughout the organization, leveraged the differences in GE's businesses to give people opportunities to lead in a wide variety of circumstances (e.g., growing versus plateauing markets, capital asset intensive versus human capital intensive, unionized and nonunionized), and used every speech, supplier visit, and public appearance to search out the best talent available in the open market. But he was also legendary for declaring that the task of leader development was too important to be left to human resources—in large measure because, as colleague Steve Kerr (former chief leadership officer and director for many years of GE's Crotonville management education center) argued, "Starting in 1992 Welch decided it was folly to try to prepare for a future that was so uncertain. We decided instead that most of our efforts would be spent making leadership of change a core competence of the firm."

The key phrase from Kerr is "a core competence of the firm." In other words, it's not just about growing a stratum of leaders; it's about increasing the number of leaders at all levels. Rather than limit the objective to senior management, Welch (and subsequently his successor, Jeff Immelt) pledged to drive leadership of change deeply into the organization—to create what Joseph Raelin refers to as a "leaderful organization"—and to do so by adroitly combining learning and doing.[10] The Work-Out methodology—lionized for its contributions to performance improvement—is just as significant for the combination of hands-on experience and the training it gives to line employees, first- and second-level supervisors, and managers in how to collaborate in solving problems and how to make and implement effective decisions in a timely way. The experience gained in Work-Out lasts a very long time; hence, the investment in training pays out year after year. The same can be said for GE's dedication to Six Sigma and Change Acceleration: while ostensibly focused on continuous performance improvement, each builds off a robust philosophy of structured experimentation, analysis, and learning.

Like many professional services organizations, management consultancies live or die by their intellectual capital—not just what they've documented in software or manuals, but also in the know-how, the tacit skills that employees carry in their heads (and take home with them at night). Poor or inexperienced or inflexible leadership can drive intellectual assets out of the firm literally overnight. For this reason, some, like Accenture and Deloitte, strive to grow leaders at the same time that they solve client problems.

Accenture and Deloitte Touche Tohmatsu

Like many professional services firms, Accenture (my current employer) and Deloitte Touche Tohmatsu organize themselves around projects. But unlike many peer organizations, they use projects not just to deliver services to their clients, but also to grow and test leaders.

Consulting engagements vary in length from a few months to a year or more, but in that time consultancies like Accenture use team and peer reviews to provide project leaders with a continuing stream of feedback on their performance and that of their teams. Given the intense pressures created by deadlines and client expectations, these firms cannot afford to let problems arise without being quickly resolved. Feedback that is fast, honest, and constructive is absolutely essential. So, too, is managers' ability to incorporate the feedback immediately into changed practice. That's why in these two companies, in recent years significant investments have been made in growing both the interpersonal and the technical skills of leaders at the project level.[11]

Accenture's MyLearning and Deloitte's Global Learning technology platforms are aimed at providing a wraparound resource for their professional staffs. That is, they create an Internet-based storehouse that allows individuals to locate their personal learning plans (often constructed in collaboration with career counselors), to access a rich portfolio of online training materials at a moment's notice, to identify projects (both internal and client-facing) that will provide a chance to acquire or practice specialized skills, and to catalog their accomplishments.

Deloitte's Career Value Map is an interactive online career development tool that seeks explicitly to align individual interests with experiential opportunities as they arise—for example, openings in new or ongoing client projects. According to Nick van Dam, Deloitte's chief learning officer, "Half the task is helping individuals get clear about what they want to accomplish in their careers. When they can state their interests and ambitions more clearly, we can guide their search for relevant experiences."[12] Accomplishing that within a global network of over ninety thousand employees is no simple job.

Just as it has become apparent that change is a continuous process in most organizations (and certainly business organizations), so too must learning be a continuous process, especially for leaders. To treat learning as episodic—which a curriculum of periodic seminars inevitably does—says that learning occurs only during prescribed times. In experience-based leader development, renewal is a continuous activity.

Renewing

Geeks and Geezers introduced the term *neoteny* to characterize lifelong learners: men and women who march through their lives (not just their work) with their "eyebrows arched in surprise."[13] They delight in learning new things, especially when insight leads to enhanced performance. Leaders who exhibit neoteny are never bored and never tire of change; they routinely interpret a disruption in the status quo as a challenge to grow.

The challenge for most organizations, it seems, is that they are paralyzed when confronted by equally compelling but seemingly contradictory demands. Either they freeze or they pursue one purely out of frustration with not being able to do both (or alternate between them). Thus, faced with the dilemma of promoting stability through shared mind-sets on the part of the leadership cadre while, at the same time, promoting change through divergent thinking, many will opt for the former until such time as it fails—and then they will turn 180 degrees to salute the flag of divergent thinking as they usher in an outsider as CEO.

Fortunately, several organizations have found a way to create experiences that renew and refresh leaders even as they strive to keep on a stable course. Toyota is a powerful example.

Toyota

At Toyota, much of the training that helps individuals learn and grow as leaders is embedded in initiatives and programs that have, on the surface at least, little to do with leadership. For example, according to Jeffrey Liker's book about the company, supervisors and managers are routinely handed assignments that require them to reach out to others for information, resources, labor, and political support if they are to be successful.[14] These tasks are not just obstacle courses that regulate movement up the ranks; they are opportunities to be coached or mentored and to experiment with new styles of managing and leading. Though referred to casually by some as a manifestation of Toyota's deep "paranoia," the discipline of continuous renewal applies to individuals, teams, technologies, products, and the organization as a whole.[15] It's a culture and a leadership philosophy dedicated to learning as a way to avoid the traps of success.

In fact, Toyota embeds four fundamental principles into its production system in a creative illustration of the power of renewal through experience. According to Steven Spear's research at Toyota:[16]

- *There is no substitute for direct observation.* When it comes to diagnosing the ailments of a mechanical process, a business function, or a management practice, the ability to observe and document is essential. While not eschewing aggregate data, statistics, or the like, Toyota managers learn early on to watch people and processes rather than jump to conclusions. Doing this effectively demands discipline; it's far too easy to jump to conclusions and, therefore, far too easy to overlook vital clues and surprises.

- *Proposed changes should be structured as experiments.* That is, disciplined approaches not only increase understanding but also make learning more efficient. Again, nothing is taken for granted. But employees at all levels must also have a facile understanding of what an experiment requires in the way of planning and controls.

- *Workers and managers should experiment as frequently as possible.* Small, simple experiments not only accelerate the pace of improvement and learning, but they also increase comfort and confidence with putting ideas at risk.

- *Managers should coach, not fix.* Leaders need to be open to learning, and they must encourage others to learn, too. As Spear observed, "Indeed, the more senior the manager, the less likely he was to be solving problems himself . . . The result of this unusual worker-manager relationship is a high degree of sophisticated problem-solving at all levels of the organization."

No single one of the Toyota principles, by itself, seems remarkable. Taken together, however, they constitute an approach to learning from experience that is simple, adaptable, and inclusive. More important, it is a learning process that Toyota relies on, in order to keep ahead of the competition by means of rapid technological change, a continuously refined product development process, and work methods, that has successfully transferred throughout the world.

Now let's look at another car company that also offers lessons in renewing.

Ford Motor Company's Virtual Factory

One popular way to help seasoned veterans see the world differently is to pull them out of familiar surroundings. Off-sites in the woods and courses in the pastoral setting of a corporate university encourage everyone to breathe deeply and slip free from the tunnel vision of work where everything-is-so-urgent-you-can't-stop-to-think. Or maybe not.

In 2001, Ford Motor Company founded and built the Virtual Factory and housed it in the basement of a nondescript brick building just off the crowded and perpetually under-repair South-field Freeway in Dearborn Heights, Michigan. The "factory" resides in a single room, and the assembly operation consists of a network of personal computers arrayed in a large circle and partitioned into stages that mirror an assembly plant: chassis, body-in-white, interior assembly, and final assembly. There are no cars in sight, except as subassembly cartoons that slowly march their way across the screen of each computer. Each computer represents a workstation—for example, where doors are hung on the naked chassis before painting. Simulated forklift trucks (dollies for carrying floppy disks that replenish the inventory of parts for each workstation), a tool crib, and an infirmary (a chair off to the side of the "factory floor") complete the scene.

Since its inception, the factory has "graduated" over four thousand Ford employees to rave reviews. Everyone who passes through the virtual gates—whether they are assemblers and machine operators, first-level supervisors, engineers, or plant managers—walks away with a firsthand exposure to what the company hopes will be its factory of the future, based on the principles and practices of lean engineering and lean manufacturing. They don't just play a video game; they rotate through roles: supervisor, line worker, skilled tradesman, union committeeman, and engineer. Pressure, noise, stress, and time constraints are re-created through elaborate but, according to participants, very realistic artifices, like simulated material shortages, physical accidents, machine breakdowns, surprise visits by the plant manager, and eight-hour shifts in a windowless environment. After-shift meetings focus on process improvement, as well as on team building and one-on-one coaching and feedback from trained observers. Veteran "factory rats" praise the simulation for its authenticity, but then marvel at the differences in their own behavior brought about by minor shifts in rules and roles. (Remember Penn and Teller's approach to magic?)

The objective of the virtual factory is nothing less than to create "a paradigm shift in pedagogy that focuses on *learning*, not *teaching*," according to Hossein Nivi, one of its principal designers. "Typical teaching techniques create disengaged students who are eager to escape an instructor reciting canned material. In the Virtual Factory, students learn by discovering the material through simulation and they develop the mental muscles needed to apply their discoveries."

The core premise in the design of the factory is simple and familiar: production leaders have few, if any, opportunities to practice new skills or ways of working. Simulation provides the time and the methods to help participants renew themselves with challenging new practices, to think about alternative realities while enmeshed in a convincing simulation, and to refresh their enthusiasm for learning.

LOOKING BEYOND
CONVENTIONAL BOUNDARIES

Although each organization described in the preceding section offers valuable examples and insights, none is a complete example of experience-based leader development.[17] Yet by expanding the scope of exploration to the less conventional ("closed" or highly selective organizations as well as those that engage in activities that require secrecy and/or substantial bonds of trust), I found two organizations that do, in fact, offer a closer approximation of what I refer to as experience-based leader development. These two organizations rely heavily on experience—and on learning from experience—as a central part of their practice of growing leaders. In fact, they are organizations that *must* "grow their own" because of self-imposed restrictions on their ability to recruit leaders from the outside.

In the two organizations—the Church of Jesus Christ of Latter-day Saints (the Mormons) and the Hells Angels motorcycle club—

there is a strong need for leadership, particularly during periods of growth or attack from the outside. Likewise, in both religious organizations and outlaw gangs in general, members often operate over large territories, requiring them to both grow and populate an administrative structure of some sort.

Given that neither is unlikely to be in the leader development business—and that both are likely to be wary of outsiders—where do they go for leaders? How do they combat the tendency toward a weak leadership "gene pool"? What alternative approaches to leader development might they use?[18]

Before I begin to answer those questions, consider too that both organizations are large, durable, complex, multiunit, multinational entities that have experienced periods of rapid growth in the past three decades. Both have elected, for different reasons, to not go outside for leaders. Yet neither has suffered an obvious shortage of leaders. Both have closed borders and engage in selective recruitment of new members; and they rarely admit converts into the top leadership ranks. Yet neither suffers from a weak leadership gene pool. Most importantly for our purposes, both use crucible experiences as a central part of leader development. The most visible crucible for members and leaders of the Mormon church is the missionary experience: an eighteen-month to two-year test of faith, identity, and leadership talent that also serves as the principal growth engine for church membership. For the Hells Angels, it takes the form of the motorcycle run: an event remarkable for its functional similarity to that of a missionary tour of duty, but also a period of time in which important leadership and learning lessons can be achieved.

A brief analysis of these organizationally instigated crucibles provides the final piece of the puzzle for what I have been calling experience-based leader development.

The Missionary Experience

With 12 million members, the Church of Jesus Christ of Latter-day Saints is well on its way to becoming a world religion. Especially notable is the fact that church membership doubled between 1985 and 2005 and has averaged 53 percent expansion per decade since 1945.[19] The principal mechanism through which the Mormon church grows is proselytizing (or what members refer to as "proselyting") largely through missionary work. In 2005, the Mormon church had over 52,000 men and women serving as missionaries in 162 countries. Since missions last two years for men and eighteen months for women, nearly 30,000 new missionaries must come forward each year.

Mission work—in the form of teaching, service, conversion, and baptizing—is critical to fulfillment of the members' and the church's spiritual obligation. But the mission is also fascinating from a sociological perspective. The mission is, at one and the same time, a critical organizational function, a rite of passage for young men and women (ages nineteen to twenty-six), and a leadership crucible. Missionary work grows the church and helps fulfill its earthly and spiritual objectives. It provides a capstone experience for young people—something they've been anticipating since childhood that cements them as adult members of the community. And it serves as a leadership crucible—a time of test or trial from which an individual emerges with a new or an altered sense of identity and from which also emanate the future leaders of the church.[20]

Mission work can easily be compared to a classic international assignment. Individuals are selected and assigned, prepared for the culture and the unique requirements of the job, deployed and managed while on-site, and renewed or reincorporated with new skills and perspectives. Yet, in order to capture the most from the experience, the Mormon process goes deeper on every level. Each phase emphasizes the acquisition of technical skills *and* learning skills. For example, before they leave for their particular posting, missionaries get intense training in language, culture, and pedagogical technique (the stages of conversion referred to as the *commitment pattern*). Those are the technical skills. In addition, missionaries are also steeped in methods for reading situations, judging the sincerity of someone on the journey to conversion, resolving conflicts and maintaining productive relationships with their missionary companions (with whom they live and work 24/7 for upwards of six months), and practicing in very practical terms the personal resilience necessary to withstand frequent rejection. Many missionaries keep journals during their time away and record their impressions, insights, and lessons learned so that they can revisit them later and gain insight through reflection.

Mission is a time for deploying skills and for experimenting, if only in small ways, with the words, gestures, images, and stories at the heart of the proselytizing process. It's also a time for testing, exploring, and shaping one's own identity. Indeed, it's nearly impossible not to do so when, in the words of one missionary I spoke with: "You go to the door and for the ten-thousandth time you're greeted with 'Oh, you guys are crazy' or 'No thanks, I'm all set' and the door slams in your face . . . The mission definitely teaches you how you can take a bad day and turn it into the most wonderful day of your life. It teaches you not to let the negative things that happen to you shape your decisions and your actions that day. You can use that negative and turn it into a positive."

Successfully deploying a particular set of skills, whether you measure that success in the number of conversions or length of service, reinforces and extends the lessons learned in preparation and adds new ones. Support, in the form of senior companions like Major Rupp's zone leader (described in chapter 2), enables missionaries to navigate through uncertain times and situations.

Return from the mission is a time of renewal for the individual and for the organization. Special parties are organized to welcome missionaries home. Families are counseled to give returning members time and space to collect themselves and to fit their new identity into an environment that will appear to them as having changed dramatically in their absence. Individuals find themselves displaying a newer, more mature and confident persona: someone both more worldly and more parochial (or dedicated to the church and the Mormon community). Alumni networks are formed among cohorts of returnees—many of whom will have gone through the Missionary Training Center together—and these serve not only to ease reentry but to periodically reunite and celebrate the experience.

As a result of the mission, then, the organization has new members and a fresh supply of dedicated individuals who represent the pool from which the next generation of lay leaders can be recruited. Let's look now at how the Hells Angels accomplishes experience-based leader development.

The Motorcycle Run

The Hells Angels began in 1948 in Oakland, California, and claims upwards of 2,500 members spread across 227 chapters in the United States and around the world. Alternately reviled and mythologized, the Hells Angels is perhaps best known for two things: its violent past—including murders, drug wars, and gang fights—and its longevity. This last point is fascinating because only a small handful of other groups involved in organized crime in the United States have remained viable entities for over fifty years. The Hells Angels has not only grown in number and complexity—there are, for example, dozens of branded products for sale, and the gang recently sued Walt Disney for copyright infringement—but it has also demonstrated remarkable stability and flexibility as an organization, despite the periodic arrest of large fractions of its leadership.

Like many network-based organizations, the Hells Angels maintains a strong core leadership and a relatively flat, multinodal (chapter) structure. This enables it to be both centralized, with a constitution and a clearly defined division of labor between the international organization and the chapters, and decentralized—for example, to protect itself from decapitation with the arrest and incarceration of top leaders.

Contrary to its media image as ruthlessly violent and anarchic, the Hells Angels shares in common with the Mormon church certain core attributes and practices. Leaders are rarely recruited from the outside, and candidates undergo both a careful screening process and critical crucible experiences. The most relevant crucible experiences involve organizing and successfully managing motorcycle runs. The run, according to retired Angels president Sonny Barger, "is a real show of power and solidarity when you're an Angel. It's being free and getting away from everything. Angels don't go on runs looking for trouble; we go to ride our bikes and to have a good time together."[21]

Organizing a run is no simple affair. Runs typically stretch hundreds of miles along public thoroughfares. The extraordinarily loud and deep rumble of dozens (occasionally hundreds) of un-muffled Harley-Davidson motorcycles can be heard for miles—no small source of delight to the riders. Though legal in most juris-dictions, runs nonetheless attract a great deal of attention from local law enforcement agencies and civic officials anxious to divert the event if possible. Moreover, runs invariably cross territorial boundaries between different clubs, many of which are hostile. Hence, negotiating a run is a challenge, and in some chapters it is a task rich with opportunities for learning about leadership.

A Hells Angels chapter president I interviewed leads a major California chapter, and though he refused to be identified pub-licly, he talked to me out of interest in the leadership topic. From his perspective, a run is a testing ground for future leaders: "The run organizer's got to figure out the route and who we're going to have to negotiate with to get it done. Sometimes it's cops who've got it in for us and don't want us near their town. So he's got to figure out if it's worth it to challenge them or whether to take a detour. If the guys in the chapter smell a little fear or whatever, they might push back and say, 'Hell, let's scare them!' So, he's gotta balance a lot of things. Keep in mind, it's gotta be fun but it's serious, too, because we got guys that are on parole so they can't be outrageous. Unless they want to."

A successful run requires imagination, negotiating skill, a sur-prise or two (e.g., an unusual camping spot or entertainment), and attention to history. Veteran members recall past runs and judge current ones accordingly. Run organizers benefit from build-ing on legend and venturing to enable new ones. For example, one member discovered that bicycle paths could be used for legal passage when two towns refused to allow parade permits for a planned run.

Runs are organized several times a year in this leader's chap-ter, and he allocated responsibility for organizing and managing them to men he considered "leadership material." He explicitly counseled organizers to talk with veterans about what lessons they'd learned in previous runs and to prepare themselves for any of a host of contingencies, including accidents, brushes with the law, and inclement weather. Reflecting on his own experiences, the chapter president recalled, "It never occurred to me how organized we had to be in order to appear *disorganized*," he said. "We have rules about lots of things—like when we carry guns and what time of day it's allowable to shoot them. But you have to know town rules and laws, you have to be a lawyer to know whether crossing some county lines will violate a guy's parole or something. It opened my eyes even more to what it takes to keep your freedom to do what you want."

Every run, like every major Angels event (including the death of a member), is followed by a leadership meeting in which every detail is reviewed with a level of candor that journalist Hunter S. Thompson described forty years ago in the *Nation* as a "group-therapy clinic." Refusing to go into detail, the chapter president depicted these meetings to me as "an important part of a guy's education. Who else is going to tell him that he fucked up but his family? We're his family."

Paradoxical as it may seem for an organization widely regarded as anarchic, the Hells Angels is exemplary in its use of critical experiences to grow leaders.

Crucibles are transformative events through which people learn powerful lessons about what it takes to be a leader: how to adapt, how to engage others, how to live (not just to display) their integrity. *And* they learn a great deal about how they learn and how they can keep on learning. Crucibles are complex, demanding, and daunting, but they are frequent and they are free. The challenge, as I've tried to portray it in this chapter, is in how organizations can leverage and even foster the experiences that help aspiring leaders become adept or even outstanding leaders.

Fortunately, the power of experience is not lost on organizations that have set for themselves the task of growing leaders. But few organizations carry the task through all phases of the learning cycle. Some excel at preparing or deploying but have yet to extend the process to renewal. Others strive to renew but have yet to connect those efforts to preparing. And then some—indeed, the majority, I would argue—deploy potential leaders into assignments and geographies pregnant with the potential to learn from experience, but largely fail to prepare them and almost always neglect to renew them.

A brief side trip in my quest for an experience-based approach to leader development provided glimpses at a solution that more mainstream businesses and governments might consider applying. As we saw, the Mormons and the Hells Angels demonstrate how it is possible to craft or to convert core activities to serve as practice fields for leaders. In both cases (though in very different ways), the Mormons and the Hells Angels engage in elaborate preparation before sending would-be leaders out into the field. They teach technical skills, certainly, but as important are the learning skills: the rules of the road, the watch-outs for oncoming trouble, and the ways to preserve one's identity and sense of wholeness while engaging with others.

The Mormons and the Hells Angels also provide a supporting infrastructure while members are in the midst of a crucible. There are senior, seasoned companions and supervisors who know when to say no. Coach or mentor, the role is not just a job. It is a statement of commitment to the individuals in need and to the mission of the organization, as well.

Finally, both the Mormons and the Hells Angels recognize the need for renewal in both individuals and the organization. They organize to accomplish both stability and change by investing in crucible events. Crucibles foster a new generation of leaders, enable each organization to replenish and even to expand its ranks, and provide a selective membrane that screens new ideas and new technologies before they enter the organization.

Five criteria for effective experience-based leader development can be extracted from GE, Toyota, Ford, Accenture, Deloitte, MIT, the Hells Angels and the Mormon church:

- Helping individuals clarify their aspirations and values will strengthen their ability to mine experience for insight.

- Leaders need to learn technique and judgment, and organizations can foster both.

- Feedback needs to be fast, honest, and immediately incorporated into changed behavior.

- Practice needs to be encouraged as a lifelong pursuit.

- Adaptive capacity is essential for individual leaders and for the organizations that want to grow them.

Now it is time, in the next chapter, to merge the two models at the heart of experience-based leader development. For individuals: the model of expert performance with a Personal Learning Strategy at its core; for organizations: prepare, deploy, renew.

$$\left[\ 9\ \right]$$

INVIGORATING THE PRACTICE
OF LEADERSHIP

Aligning Organizational Needs
with Individual Capabilities

Learning is not compulsory . . . neither is survival.
—W. Edwards Deming

*You cannot teach a man anything; you can
only help him find it within himself.*
—Galileo Galilei

DEMING AND GALILEO CAPTURE precisely the double bind that many organizations face. Learning *is* compulsory, but it cannot be forced. Individual leaders need to grow and develop, to deepen their skills and their capabilities, and to extend the range of situations they can address. And organizations need them to do those things—not because organizations are particularly enlightened, but because great leadership is *necessary*.

Organizations cannot teach people to lead, though they can and should provide the means through which technique can be learned and practiced. Organizations cannot compel individuals to strive for eminence, but they can encourage and support aspiring leaders to look inward and find the insights and the distinctive perspective that could make them great. Organizations should not provoke adversity, but they do need to recognize the transformative potential of crucible experiences and to provide the resources people need to extract insight from them.

Alas, this double bind comes with a twist: organizations of all sorts—public and private, large and small—confront futures riddled with uncertainty, complexity, and potential for disruption. Uncertainty demands a strong sense of direction and the fortitude to stick with it. Complexity demands leaders who can mobilize *networks* of expertise—rather than fortifying pyramids dedicated to stability and routine.[1] And disruptive change—driven by technology, competition, geopolitics, or a mixture of all three—will require organizations to find people capable of fostering both adaptation and innovation.

In other words, what's needed is *more* leaders, not fewer; leaders who can mobilize networks, not just command departments; and leaders who are dedicated to continuous, productive change. What's needed are learning leaders.

This chapter will introduce an experience-based approach to leader development that can help organizations grow more leaders, over a larger terrain and faster than ever before. We begin with a brief review of key findings from the book—not so much as a summary, but as a prelude that reminds us of how challenging the task is for organizations. The focus then shifts to an action agenda for the organizational leaders and professionals who must bend, shape, and redirect existing resources to make an experience-based approach work. Throughout that section I will underscore the role that a Personal Learning Strategy can play in bridging individual and organizational needs. Finally, the chapter—and this book—concludes with a charge to the current generation of leaders:

to take responsibility for the next generation of leaders and, more importantly, for the generation after that.

WHAT WE'VE LEARNED
ABOUT LEARNING TO LEAD

Accomplished leaders say that experience is their best teacher. They learned their most meaningful and important leadership lessons—lessons that they've integrated into their own leadership style—through *crucibles*. These were critical events and experiences, times of testing and trial, failure more often than grand success, that grabbed them by the lapels and demanded to know "What do you stand for?" and "What are *you* going to *do*?" A situation arose that did not respect age, gender, generation, nationality, talent, or charisma; all it asked was that a person step up and be someone or do something they'd never been or done before.

Crucibles are hard to predict, and the events themselves are likely to be idiosyncratic. Sometimes they take place at work, but work is often the backdrop, the place where learning happens, not the place in an individual's internal landscape most affected by the lessons or the reason why learning occurred. Business school cases may feature solitary decision makers gazing at an oncoming rush of storm clouds and pondering make-or-break choices; but when you ask people to tell you about their personal defining moments, you're more likely to hear about something that occurred on a much smaller and more personally meaningful stage, in the off-hours, the unscheduled time, in the ROL (the rest of life). Regrettably, you can never tell when you might learn something important about leading.

A key characteristic of leaders who leverage experience, I found, is their alertness to learning opportunities. Like tennis players anticipating a serve, they are always on the balls of their feet, weight shifting back and forth, ready to spring in one direction or the other in a fraction of a second. That level of preparedness, that ability to read subtle clues about direction and intent, is the product of practice. It does not matter whether the ability is inherited or learned; it loses its edge without practice. The same goes for recognizing learning opportunities, particularly crucible experiences. Practice matters.

Practice is not something these leaders do just in the off-hours, because, as we know, there are so few off-hours. True learning leaders practice all the time, while they perform and while they are offstage. They experiment in real time in much the same way a consummate violinist or dancer or athlete might vary her performance in order to achieve a more elegant or unprecedented effect.

These leaders share one more critical characteristic: a Personal Learning Strategy. Whether consciously recognized or not, whether it even has a name, whether it is better described as a signature or a style, what they have achieved is a unique understanding of how they learn and improve best and why. As I've attempted to show, a PLS is a deeply personal covenant—a truly individual awareness of aspirations, motivations, and learning style. It is not a strategy that can be imposed; it must be discovered. However, as we have also seen through comparing the experiences of consummate leaders and performers, a PLS can be seeded through an explicit process of self-examination, mastery of underlying moves, instruction, feedback, and practice, practice, practice.

WHAT THIS MEANS FOR ORGANIZATIONS

Experience is an underused asset in organizations. Not that experience is devalued—not by a long shot, if you judge by the weight that employers give to résumés and past performance—but it is to suggest that experience is seriously underleveraged. People are often sent on assignment with the blind hope that while accomplishing the task set before them, they will also learn something important, something that will impart wisdom and insight and judgment. Organizations establish rotational programs in the hope that general management skills and cross-functional thinking will emerge. Managers are trained and rewarded to keep things under control—budgets, processes, and people—and then we grimace in frustration when those same people can't switch effortlessly to being leaders of change. Managers are elevated into the executive ranks with the hope that they will intuit how to shift from a focus on problem solving to a focus on vision and strategy. But blind hope is not a wise investment strategy.

What, then, would be a better investment strategy?

To answer that question, we must venture into a world that does not exist . . . yet. As I tried to show in the last chapter, companies like Toyota and GE and institutions like MIT foreshadow what's possible. Research carried out by the Accenture Institute for High Performance Business over the past two years has found that organizations as diverse as State Farm Insurance, Schlumberger, John Deere, Honda, Caremark, Tata Engineering, National Australia Bank, BMW, UBS, Medtronic, Teach For America, the Peace Corps, City Year, and the Girl Scouts all have worked to more closely tie work experience and leader development.[2] More and more organizations employ action-learning projects as a way to link learning and doing. And though the connection between the task and the learning sometimes seems a bit contrived, participants in those projects almost always walk away with a greater appreciation for what can be learned through collaborative problem solving. And finally, it is common to find organizations encouraging (or requiring) employees to compile long-term personal development plans—not just cursory annual objectives.

Organizations that pursue an experience-based approach to leader development, however, will demonstrate a fundamentally different attitude toward leading and learning. Experience-based leader development equips employees to mine experience—continuously and intensively—for insight on what it takes to lead, what it takes to grow and adapt as a leader, and what it takes to cultivate the leader in others (peers and superiors as well as subordinates). Such leader development links activities that most organizations already have in place—for example, classroom-based

training, assessment centers, career development, succession planning, and performance management—with real work assignments and innovative uses of information technology to create a
comprehensive process for developing leaders at all levels of an
organization.

In chapter 8 we began to look at how experience-based leader
development comprises three major processes: preparing, deploying, and renewing (see figure 9-1). In this chapter we'll explore
how organizations might actually use these concepts in practice.

Prepare

Learning to lead requires individuals to prepare in several important ways. For example, to prepare a potential leader to make the
most of a rotational assignment and through that assignment learn,
say, effective decision making and communication, organizations
need to help individuals learn fundamental (though by no means
rudimentary) skills like how to separate fact from perception, ask
penetrating questions, and assess risks and consequences. How
else will they be positioned to notice the vital messages about
agreement or disagreement, trust, and engagement that are so

FIGURE 9-1

Processes of experience-based leader development

often culturally encrypted—that is, hidden in the choice of words, body language, and facial gestures among peers, subordinates, alliance partners, and customers in unfamiliar settings?

To be capable observers, aspiring leaders need to take into account how their own motives, aspirations, values, stereotypes, and expectations shape what they see, and how their individual learning styles can be best engaged to aid them in the process of adapting to change. Recall, for example, how Mormon youths are prepared for their missionary experience through a combination of intense study and role playing (language, conversation, planning, resilience). That kind of preparation requires that time be set aside for well-conceived assessment of one's deeper aspirations and motives—not a twenty-item personality inventory that captures little more than one's mood on a given day and time. Preparation and awareness flourish when individuals are not only allowed but encouraged to question others about the meaning of taken-for-granted words and practices. The converse is also true.

Deploy

Experiences on the job and off provide, as we've seen, a remarkably fertile ground for learning—if they are perceived as such. In simplest terms, if performance improves through practice, then practice needs to be legitimated as an essential and valued activity for leaders. "If everyone knew how to practice, everyone would be a genius!" declared Wanda Landowska, who helped initiate the revival of the harpsichord in the twentieth century, and she's not wrong.[3] Individuals need to practice leadership technique in real time with real consequences. But they also need to understand that each performance, like each concert or each surgery, is a learning opportunity, a time in which to notice the effects of practice and the places where more deliberate effort is required. And superiors and peers need to encourage this merging of performance and practice. Indeed, in the absence of encouragement to both act and reflect, it's unlikely that individuals will evolve their own distinctive leadership perspective.

Organizations thus need to provide training in technique, opportunities to experiment and to practice, and guidance in how to evolve an individual perspective on leading. Assignments need to be evaluated not only in terms of tasks that need to be accomplished, but also in terms of what the tasks or the role offers in the way of experience for individuals to learn from. In much the same way that Boeing, State Farm, and other firms have begun to catalog the leadership lessons learned from various kinds of assignments, organizations will need to be far more attentive to the learning opportunities that commonly attend different roles and assignments. These can vary from major, crucible-like events (e.g., recovering from financial disaster, reenergizing a demoralized workforce, launching a radical innovation in product or process) to more conventional challenges (like foreign postings), to the prosaic yet vital things we expect from leaders on a daily basis (e.g., coaching a talented but disgruntled employee, carrying out incremental change, or providing an example worth following).

Renew

Just as a photographer must "fix" an image to preserve it, both organizations and individuals need to find ways to preserve and renew what they've learned. Inspired by their observation of great leaders in a variety of settings, scholars like Noel Tichy emphasize the importance of having a teachable point of view. At its best, a teachable point of view is the distillate of effective preparation and deployment. In much the same way that young Mormon missionaries are consciously reincorporated in the church community as teachers on their return from the field, aspiring leaders need to be encouraged to shape experience into part of their personal leadership perspective. But a personal perspective or a teachable point of view must also be open to adaptation, amendment, and change as different experiences and challenges emerge. Some of those challenges will derive from the individual leader's life, but they can and should be supplemented by the lessons shared among a community of leaders.

Leaders, by the very nature of their role, rarely work alone or learn alone. Indeed, the experience of the Leaders for Manufacturing program at MIT and the Young Presidents' Organization suggests that the most effective learning takes place when the individual leader has access to others who care enough to challenge, cajole, critique, and care. Thus, in preparation, organizations need to make explicit provision for leaders to build their own advice networks—people to whom they can turn for honest, critical, and timely advice. In deployment, these same people can serve as a learning community, a place where insights can be shared and where personal dilemmas, problems, and achievements can be presented, analyzed, and understood.

ALIGNMENT THROUGH A PERSONAL LEARNING STRATEGY

The problem with career plans or personal development plans (PDPs) for aspiring leaders is that they provide at best a weak link between an individual's aspirations and motivations and an organization's formal and informal human resource processes. In far too many instances, career plans or PDPs are an exercise indistinguishable from annual objective setting, carried out by managers not trained well enough to dig beneath the surface to explore real motivations and aspirations.

A Personal Learning Strategy, on the other hand, can be a vital connection between individuals and organizations in an experience-based approach to leader development. Although a PLS may be a deeply individual covenant, it is enacted in and through organizations. Organizations are the playing field, the stage, and the studio. Organizational peers are the teammates, the ensemble cast, and the audience. Customers, shareholders, subordinates, and bosses are the critics. And no matter how elegant the performance from the perspective of the performer, organizations and their stakeholders write the review.

For this reason, it is essential that organizations do more than compose lists of desired leadership competencies and address them through a menu of courses and workshops. They must also encourage each individual—or, at a minimum, each individual who aspires to a leadership role—to craft a PLS and to use it as a living document, not something sketched once and set aside. Further, organizations need to treat leadership as a profession built on a foundation of both technique and perspective (see figure 9-2). That is, individuals should be expected to acquire deeper skill in leadership technique through structured, deliberate practice. Skills can stagnate from underuse; they can be blunted through misuse; and they can be superseded by advances in the field. They must, therefore, be renewed.

Indeed, one constant in the relationship between individual leaders and the organizations that employ them will be a mutual expectation that learning is a necessity throughout a career. Organizations will expect individuals to learn in order to remain effec-

FIGURE 9-2

Personal Learning Strategy

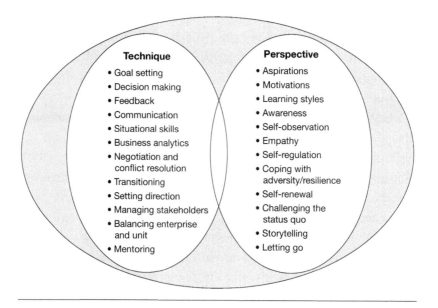

tive in their roles. Individuals, in turn, will expect organizations to provide them with experiences and resources through which to learn—irrespective of the positions they occupy in the organizational hierarchy. Thus, expectations about the fact of learning should have little to do with hierarchy: preparing, deploying, and renewing should cut across organizational levels.

Leadership perspective, like wisdom and judgment, grows with experience and with acuity at mining experience, not just with age or seniority. Therefore, organizations will need to target opportunities and resources for enhancing *both* technique and perspective in parallel.

For example, novice leaders (no matter what their age or career stage) need both technique and perspective. Conventional leader development models focus heavily—and appropriately—on techniques applicable in small groups or work teams, like goal setting, decision making, and feedback. But what cannot be overlooked are the questions that help a novice gain perspective on both the role of leader and his or her aspirations, motivations, and learning style. Perhaps the most important question to be answered at this stage is simply, "Why lead?"

Adept leaders (whether they are twenty-five years old or twice that) need to practice a larger repertoire of techniques and to extend the scope of their responsibility. But they also need to expand their ability to read situations and the effect they personally have well beyond their immediate surroundings. Adept leaders often rise in the organizational hierarchy and gain greater scale and scope of responsibility—but it doesn't necessarily follow that anyone placed in a high rank is adept as a leader.

Eminent or outstanding leaders must keep learning new technique, lest they stagnate (with negative consequences for others, not just themselves). So, too, must they be encouraged to renew their own energies and aspirations, spread their insights through mentoring, and let go so that others may test themselves. At the risk of repetition, a reminder is appropriate here: eminent leaders can be found (and, in what Joseph Raelin delightfully calls "leaderful" organizations, they ought to be found) at *any* hierarchical level.[4]

This brings us to the challenge of working with the experiences that have the potential to transform a leader's identity and self-concept.

CRAFTING CRUCIBLES

At the outset of the chapter, I discouraged organizations from "provoking adversity" in their zeal to develop leaders through crucible experiences. We create enough pressures to perform that we don't need to invent new ones just so we can accelerate leader development. The trick is to harness the crucibles that life sets in motion so the opportunity for learning is not squandered. To harness crucibles, we need to recognize two essential points: first, although many crucibles do not occur on the job, they are nonetheless an important part of a leader's development; and, second, irrespective of where they take place, crucibles generally have a deep personal impact—for example, they tend to stir up very strong emotions, and so harnessing their power is not a simple undertaking. Let's consider the implications of each point.

Off the Job or on the Job?

Recall that in chapter 8 I quoted the chief leadership officer of a pharmaceutical company who claimed that it was "taboo" to bring nonwork experiences, particularly times of personal adversity, into the workplace even if they were relevant to leader development. I, too, have heard and experienced the same taboo. Yet whenever I've had the opportunity to talk about my research with workplace audiences, including audiences with participants from many different layers in a hierarchy, I have been astounded by the willingness—indeed, the eagerness—with which people talk about powerful personal experiences. Sometimes those conversations take place in twos and threes; but just as often they are shared with a larger group. Senior executives have talked about the challenge of being a child of divorce at a very early age and what it taught about learning to be independent while wanting very much to depend on others. They've talked about failure and the lingering specter of depression that challenged them to step out of a funk and to take responsibility because others depended on them. These were things that were not generally known but, once known, emboldened the teller and encouraged others to explore their own crucibles for lessons learned.

The nugget here is that people are actually much more willing to share and to explore topics that we refer to as taboo than most of us imagine. Obviously, there are many things that good taste and the law prohibit. But when people understand that the intent is to explore how men and women learn to lead—not to embarrass or to vilify—and when they gain insight into how they and others actually learn, off-the-job experiences become a legitimate part of the process of leader development. For this reason, I often encourage leaders who want to initiate conversations about learning from experience to begin with a crucible story of their own. It's also why I encourage coaches and mentors to recommend to their clients and mentees that they take up an avocation, something outside of work, that will cause them to learn something new and that will force them to find a community of others also pursuing that avocation, so that they can gain comfort in being "an absolute beginner" with nothing to hide or to claim other than a desire to learn.

The Emotional Side of Learning

The second point is, in many respects, a cautionary tale with regard to the first one. That is, crucible experiences quite often set loose (or, in the retelling, resurrect) strong feelings. It's a bit misleading to label such feelings as "good" or "bad" or "positive" or "negative"—that's entirely in the eye of the beholder. But they are undeniably there. If you doubt what I say, then think of a time when you learned a lesson that's really stuck with you; it doesn't have to be about leadership. It could be a moment of contradiction—you never thought things could be any other way—or it could be a moment of revelation in which a puzzle that had bedeviled you suddenly reveals its inner secret. Relief, frustration, anger, betrayal, panic, exhilaration, sorrow—they are all very strong emotions and certainly not the sort of thing we associate with the even-tempered or stoic behavior we expect to encounter in the modern workplace. All the more reason why, when you read about management writers extolling the virtues of organizational learning and continuous change, you have to wonder how prepared workplaces (and managers) are for all the strong emotions they are inviting.

If deep learning of the sort we encounter in crucibles is an important part of a leader's journey, and if strong emotions commonly accompany deep learning, then we need to know that strong emotions are very likely to be a part of leader development. If learning from experience is not a desirable part of leader development, then we can ignore it and hope it goes away; if we elect to pursue an experience-based approach to leader development, our only alternative is to find ways to work with emotions.

Though inelegant, an analogy exists in the way toxic waste is managed in industry. Organizations commonly choose to do one of three things: they bury it, they try to find a way to filter it out at the end (what's often referred to as the "end of pipe" solution), or they try to process it at the source—for example, to avoid producing it in the first place. Strong emotions that are unmanaged share a lot with toxic waste: they are often corrosive and destructive to the individual and to those around him or her if they are not treated properly, and even when buried, they tend to resurface, often at the most inopportune times. End-of-pipe solutions are often selected because they don't require significant alterations to an existing process; but what tends to get missed is the extraordinary energy and resources that get consumed in partial and unsatisfying efforts to filter out unwanted things before they impact the public. They really do need to be managed at the source. If strong, difficult, or taboo emotions are being generated because crucibles and other powerful learning experiences inevitably happen, then it is the wise and ultimately the efficient organization that finds ways to work with strong feelings.

To that end, there are no easy solutions. What's required is a significant investment in helping—through what I've referred to in earlier sections as preparing—individuals to recognize their own crucible situations, to practice the learnable dimensions of resilience (from chapter 3), and to help managers and professionals responsible for leader development to coach and mentor aspiring leaders through emotionally turbulent times. This challenge is implicit in the best work on emotional intelligence, such as Daniel Goleman's work and that of Richard Boyatzis and Annie McKee, even if it is only rarely addressed directly.

What, then, can organizations do to harness the power of experience? Organizations should strive to create experiences that can be mined for leader development and to leverage the ones that occur without warning. Three types of experiences, corresponding to the types of crucibles we discussed in chapter 2, are most relevant: new territory, reversal, and suspension (see table 9-1).[5]

Experiences that involve new territory are best preceded and/or accompanied by an individual's gaining greater insight into his personal motivations, aspirations, and values, and by a deeper understanding about how he learns (and learns best). Experiences that involve reversal are best leveraged if the individual has greater comfort at self-observation and self-regulation, has the ability to cope with adversity, and is capable of exercising empathy. Experiences that involve suspension are best leveraged if the individual has gained insight into what it takes him to renew himself (e.g., physically, intellectually, and/or spiritually); quite often, it also requires the ability to effectively communicate to others what he has learned (e.g., as part of a true mentoring process).

Optimally, the professionals responsible for leader development would be in a position—along with the aspiring leader and in conjunction with his or her PLS—to understand which aspects of leadership technique and perspective would be enhanced by a particular experience. Simpler said than done, of course, but if the

TABLE 9-1

Experiences for leader development

	Work	Life
New territory	• Early work	• Military service
	• First supervision	• New kid on the block
	• Foreign assignment	• Music camp
	• Staff assignment	• Lost in the woods
Reversal	• Project failure	• Bankruptcy
	• Bad quarter	• Divorce
	• Audit	• Election defeat
	• Death of a coworker	• Loss of a loved one
Suspension	• Sabbatical	• Long-term illness
	• After-action review	• Long-term unemployment
	• Night or rotating shifts	• Going back to school
	• Temporary layoff	• Extended retreat

aspiring leader is a partner in the exercise, not just a client, then what's involved would more closely resemble a redirection of effort rather than a whole new effort.

There is also a partner, sponsor, and champion without whose involvement an experience-based approach to leader development is impossible. Fortunately, that partner/sponsor/champion has a deep personal prestige and financial stake in growing more leaders faster. I refer to the current generation of leaders.

A CHALLENGE TO THE CURRENT GENERATION OF LEADERS

We've known for decades that top leaders can have enormous symbolic as well as practical impact on an organization's performance—even though it's often not clear whether individual CEOs or executive directors or agency chiefs deserve all the credit (or blame). But speculation about the relationship between their behavior and outcome measures like share price movements can divert attention from much more important effects that top management can have on the long-term viability—and therefore the long-term value—of an enterprise: namely, the depth and quality of its leadership talent.

Top management behavior sets the tone (and the morale) of leaders at all levels—something evidenced most dramatically in the devastating impact that top management failures have had on companies like Tyco, WorldCom, Adelphia, and Enron in both the short and the long run. Successor CEOs in those organizations find themselves saddled with the enormous task of resuscitating morale, rejuvenating middle management, and finding ways to recruit new talent to what might appear to be tainted soil. Conversely, the depth of leadership talent at companies like GE, UPS, Marriott, and Microsoft is an intangible asset that institutional investors often cite when discussing the drivers of shareholder value.

To enjoy increasing returns from leadership investments, top management must actively *cultivate* next-generation leaders: their immediate successors and *at least two generations beyond them.* That is, in addition to investing in the infrastructure necessary to support leaders at all levels and championing experience-based leader development, top management must take personal responsibility for recruiting and mentoring future leaders, whether they do it intuitively or programmatically. It's a challenging task, considering the incessant drumbeat of quarterly performance, but it's difficult to imagine who besides top management could do the job.

Cultivating next-generation leaders requires that today's leaders, beginning with the CEO, the executive director, and the agency chief, be connoisseurs of talent, capable of identifying and courting employees who have gifts the organization needs and that they themselves may lack. There is no room in an economy dependent on ideas for a leader who is threatened by the greatness of others.

One form of leadership that will increasingly develop is a partnership, formal or informal, between a lion in winter eager to share what he or she has learned and a young leader who's eager both to learn and to teach. In such lash-ups, the older individual may inspire greater trust than a younger colleague who might be viewed as a potential competitor. Yet the collaboration is mutually beneficial, since the older leader gains the satisfaction of mentoring and benefits from an inside view of a new generation at work. The younger leader gets to mentor as well and gains invaluable access to a broader perspective.

Though by no means exhaustive, the following questions ought to stimulate some reflection on any leader's preparedness to cultivate the next generations:

- Are you and your organization doing enough to choose the right people to be candidates for the next generation of leaders?

- Are you selecting candidates on the basis of today's success criteria or tomorrow's?

- If you believe that experience is the best teacher of leadership, what are you and your organization doing to help people at all ages and levels to make the most of their experiences?

- How much do you know about the generation of leaders after the next one? Who are they? What do they value? Have you done enough to motivate them to step up and take the mantle?

Leaders don't become leaders on talent alone. No matter how intellectually or emotionally gifted or economically advantaged or socially privileged, no one is prepared for all the uncertainty and newness that organizational life will throw at them. Leaders must adapt and learn if they are to fulfill what we expect of them, and—if this study is any guide—if they are to fulfill what they expect of themselves. Albert Einstein put it best when he said, "Wisdom is not a product of schooling but of the lifelong attempt to acquire it."

My hope is that this book has drawn the disciplines of learning and leading a little closer together and that it may serve, by documenting the strategies that eminent performers and leaders have adopted, to stimulate both individuals and organizations to take their performance to a higher level.

NOTES

Preface

1. Warren G. Bennis and Robert J. Thomas, *Geeks and Geezers: How Era, Values, and Defining Moments Shape Leaders* (Boston: Harvard Business School Press, 2002).

Chapter 1

1. According to Daniel J. Levinson et al., "The life structure evolves through a relatively orderly sequence during the adult years. The essential character of the sequence in time is the same for all the men in our study . . . It consists of a series of alternating stable (structure-building) and transitional (structure-changing) periods." Daniel J. Levinson et al., *The Seasons of a Man's Life* (New York: Ballantine, 1978), 49. See also Gail Sheehy, *Passages: Predictable Crises of Adult Life* (New York: Ballantine, 2004).

2. Unless otherwise indicated, quotes throughout the book are verbatim extracts from interviews conducted by the author for the purposes of this project. Interviews were conducted between February 2000 and July 2007.

Chapter 2

1. Erving Goffman, *Asylums: Essays on the Social Situation of Mental Patients and Other Inmates* (New York: Anchor Books, 1961).

2. Noel M. Tichy, *The Cycle of Leadership: How Great Leaders Teach Their Companies to Win*, with Nancy Cardwell (New York, Harper-Business, 2002).

3. Bronwyn Fryer, "Storytelling That Moves People: A Conversation with Screenwriting Coach Robert McKee," *Harvard Business Review*, June 2003, 5–8.

4. In their seminal work on how executives learn at work, McCall, Lombardo, and Morrison make a parallel point: "So, if there is indeed a right stuff for executives, it may be this extraordinary tenacity in extracting something worthwhile from their experience and in seeking experiences rich in opportunities for growth . . . In short, the closest thing to a prescription we could find was: Make the most of your experiences." Morgan W. McCall Jr., Michael M. Lombardo, and Ann M. Morrison, *The Lessons of Experience: How Successful Executives Develop on the Job* (New York: Free Press, 1988), 122.

5. After listening carefully to the first comments people made about "how they learned," I began to understand why I'd always found speeches by leaders—particularly by celebrity business leaders talking to large crowds of MBAs in stuffy amphitheaters—to be only marginally educational. The speeches were always about what they did or what one should do, not about how they learned to do what they do. When they were jolted off-script by a probing question about themselves, real insights might be gained, but often those circumstances were limited and transitory. As a result, I now invite speakers to address my classes for a maximum of ten minutes—during which time I advise them to say what they are really dying to say—and the remainder of the visit is devoted to students asking questions about how the speaker learned to lead. The responsibility is thus put on students' shoulders to prepare questions that will lead to insightful observations.

6. It is important to note that the lessons people pointed to about learning span the spectrum of learning styles. Some are visual (learn by seeing); others are verbal/auditory (learn by hearing); others involve reading/writing (learn by processing text); and some are kinesthetic or practical (learn by doing).

7. McCall, Lombardo, and Morrison, *The Lessons of Experience*, 73.

Chapter 3

1. Edgar Allan Poe, *Complete Stories and Poems of Edgar Allan Poe* (New York: Doubleday, 1984).

2. Richard Boyatzis and Annie McKee, *Resonant Leadership: Renewing Yourself and Connecting with Others Through Mindfulness, Hope, and Compassion* (Boston: Harvard Business School Press, 2005).

3. Frederic Flach, *Resilience: Discovering a New Strength at Times of Stress* (Long Island City, NY: Hatherleigh Press, 2004), xix. Similarly, George Vaillant, a Harvard University psychologist who chronicled the lives of ninety-five men in the Grant Study, sees resilience as an underlying feature

of healthy adult adaptation to crisis and change. George E. Vaillant, *Adaptation to Life* (Cambridge, MA: Harvard University Press, 1998), 385–386.

4. Flach, *Resilience*, 34.

5. See Muriel Siebert, *Changing the Rules: Adventures of a Wall Street Maverick* (New York: Free Press, 2002).

6. Island Moving Company, "Our Mission and Vision," October 11, 2007, http://www.islandmovingcompany.org/aboutus/mission.html.

7. Vaillant, *Adaptation to Life*.

8. Betsy Morris, "Overcoming Dyslexia: Fortune Examines Business Leaders and Artists Who Have Gone Beyond the Limitations of Dyslexia," *Fortune*, May 13, 2002, http://www.fortune.com/indexw.jhtml?channel=artcol.jhtml&doc_id=207665.

9. Studies of the adaptive strategies of people with learning disabilities also shed insight on the more general process of creating a Personal Learning Strategy. For example, they emphasize the importance for individuals of gaining an intimate understanding of their learning style, their underlying motivations and aspirations, and the characteristics of a social environment that are most conducive to their comfort while learning new (and perhaps disconfirming) things. For example, see Henry B. Reiff, Paul J. Gerber, and Rick Ginsberg, "Learning to Achieve: Suggestions from Adults with Learning Disabilities," *Journal of Postsecondary Education and Disability* 10, no. 1 (1993).

10. Vaillant, *Adaptation to Life*, 338.

11. Janice A. Klein, *True Change: How Outsiders on the Inside Get Things Done in Organizations* (San Francisco: Jossey-Bass, 2004). This stance is very similar to what Heifetz and Linsky refer to as "going to the balcony" so one can observe the action at some remove. Ronald A. Heifetz and Marty Linsky, *Leadership on the Line: Staying Alive Through the Dangers of Leading* (Boston: Harvard Business School Press, 2002).

12. Martin E. P. Seligman, *Learned Optimism: How to Change Your Mind and Your Life* (New York: Free Press, 1998).

Chapter 4

1. Familiar allusions to leadership and other performing arts—not including the ever-present references to sports—include Max De Pree, *Leadership Is an Art* (New York: Doubleday, 1989) and *Leadership Jazz* (New York: Doubleday, 1992); Peter B. Vaill, *Managing as a Performing Art: New Ideas for a World of Chaotic Change* (San Francisco: Jossey-Bass, 1989); John Kao, *Jamming: The Art and Discipline of Corporate Creativity* (New

York: HarperCollins, 1996); and Rosamund Stone Zander and Benjamin Zander, *The Art of Possibility: Transforming Professional and Personal Life* (New York: Penguin, 2002).

2. Philip E. Ross, "The Expert Mind," *Scientific American* 295, no. 2 (August 2006): 68. See also M. T. H. Chi, R. Glaser, and M. J. Farr, *The Nature of Expertise* (Hillsdale, NJ: Erlbaum, 1988), xv–xviii.

3. See, for example, *Penn and Teller Go Public*, a videotape of their 1985 Public Broadcasting performance (Stamford, CT: Vestron Video, 1989). Part of their genius resides in the way Penn and Teller touch a tender paradox of the Western mind: we deny that magic is real while, at the same time, secretly hope that it is.

4. Kevin Spacey, appearing on *Inside the Actors Studio*, first aired on March 5, 2000.

5. Atul Gawande, *Complications: A Surgeon's Notes on an Imperfect Science* (New York: Metropolitan Books, 2002), 19.

6. See, for example, the fascinating studies of expert performance in sports, theater, chess, typing, card playing, and medicine depicted in K. Anders Ericsson, Neil Charness, Paul J. Feltovich, and Robert R. Hoffman, eds., *The Cambridge Book of Expertise and Expert Performance* (Cambridge: Cambridge University Press, 2006). A recent effort to extend ideas about expert performance to business can be found in K. Anders Ericsson, Michael J. Prietula, and Edward T. Cokely, "The Making of an Expert," *Harvard Business Review*, July–August 2007.

7. "To reach the status of an expert in a domain it is sufficient to master the existing knowledge and techniques. To make an eminent achievement one must first achieve the level of an expert and then in addition surpass the achievements of already recognized eminent people and make innovative contributions to the domain." See K. A. Ericsson, Ralph Krampe, and Clemens Tesch-Romer, "The Role of Deliberate Practice in the Acquisition of Expert Performance," *Psychological Review* 100, no. 3 (1993): 366.

8. Howard S. Becker, *Art Worlds* (Berkeley: University of California Press, 1982); and Harrison White, *Careers and Creativity: Social Forces in the Arts* (Boulder, CO: Westview Press, 1993).

9. Warren G. Bennis and Robert J. Thomas, *Geeks and Geezers: How Era, Values, and Defining Moments Shape Leaders* (Boston: Harvard Business School Press, 2002); see especially chapter 5.

10. The topic of renewal—on the individual as well as the organizational level—is critically important and is finally receiving the attention it deserves, particularly in the aftermath of the dramatic rise and fall of dot-com-era entrepreneurs and CEOs and their companies. For insightful treat-

ments of renewal at the individual level, see John William Gardner, *Self-renewal: The Individual and the Innovative Society* (New York: Harper & Row, 1964); and Richard Boyatzis and Annie McKee, *Resonant Leadership: Renewing Yourself and Connecting with Others Through Mindfulness, Hope, and Compassion* (Boston: Harvard Business School Press, 2005). At the organizational level, see Robert J. Thomas, Fred Harburg, and Ana Dutra, "How to Create a Culture of High Performance," *Outlook*, November 2007, 1–6; and Gary Hamel, *Leading the Revolution* (Boston, Harvard Business School Press, 2000).

11. Michelene T. H. Chi, "Two Approaches to the Study of Experts' Characteristics," in K. Anders Ericsson, Neil Charness, Paul J. Feltovich, and Robert R. Hoffman, *The Cambridge Handbook of Expertise and Expert Performance* (New York: Cambridge University Press, 2006), 21–30; and Ericsson, Krampe, and Tesch-Romer, "The Role of Deliberate Practice," 366.

12. Eric Clapton, in Terry Gross, *All I Did Was Ask: Conversations with Writers, Actors, Musicians, and Artists* (New York: Hyperion, 2004), 278.

13. In other words, what's needed is not just an accumulation of experiences but a process for organizing, testing, and applying them. Experts, to paraphrase Feltovich and colleagues (in Ericsson et al., *The Cambridge Handbook of Expertise and Expert Performance* 57), "know more and know differently than novices."

14. See, for example, the first chapter in Peter Guralnick, *Last Train to Memphis: The Rise of Elvis Presley* (Boston: Back Bay Books, 1995); and *Rolling Stone Encyclopedia of Rock & Roll* (New York: Fireside, 2001), 783.

15. See Noel M. Tichy, *The Cycle of Leadership: How Great Leaders Teach Their Companies to Win*, with Nancy Cardwell (New York: HarperBusiness, 2002); Dave Ulrich and Wayne Brockbank, *The HR Value Proposition* (Boston: Harvard Business School Press, 2005); Ram Charan, Stephen Drotter, and James Noel, *The Leadership Pipeline: How to Build the Leadership-Powered Company* (San Francisco: Jossey-Bass, 2001); and William C. Byham, Audrey B. Smith, and Matthew J. Paese, *Grow Your Own Leaders* (Upper Saddle River, NJ: Prentice Hall, 2002).

16. Of course, extrinsic motivation plays a role, and, particularly in young beginners, it's difficult to distinguish from personal ambition. For example, parental expectations and attention, along with peer pressure, rank high among the reasons children and adolescents give when asked why they take up music, sports, chess, and/or theater. See, for example, Benjamin S. Bloom, "Generalizations About Talent Development," in *Developing Talent*

in Young People, ed. Benjamin S. Bloom (New York: Ballantine, 1985), 507–549; Mihaly Csikszentmihalyi, Kevin Rathunde, and Samuel Whalen, *Talented Teenagers: The Roots of Success and Failure* (New York: Cambridge University Press, 1997); and Mihaly Csikszentmihalyi and Barbara Schneider, *Becoming Adult: How Teenagers Prepare for the World of Work* (New York: Basic Books, 2000).

17. Johnny Cash, in Gross, *All I Did Was Ask*, 31.

18. Ericsson, Krampe, and Tesch-Romer, "The Role of Deliberate Practice," 371. For those who continue, the meaning of practice itself evolves; most importantly, as we will discuss in greater detail in chapter 5, the distinction between practice and performance fades into the background. That is, they may be separated temporally—there's performance on the weekends for a dancer or an athlete and practice on the weekdays—but practice and performance become part of an integrated whole. One does not really make sense without the other.

19. Attributed variously to Doc Severinsen, Miles Davis, Igor Stravinsky, and Johann Sebastian Bach: "If I don't practice for one day, I can hear a difference. If I don't practice for two days, other musicians can hear a difference. If I don't practice for three days, anybody can hear a difference."

20. James Champy and Nitin Nohria, *The Arc of Ambition: Defining the Leadership Journey* (Cambridge, MA: Perseus Books, 2001).

21. Indeed, most organizations choose leaders through something James Rosenbaum called a *tournament model*; James E. Rosenbaum, "Tournament Mobility: Career Patterns in a Corporation," *Administrative Science Quarterly* 24 (1979): 220–241. A tournament is a series of implicit competitions for promotion that progressively differentiate a cohort of employees throughout their careers. Simply put, "winners"—for example, those who individually outperform their peers or manage units that achieve superior results—are qualified to go on to the next round. At some point, having won enough times, they are no longer called managers. They are called leaders. There are two dangers associated with the tournament approach. First, it can orient young managers to do only what it takes to win and cause them to miss the fact that leading often encompasses a great deal more than managing, like investing in people, relationship building, and mastery of core skills like influence and communication. They may also neglect investing in themselves as leaders. Second, it can, as Rosenbaum points out, create a potentially devastating self-fulfilling prophecy: "The 'instant death' character of a loss in the tournament will tend to discourage innovation and to encourage conformist 'safe' strategies."

22. Jodie Foster, in Gross, *All I Did Was Ask*, 160–161.

23. It's important to note that teachers/mentors must also be recruitable—i.e., they must be open to sharing and to caring about the accomplishments of the protégé. See Robert Kegan, *The Evolving Self: Problem and Process in Human Development* (Cambridge, MA: Harvard University Press, 1982). As I'll point out in a later chapter, a common failing of formal mentoring programs is that organizations don't assess how recruitable mentors are. Too often, age, seniority and title are used as predictors of an individual's ability to mentor effectively.

24. American Society for Training and Development, *State of the Industry Report* (Alexandria, VA: ASTD, 2006).

25. Edgar H. Schein, *Organizational Culture and Leadership*, 2nd ed. (San Francisco: Jossey-Bass, 1992).

26. Pablo Picasso, cited in Howard Gardner, *Artful Scribbles: The Significance of Children's Drawings* (New York: Basic Books, 1982), 141.

27. Something similar happens when you ask most leaders to relate their philosophy of leadership: those who don't get tongue-tied often end up sharing vague platitudes that neither they nor their audiences find especially satisfying. Fact is, most have been too busy leading to come up with a theory of leadership. This is why Tichy's notion of hammering out one's own "teachable point of view" is such a valuable exercise. It not only forces individuals to come to closure on what they stand for, but it reminds them that, like it or not, effective leaders are also teachers. See Tichy, *The Cycle of Leadership*.

28. PBS's *Creativity* series, moderated by Bill Moyers; the episode with Pinchas Zukerman first aired in 1981.

29. Bill Russell, *Russell Rules: 11 Lessons on Leadership from the Twentieth Century's Greatest Winner*, with David Falkner (New York: Dutton, 2001), 19–20.

30. See, for example: Warren G. Bennis, *On Becoming a Leader* (Cambridge, MA: Perseus Books, 1989); Noel M. Tichy, *The Leadership Engine: Building Leaders at Every Level* (Dallas: Pritchett & Associates, 1998); Ram Charan, Stephen Drotter, and James Noel, *The Leadership Pipeline: How to Build the Leadership-Powered Company* (San Francisco: Jossey-Bass, 2001).

31. Daniel Goleman, *Emotional Intelligence* (London: Bloomsbury, 1996); and Daniel Goleman, Richard Boyatzis, and Annie McKee, *Primal Leadership: Realizing the Power of Emotional Intelligence* (Boston: Harvard Business School Press, 2002). According to Langer, mindfulness, especially when it comes to learning, consists of five overlapping qualities, almost all of which we will reencounter in chapters 5 and 6 as facets of a

Personal Learning Strategy: openness to novelty; alertness to distinction; sensitivity to different contexts; implicit, if not explicit, awareness of multiple perspectives; and orientation in the present. See Ellen J. Langer, *The Power of Mindful Learning* (New York: Addison-Wesley, 1997), 23.

Chapter 5

1. Assumed, but not overlooked, in the Personal Learning Strategy are the technical and theoretical foundations of leadership as a performing art. These are the things that in chapter 4, in the language of expert performance, I referred to as "grasp of method." This basket of competencies is the minimum price of entry into leadership and includes skills such as planning and goal setting, decision making, communication, soliciting feedback, professional/business acumen, conflict resolution, and stakeholder management. These skills compose an important part of a Personal Learning Strategy, but I give them less direct emphasis because most organizations invest heavily (and appropriately) in devising their own leadership competency models—many of which are designed to incorporate values distinct to the enterprise—and with them processes for training and rewarding leadership candidates who demonstrate these kinds of competencies. See Noel M. Tichy, *The Leadership Engine: Building Leaders at Every Level* (Dallas: Pritchett & Associates, 1998); and Ram Charan, Stephen Drotter, and James Noel, *The Leadership Pipeline: How to Build the Leadership-Powered Company* (San Francisco: Jossey-Bass, 2001).

2. As Jim Loehr and Tony Schwartz, "The Making of a Corporate Athlete," *Harvard Business Review*, January 2001, 120–128; and Jack Groppel, *The Corporate Athlete: How to Achieve Maximal Performance in Business and Life* (New York: Wiley, 2000), emphasize in their works on "corporate athletes," sticking to a practice regimen, like getting up at 4 a.m. to strap on the ice skates, is not always the toughest part about improving one's performance, but it is the most commonly mentioned explanation for why improvement efforts fail. I take this up explicitly in a later chapter.

3. As told to me by Rajarshi Chowdury, Tufts University undergraduate, February 2006.

4. Likewise, the point of envisioning your current reality and enumerating your defenses and diversions was to generate even more data with which to analyze your underlying motives.

5. David C. McClelland, *The Achieving Society* (Princeton, NJ: Van Nostrand, 1961); David C. McClelland, *Power: The Inner Experience* (New York: Halstead Press, 1975); David C. McClelland et al., *The Achievement*

Motive (Princeton, NJ: Van Nostrand, 1953); David C. McClelland et al., "A Scoring Manual for the Achievement Motive," in *Motives in Fantasy, Action and Society*, ed. John W. Atkinson (Princeton, NJ: Van Nostrand, 1958); and David C. McClelland and David Burnham, "Power Is the Great Motivator," *Harvard Business Review*, March–April 1976. For a detailed review of the critiques and controversies surrounding McClelland's model, see John Raven, "The McClelland/McBer Competency Models," in *Competence in the Learning Society*, eds. John Raven and John Stephenson (New York: Peter Lang, 2001).

6. Myers-Briggs and FIRO-B assessments have been accused of providing fickle and transient results; but despite that, I believe they can trigger valuable exploration of the consequences of being introverted versus extraverted for such things as your openness to experiencing new things, to conflict (especially in the realm of deeply held values), and to the ways in which you prefer to assimilate new information.

7. McClelland used the Thematic Apperception Test (TAT) as a tool to measure the individual needs of different people. The TAT is a test of imagination that presents the subject with a series of ambiguous pictures, and the subject is asked to develop a spontaneous story for each picture. The content of those stories is then coded with a scheme developed by McClelland and his coauthors (which has been refined over the years). The assumption is that the subject will project his or her own needs into the story. McClelland et al., "A Scoring Manual for the Achievement Motive."

8. The distinction between institutional and interactive leaders is based on findings from research carried out by David Burnham and his associates in recent years. They ascribe the difference to an emergent recognition on the part of leaders that changes in environmental conditions—most important among them being rapid change in technology, competitive strategies, and workforce demographics—have forced a shift in the way that successful leaders think about their role. See David H. Burnham, "Inside the Mind of the World-Class Leader" (white paper, Burnham Rosen Group, Boston), http://www.burnhamrosen.com/Publications/Inside_the_Mind.html.

9. Michelene T. H. Chi, "Two Approaches to the Study of Experts' Characteristics," in *The Cambridge Handbook of Expertise and Expert Performance*, eds. K. Anders Ericsson, Neil Charness, Paul J. Feltovich, and Robert R. Hoffman (Cambridge: Cambridge University Press, 2006), 21–30; and Donald A. Schon, *The Reflective Practitioner: How Professionals Think in Action* (New York: Basic Books, 1983).

10. Chris Argyris described this paradox in his distinction between espoused theory and theory in use: "Ask people in an interview or questionnaire

to articulate the rules they use to govern their actions, and they will give you what I call their 'espoused' theory of action. But observe these same people's behavior, and you will quickly see that this espoused theory has very little do with how they actually behave" (i.e., their theory in use). See Chris Argyris, "Teaching Smart People How to Learn," *Harvard Business Review*, May–June 1991, 6.

11. Educational theorists summarize these differences in the VARK model: visual (learn by seeing), verbal/auditory (learn by hearing), reading/writing (learn by processing text), and kinesthetic or practical (learn by doing). See John Bransford, Ann L. Brown, and Rodney R. Cocking, *How People Learn: Brain, Mind, Experience, and School* (Washington, DC: National Academy Press, 2000). In all honesty, however, there is considerable disagreement about whether learning styles are an effective predictor of learning performance, particularly in classroom settings. As in every effort to move from theory to practice, certain assumptions have to be made. In this case, I assume that learning styles provide insight into learning accelerators and impediments that can be used by individuals to devise an effective, though hardly immutable, Personal Learning Strategy. For critiques of the learning styles approach, see Robert J. Sternberg, *Thinking Styles* (Cambridge: Cambridge University Press, 1999); L. Curry, "A Critique of the Research on Learning Styles," *Educational Leadership* 48 (1990): 50–56; and Steven A. Stahl, "Different Strokes for Different Folks?" in *Taking Sides: Clashing Views on Controversial Issues in Educational Psychology*, ed. Leonard Abbeduto (Guilford, CT: McGraw-Hill, 2002), 98–107.

12. Paulo Freire, *Pedagogy of the Oppressed* (New York: Herder and Herder, 1971).

13. David A. Kolb, *The Learning Style Inventory: Technical Manual* (Boston: McBer and Company, 1976); David A. Kolb, "Learning Styles and Disciplinary Differences," in *The Modern American College*, ed. A. W. Chickering (San Francisco: Jossey-Bass, 1981); and David A. Kolb and Ronald E. Fry, "Toward an Applied Theory of Experiential Learning," in *Theories of Group Process*, ed. Cary L. Cooper (London: Wiley, 1975).

Chapter 6

1. These exercises were derived from fifteen years of intense collaboration with industry executives, faculty, and students at the Massachusetts Institute of Technology and Tufts University's Fletcher School of International Affairs. That collaboration resulted in a process for learning leadership founded on the premise that practice has to be intimately connected to

the day-to-day experience of leadership. The process has subsequently been validated in a dozen years' work as a coach to executives in the automobile, electronics, and metals industries.

2. John Berger, *Ways of Seeing* (London: British Broadcasting Corporation and Penguin Books, 1972), 7.

3. In the interest of extending the range of practice fields available, I depict in this and subsequent sections exercises that can be carried out at work and away from work, and at different levels of engagement: technical, background, rehearsal, and practicing while you perform (see the box, "Practicing While You Perform").

4. Bronwyn Fryer, "Storytelling That Moves People: A Conversation with Screenwriting Coach Robert McKee," *Harvard Business Review*, June 2003, 6.

5. Robert Kegan, *The Evolving Self: Problem and Process in Human Development* (Cambridge, MA: Harvard University Press, 1982), 16.

6. Fryer, "Storytelling That Moves People," 6.

7. Of the many books available now on storytelling, particularly for people in business, the ones I have found most useful are Jack Maguire, *The Power of Personal Storytelling: Spinning Tales to Connect With Others* (New York: Tarcher/Putnam, 1998); and Julie Allan, Gerard Fairtlough, and Barbara Heinzen, *The Power of the Tale: Using Narratives for Organisational Success* (West Sussex, England: Wiley, 2002).

8. Edgar Schein, in his classic work *Organizational Culture and Leadership*, underscores the role of the founders' story in helping explain how organizations come to have distinctive cultures. See Edgar H. Schein, *Organizational Culture and Leadership* (San Francisco: Jossey-Bass, 1985). His most recent book, *DEC Is Dead, Long Live DEC* (San Francisco: Berrett-Koehler, 2005), provides a rare insider's account of the rise and fall of one of the most influential organizational cultures in the late twentieth century.

9. *Wall Street Journal*, "Elder Man Drafts Slippage Note, But His Friends Don't Fall for It," December 9, 1997.

Chapter 7

1. I encourage you to duplicate the three assessments from chapter 6 and share them with people who you can rely on to give you a candid assessment. The added information you can get from partners, spouses, and associates can help you make a more considered judgment of your personal strengths and weaknesses. Keep another set handy as you complete part 2 of the PLS.

2. Shoji Shiba, Alan Graham, and David Walden, *A New American TQM: Four Practical Revolutions in Management* (University Park, IL: Productivity Press, 1993).

3. Richard Boyatzis and Annie McKee, *Resonant Leadership: Renewing Yourself and Connecting with Others Through Mindfulness, Hope, and Compassion* (Boston: Harvard Business School Publishing, 2005).

4. Edgar H. Schein, *Process Consultation Revisited: Building the Helping Relationship* (New York: Prentice-Hall, 1998).

5. The eight themes are technical/functional, general managerial, autonomy/independence, security/stability, entrepreneurial creativity, service/dedication to a cause, pure challenge, and lifestyle. For more detail, see Edgar H. Schein, *Career Anchors: Discovering Your Real Values* (San Francisco: Jossey-Bass Pfeiffer, 1990).

6. In the PBS video series on creativity, there are some captivating moments when creative people are overheard talking as they create. One particular segment in the episode devoted to Pinchas Zukerman and the St. Paul Chamber Orchestra nicely portrays the way in which collaboration can enhance individual creativity: it features two cellists swapping insights on how they learned different finger placements and how each could enhance the depth and the quality of sound the other created.

Chapter 8

1. John Dewey, *Experience and Nature* (New York: Kessinger Publishing, 2003); Kurt Lewin, *Field Theory in Social Science: Selected Theoretical Papers* (Washington, DC: American Psychological Association, 1997), chapter 4, Field Theory and Learning; Edgar H. Schein, *Organizational Culture and Leadership* (San Francisco: Jossey-Bass, 2004); David A. Kolb, *Experiential Learning: Experience as the Source of Learning and Development* (Upper Saddle River, NJ: Prentice Hall, 1984); Warren Bennis, *On Becoming a Leader* (Cambridge, MA: Perseus Publishing, 2004); and Morgan W. McCall Jr., Michael M. Lombardo, and Ann M. Morrison, *The Lessons of Experience: How Successful Executives Develop on the Job* (New York: Free Press, 1988).

2. James E. Rosenbaum, "Tournament Mobility: Career Patterns in a Corporation," *Administrative Science Quarterly* 24 (1979): 220–241.

3. The gang spells its name as Hells Angels (without an apostrophe) for the following reason, according to its Web site: "Should the Hells in Hells Angels have an apostrophe, and be Hell's Angels? That would be true

if there was only one Hell, but life and history has taught us that there are many versions and forms of Hell." Hells Angels Motorcycle Club FAQ page, http://hells-angels.com/faq.htm.

4. Loren Gary, "Pulling Yourself Up Through the Ranks," *Harvard Management Update*, October 2003; Paul R. Yost and Mary Mannion Plunkett, "Turn Business Strategy into Leader Development," *Training and Development 56*, no. 3 (2003): 49; Robert B. McKenna and Paul R. Yost, "The Differentiated Leader: Specific Strategies for Handling Today's Adverse Situations," *Organizational Dynamics* 33, no. 3 (2004): 292–306; and interviews conducted with Boeing Leadership Center staff, January 4, 2006, and June 14, 2004.

5. See especially McCall, Lombardo, and Morrison, *The Lessons of Experience*; Marian N. Ruderman and Patricia J. Ohlott, *Learning from Life: Turning Life's Lessons into Leadership Experience* (Greensboro, NC: Center for Creative Leadership, 2004); and Maxine A. Dalton, *Becoming a More Versatile Learner* (Greensboro, NC: Center for Creative Leadership 2005). The Boeing researchers focused on two principal questions in their interviews: What situations enabled you to develop? What factors supported or challenged you?

6. They went so far as to title one of their white papers "Development Plans That Are Not a Waste of Time." It became a virtual best seller on the Waypoint intranet portal. Interview with Rob McKenna and Paul Yost, May 22, 2006.

7. Michael L. Dertouzos et al., *Made in America: Regaining the Productive Edge* (Cambridge, MA: MIT Press, 1989).

8. In Accenture's 2005 High Performance Workforce survey, executives placed their concern about an inadequate supply of leaders as among their top five worries.

9. If recent research on the utility, oil, and chemical industries and in governments in the United States and Europe is any indication, there is soon to be a profound shortfall in the supply of next-generation leaders and managers. See David Delong, *Lost Knowledge: Confronting the Threat of an Aging Workforce* (New York: Oxford University Press, 2004), on the aging workforce in the oil and chemical industries, and Ken Dychtwald, Tamara J. Erickson, and Robert Morison, *Workforce Crisis: How to Beat the Coming Shortage of Skills And Talent* (Boston: Harvard Business School Press, 2006). See also The Conference Board, *Maximizing Rotational Assignments* (New York: The Conference Board, 2005), for useful insights on how some companies treat rotational postings as opportunities for imparting leadership skills.

10. Joseph Raelin, *Creating Leaderful Organizations: How to Bring Out Leadership in Everyone* (San Francisco: Berrett-Koehler, 2003).

11. See, for example, the detailed assessment of the economic return on training and learning achieved at Accenture in Donald Vanthournout et al., *Return on Learning: Training for High Performance at Accenture* (Chicago: Agate Publishing, 2006).

12. Nick van Dam, "Strategic Capability Building Through Talent Management" (presentation at the International Consortium for Executive Development Research, Seattle, WA, May 23, 2006).

13. *Neoteny* derives from the Greek *neo*, meaning "young," and *teinein*, meaning "to extend"; literally, it means to extend youth. *Online Etymology Dictionary*, s.v. "neoteny," http://dictionary.reference.com/browse/neoteny.

14. Jeffrey K. Liker, *The Toyota Way: 14 Management Principles from the World's Greatest Manufacturer* (New York: McGraw-Hill, 2003).

15. David Welch, "Staying Paranoid at Toyota," *BusinessWeek*, July 2, 2007.

16. Steven Spear, "Learning to Lead at Toyota," *Harvard Business Review*, May 2004.

17. And, to be truthful, not all survive long enough to bear fruit. For example, the Boeing Waypoint project has been scaled back significantly while the company explores other approaches to leader development.

18. Military organizations are an obvious choice, too. However, I did not include military organizations, like the U.S. Army, in this comparison, because they have at the core of their mission the development of leaders. I was much more interested in how organizations that don't see themselves in the leader development business go about addressing the challenge of maintaining a supply of leaders without going outside for new blood.

19. *Deseret News Church Almanac, 1997–1998*, cited in Gary Shepherd and Gordon Shepherd, *Mormon Passage: A Missionary Chronicle* (Urbana: University of Illinois Press, 1998), 3; and most recent church figures, available from Church of Jesus Christ of Latter-day Saints, Newsroom page, http://www.lds.org/newsroom.

20. According to Shepherd and Shepherd, *Mormon Passage*, xii: "Historically, the majority of Mormonism's most prominent officials have commenced their advancement through the ecclesiastical ranks after completing a period of mission labor."

21. Ralph "Sonny" Barger, *Hells Angel: The Life and Times of Sonny Barger and the Hells Angels Motorcycle Club* (New York: HarperCollins, 2000).

Chapter 9

1. I am currently at work on a book with Rob Cross that addresses the role that networks play in creating organizational adaptability and the role of leaders in creating and sustaining those networks. The book is tentatively titled *Leading in a Connected World*.

2. See Robert J. Thomas and Rajan Srikanth, "Leadership and High Performance" (white paper, Accenture Institute for High Performance Business, Boston), http://www.accenture.com/Global/Research_and_Insights/Institute_For_High_Performance_Business.

3. Cited in Glenn Kurtz, *Practicing: A Musician's Return to Music* (New York: Knopf, 2007).

4. Joseph Raelin, *Creating Leaderful Organizations: How to Bring Out Leadership in Everyone* (San Francisco: Berrett-Koehler, 2003).

5. In constructing this table, I drew heavily from McCall and colleagues' seminal work, *The Lessons of Experience*, and its masterful depiction of some of the crucible-like challenges that are so much a part of day-to-day work. See Morgan W. McCall Jr., Michael M. Lombardo, and Ann M. Morrison, *The Lessons of Experience: How Successful Executives Develop on the Job* (New York: Free Press, 1988).

INDEX

ABOUT THE AUTHOR

ROBERT J. THOMAS is executive director of the Accenture Institute for High Performance Business based in Boston, Massachusetts, and the John R. Galvin Visiting Professor of Leadership in International and Organizational Management at the Fletcher School of International Affairs at Tufts University. He writes, teaches, and consults in the areas of leadership, organizational design, and transformational change. In 2002, he coauthored with Warren Bennis *Geeks and Geezers: How Era, Values, and Defining Moments Shape Leaders*, which explores the motivations and aspirations of leaders under age thirty-five and over age seventy.

Bob has also published articles on leadership and change in the *Harvard Business Review*, *Harvard Management Update*, and *Fortune* magazine. He is the coauthor with Peter Cheese and Elizabeth Craig of *The Talent Powered Organization*, one of the first systematic efforts to chart a strategy for talent management in the global enterprise. His first major book, *What Machines Can't Do: Politics and Technology in the Industrial Enterprise*, won the 1994 C. Wright Mills Award of the Society for the Study of Social Problems.

An Eagle Scout whose upbringing in central California left him with a lifelong passion for fast cars and fresh vegetables, he lives in Brookline, Massachusetts, with his wife Rosanna, chair of the Women's Studies Department at Wellesley College, and their daughter Alyssa.